I0820957

The Cradle of Citizenship

ALSO BY JAMES TRAUB

True Believer: Hubert Humphrey's Quest for a More Just America

Judah Benjamin: Counselor to the Confederacy

What Was Liberalism? The Past, Present, and Promise of a Noble Idea

John Quincy Adams: Militant Spirit

The Freedom Agenda: Why America Must Spread Democracy (Just Not the Way George Bush Did)

The Best Intentions: Kofi Annan and the UN in the Era of American World Power

The Devil's Playground: A Century of Pleasure and Profit in Times Square

City on a Hill: Testing the American Dream at City College

Too Good to Be True: The Outlandish Story of Wedtech

The Cradle of Citizenship

HOW SCHOOLS CAN HELP SAVE OUR DEMOCRACY

JAMES TRAUB

W. W. NORTON & COMPANY
Independent Publishers Since 1923

Printed in the United States of America
First Edition

For information about special discounts for bulk purchases, please contact W. W. Norton Special Sales at specialsales@wwnorton.com or 800-233-4830

Manufacturing by Lakeside Book Company
Book design by Chris Welch
Production manager: Lauren Abbate

Library of Congress Control Number: 2025946304

ISBN 978-1-324-07951-4

W. W. Norton & Company, Inc., 500 Fifth Avenue, New York, NY 10110
www.wwnorton.com

W. W. Norton & Company Ltd., 15 Carlisle Street, London W1D 3BS

Authorized EU representative: EAS, Mustamäe tee 50, 10621 Tallinn, Estonia

10 9 8 7 6 5 4 3 2 1

To the great educators I met:

Kelly Rose, Peter Brown, Jason Caros, Sheryl Hopfer

It is evident, then, that there is a certain kind of education that children must be given not because it is useful or necessary, but because it is noble and suitable for a free person.

—ARISTOTLE, *POLITICS*

CONTENTS

Introduction: Why Civics Matters 1

1 Civics Without Knowledge 11

2 How History Became Social Studies, and Meat Became Meatloaf 29

3 Beautiful Content: THE MODEL OF THE CLASSICAL SCHOOL 48

4 1619 v. 1776: THE WAR OVER THE AMERICAN PAST 68

5 *Hamilton* on the Stage and in the Classroom 89

6 The History Wars in a Purple State 105

7 You Realize That Everyone Has Reasons for What They Think 123

8 The One True Curriculum—or, Failing That, a "Roadmap" 134

9 The New Vision Struggles to Be Born 153

10 In Florida, American History Is What the Governor Says It Is 168

11 In Minneapolis, There Is Only Racism and Antiracism 187

12 Great Books Can Set You Free 209

13 The War Over African American Studies: TWO IRRECONCILABLE NARRATIVES 219

14 Culturally Responsive Teaching 228

15 Mrs. Hopfer's History Catechism 243

16 What Is to Be Done? 254

Acknowledgments 261

Notes 263

Index 275

The Cradle of Citizenship

Introduction

Why Civics Matters

In one of the lectures he delivered periodically to the Massachusetts Board of Education in the 1840s, Horace Mann, the board secretary and the most zealous advocate and tireless innovator of public education in the young nation, explained the relationship between democracy and schooling as he understood it. "The theory of our government," he said, "is—not that all men, however unfit, shall be voters—but that every man, by the power of reason and the sense of duty, shall be fit to be a voter. Education must bring the practice as nearly as possible to the theory."[1] Man was beset by temptations to wrongdoing. As this stern Puritan said in another lecture, democracy had made mankind's "latent capability of evil" yet more perilous by emboldening the ordinary person with the belief that he may do as he wishes. Against this vast potential for corruption, society posed the law, the clergy, the newspapers; but none was fully effectual. Only schooling reached future citizens—all future citizens—"during the docile and teachable years of childhood."[2] For this reason, Mann made the astonishing claim, which he put in italics to emphasize how very improbable it was, that "*The common school is the greatest discovery ever made by man.*"[3]

Education in America—public, universal, and secular—has always been understood as the handmaiden of democracy. Schools make citizens. John Adams, Benjamin Franklin, Noah Webster, and of course

Thomas Jefferson wrote about, and advocated for, the diffusion of knowledge through schools. In the middle of the Revolutionary War, when they might well have been distracted by more pressing matters, several of the thirteen colonies added clauses mandating universal education to their constitutions. The diffusion of schooling *was* an urgent matter, though Jefferson, a sunnier figure than Mann, worried less about our sinful nature than about the contrivances of tyrants. Only through the study of history, he wrote, could citizens "be enabled to know ambition under all its shapes, and prompt to exert their natural powers to defeat its purposes."[4]

The civic machinery that those prophets set in motion has long since attained the universality of which they dreamed. All American children go to school through the age of sixteen. Close to four-fifths of us graduate from high school; more than two-fifths graduate from a four-year college. All Americans study history; virtually all take one or more courses in government. Yet education has not imparted the power of reason nor armed Americans against tyranny. Not since the Civil War have Americans hated one another as they do today. Not since then, if ever, have so many Americans fallen prey to conspiratorial views of their government and of one another. Rarely have so many been prepared even to discard democracy in favor of strongman rule or some other system.

In reelecting Donald Trump as president, a majority of Americans chose a man whom they knew to be indifferent to the truth and contemptuous of the rule of law. Those voters were angry and frustrated over an economy in which they felt like they could not get ahead, an immigration system that appeared broken, elites who seemed to occupy a world of their own. Yet, as in 2016 and 2020, Republicans chose Donald Trump as the vehicle of their grievance. He told them lies that they wanted to believe; two-thirds of Republicans believed that the 2020 election had been stolen. Casting off whatever restraints he had accepted in those earlier campaigns, Trump reduced his agenda to "retribution" against the "enemy from within"—the government—and his myriad foes. He vowed to serve as a dictator—though only on "Day One." He appealed openly to sexism and racism, taunting Kamala Harris, his Black female opponent, as lazy and stupid (though he treated white, male rivals with almost equal scorn). Yet this cruel, heartless, solipsistic figure, regarded as a "fascist" by some of his own former senior officials, had succeeded in reducing one of the nation's two parties to a cult of personality. Our civic culture has hit bottom.

The only time in the past that either party nominated a candidate seen as a danger to democracy—Barry Goldwater in 1964—he was decisively defeated precisely because he was seen as an "extremist." And Goldwater, unlike Trump, was a deeply honorable man. The pull of "decency" was once powerful in American life; Joseph McCarthy was all but ruined when Joseph Welch, the attorney for the U.S. Army in the televised Army-McCarthy hearings, thundered, "Have you no sense of decency?" The question would simply bounce off our current president. As I write this in the spring of 2025, Trump has already laid waste to the norms of liberal democracy and to the legal and constitutional restraints on presidential power. He has ignored the Congress, defied the courts, and deployed his enforcement powers to wreak vengeance on enemies. He appears to be conducting a terrifying laboratory experiment in our collective capacity to resist dictatorial ambitions. We do not yet know the outcome.

Schools are not the cause of our polarization. The same deep forces that afflict many Western nations have wrenched us apart: the transition to a postindustrial economy and the attendant erosion of working-class security, the demographic shift toward a "majority minority" nation, the cultural upheaval that has dethroned men, and especially white men, from their age-old dominance—and the rise of entrepreneurs of outrage eager to exploit all that free-floating anger. Schools cannot make us a more just or equal society. Nor can we expect schools to cause young people to treat one another with respect and tolerance when the larger culture is aflame with disrespect and intolerance. Nevertheless, school and society have a reciprocal relationship: just as an increasingly coarse and intemperate culture is infecting our schools, so a conscious and thoughtful effort to promote civic education can help knit us back together.

What's more, schools matter more than they have in the past. First of all, the crisis that we now face is not just partisan but cognitive. Americans don't simply disagree, as we always have, on what is and is not true; rather, we no longer have common criteria for truth. Social media imparts a specious, but very powerful, authority to our prejudices and illusions. In *The Constitution of Knowledge: A Defense of Truth*, social critic Jonathan Rauch describes an "epistemic" crisis in which institutions to which the public once looked as sources of knowledge, whether universities or newspapers, have given way to "platforms" that disseminate information not according to its accuracy but its popularity.[5] Donald Trump is not the cause but the beneficiary of our epistemic collapse. We cannot return to the world before social media; we can only seek to strengthen the institutions—above all, school—that once constituted our epistemic foundation.

That is a very great deal to ask of any institution, even one that reaches all children during their docile and teachable years. Yet we do so in part because of another new phenomenon. Schools were not traditionally expected to bear the civic burden on their own. The remarkable civic bonds to which Alexis de Tocqueville attributed the underlying strength of American democracy had been fostered far more by the astonishing profusion of newspapers and "voluntary associations" than by schools, of which he barely took notice in his great work, *Democracy in America*.[6] This civic vitality remained central to American life through the middle of the twentieth century. But local newspapers, once the heart of small-town America, have been heading toward extinction since 1970; older Americans get their news from television, younger ones from social media. At the same time, the union hiring halls and churches and PTAs and Rotary Clubs where Americans once gathered suffered a steady decline in attendance and membership.[7] We have very few civic levers other than school left to pull.

Yet today's schools are not the kind of instruments that Mann or Jefferson imagined they would be. Despite all those years of schooling, the typical American student is stunningly ignorant of her history and government. In the 2022 tests administered by the National Assessment of Educational Progress (NAEP), only 20 percent of students scored at the "proficient" level in civics; 31 percent fell "below basic." (Two percent were "advanced.") In history, the figure for proficient was an astonishing 13 percent, with 40 percent below basic.[8] Though American students do poorly on almost everything, they recorded higher levels of proficiency on every other tested subject.[9] School is scarcely the only place where Americans learn about their history and government, but adults do little better on such tests than students do. Studies regularly find that no more than one-third of Americans can pass the test administered to would-be citizens, which requires six out of ten correct answers on questions such as who the United States fought in World War II, why the colonists fought the British, or what—anything—Ben Franklin did.[10]

Ignorance is not the sum of our problem. Mann imagined schooling as a bulwark against our fallen nature; yet a universal public institution is bound to reflect the culture in which it is embedded. Red and blue America have, inevitably, spawned red and blue curricula, pedagogy, state standards, "evidence-based research," and the like. The publication by the *New York Times Magazine* in 2019 of the "1619 Project," with its claim that America is a "slavocracy" defined by white supremacy, provoked a counterblast by the Trump administration, the "1776 Report," which offered a patriotic account of America as an exceptional nation dedicated, if imperfectly, to its founding principles. There aren't, as I found, very many ideologically pure 1619 or 1776 schools out there, but there are a great many 1619 or 1776 state legislators, curriculum experts, district and state superintendents, and college professors who shape the larger debate over the schools as well as the particulars of what students learn.

The adoption of state history and civics standards, once a sleepy affair conducted by professionals, has sunk to the level of gladiatorial spectacle; so, too, with school board elections. The idea of a national narrative in which all Americans can find a place seems an artifact of a vanished era of consensus. The culture war has so deeply pervaded the schools that many states have adopted standards in history and civics that are either blatantly red, blatantly blue, or, yet more common, blatantly vapid. A 2021 study of such standards by the Fordham Institute, an education think tank and advocacy body, found only five states with "exemplary" standards and a full half of them with "inadequate" ones—a D or an F. Some states apparently concluded that the only way to escape public wrath was, as Fordham put it, to "paper over differences, avoid specifics and settle for vague generalizations."[11]

Yet despite nostalgia for a supposed golden age of civic awareness, American students are probably no more ignorant today than they were forty years ago when NAEP first administered tests of historical and literary knowledge. At that time the majority of high school juniors thought the Jim Crow laws had been enacted to *protect* Black people; only a third could place the Civil War in the second half of the nineteenth century. Yet three-quarters of those students reported that they were taking an American History class *at the time*.[12] Nevertheless, the results did not provoke fears that American democracy was going into eclipse—because it wasn't. Whatever his flaws, President Ronald Reagan spoke of democracy in mystical terms and earnestly sought to propagate it abroad. Reagan ridiculed, but never demonized, his opponents; he formed a close bond with House Speaker Tip O'Neill, an unreconstructed New Deal Democrat. Civic ignorance does not cause polarization; but civic education matters more when so many other forces pull us apart.

This book is the offspring both of my fears for the future of liberal democracy and my belief in public schooling. For the past decade—since the advent of Donald Trump—I have devoted my energies both as a teacher at New York University and as an author to the perilous state of our democracy. In my 2019 book, *What Was Liberalism?*, I examined the history of the liberal idea and asked whether it had run its course. My involvement with the schools goes back much further—to *City on a Hill*, my 1994 book about the open admissions drama at City College of New York, and then to decades of journalistic writing about the public schools and about school reform. Since 2012, I have run a volunteer tutoring program that brings writers into New York City public high schools. I am very familiar with the obstacles that schools and students face, especially in disadvantaged areas, but I am drawn to classrooms as places of hope and potential. Schools are rarely as good as we wish them to be, but when you see how education has changed the life prospects or transformed the understanding of this or that child, you can't help asking how it can do so for other children as well. Schools are not endlessly manipulable, but they are improvable. Our democracy needs them to be better.

Civic education matters. But what, exactly, do we expect it to do? For some, especially on the right, the answer is simple: instilling love of country. As one leading conservative puts it, children should study America's foundational texts and constitutional system to "take pride in what they share as Americans—an exceptional heritage of freedom, a republic that has succeeded in making liberty a fundamental principle of our government, and the joyful accomplishments of their common national culture."[13] This has the satisfying ring of tradition but sounds very close to indoctrination. What about the tragic failures of our common national culture? Less doctrinaire figures prefer to promote a "reflective patriotism" that fully takes account of our nation's terrible shortcomings.

But is civic education only a question of mastering a certain body of knowledge? The answer depends on one's conception of democratic citizenship. If citizenship can be reduced to "voting wisely," then "knowing well" is enough. But if we understand democracy as a system where each of us is responsible for our destiny, and we are called on not merely to vote and serve on a jury but to think and debate and even organize and protest, then civic education must also entail preparation for a full democratic life. Civic philosophers speak of the "dispositions" that students need to acquire: tolerance for difference, the capacity to listen, the negotiating skills that help us bring people with unlike views to agree on a common course of action. The political scientist Danielle Allen has described the ultimate goal of civic education as "participatory readiness," by which she means the ability to adopt a wide range of civic identities, whether as voter, advocate, or protestor.[14]

Civic education must impart knowledge and democratic dispositions. Should we also look to schools to shape the moral nature of children? The Founders, whose own views of citizenship were deeply shaped by the work of the classic republican thinkers, believed, like Aristotle and Cicero, that republics ultimately rested on the virtue of citizens. As James Madison put it, "To suppose that any form of government will secure liberty or happiness without any form of virtue in the people, is a chimerical idea."[15] The true patriot set aside his merely personal interest for the honor and glory of the nation. He was endowed with the virtues that enabled this ethos of self-sacrifice—prudence, courage, disinterestedness. The Founders might well say that the election of Donald Trump signals the kind of collapse of public virtue that imperils democracy. Do we think they'd be wrong? Can democracy flourish with no shared sense of decency? Can it flourish in a society that sorts everyone into winners and losers in a Darwinian competition for success? Liberals are uncomfortable with the language of virtue; the liberal understanding is that students bring different moral codes to school and should not be coerced into accepting one of them. Ought we, then, ask the schools to impart civic dispositions and skills but not civic virtues? This is one of the questions I will pursue.

Why do American schools seem to do such a poor job of teaching the subject matter of civic education? The most common explanation is that at some point, schools lost faith in their civic function and stopped teaching that material. Virtually everyone over a certain age believes that when *they* went to school, they got a firm grounding in the rudiments of American government. There is some evidence that this is true, though the chronology seems all wrong. A leading education historian concludes that the civic focus of public schools began to erode around 1950.[16] Yet even in the supposed golden age, students took on average only one more civically oriented course than they do today. What changed most drastically was not the curriculum but the pervading civic culture.

A second explanation, which clearly also contains a good deal of truth, is that teachers are now so afraid of discussing anything in detail that they content themselves, as the Fordham study put it, with vapid bromides. Yet that hardly explains why students did so poorly on tests of historical and civic knowledge forty years ago, when classrooms were not yet burning ground. It appears that we have been doing something wrong for a long time, something that applies to subject-matter knowledge more broadly. How we have failed is itself a matter of bitter contention, because the education world is every bit as polarized on questions of pedagogy as it is on content.

Pedagogical progressives believe that students are not learning history—or other topics—because most teachers are intent on jamming disjointed facts and dates into the heads of bored, passive students in an exercise mocked as "drill and kill." Schools fail because they do not encourage "critical thinking."[17] Schools shy away from the issues of identity that preoccupy non-white students, or from the controversial questions that would make young people care about their classes.[18]

The rival, "traditionalist," diagnosis is, in effect, the exact opposite: students haven't learned history or government—or science or literature—because most schools have adopted some version of the progressive pedagogy that emphasizes the acquisition of content-neutral skills such as critical thinking rather than building the foundations of understanding through the teaching of vocabulary, the reading of difficult texts, and the study of chronology and narrative.[19] Few teachers have the subject-matter knowledge that would allow them to bring their subject fully alive; their own training emphasizes skills acquisition rather than knowledge. During my time in classrooms, I saw very little evidence of drill and kill but all too many signs of flimsy understanding producing dull and empty lessons.

I spent the 2023–24 school year sitting in classrooms around the country, talking to scholars and reformers of all stripes, studying the historical development of curriculum and pedagogy, and wading into the battles over state standards in history and government. The organization of the book reflects my own experience. It begins in a classroom in September 2023 and ends in a classroom in May 2024. In the course of that year I visited schools in Texas, Illinois, Oklahoma, New York City, Arizona, Massachusetts, and Minnesota; in some cases I went back a second time. All of the schools I visited had some illustrative value: some offered unusual civics programs and some specialized in history; some were blue and some were red; some were exemplary and some very much not. When I wasn't visiting schools I was reading curricular manifestos, state standards, foundation reports, ideological screeds—and talking to their authors as well as to teachers, school board members, instructional providers, and others. I have interspersed chapters on classrooms with chapters on the history of civic education, on the debates between partisans of "1619" and "1776," on fights over state standards, and on Florida's "war on woke."

My ultimate goal was not to expose the bad but to unearth, and explain, and celebrate the good. I found that the growing concern over our civic life has produced promising new buds. Dozens of nonprofit instructional providers now provide nutritious, often winsome, curricular material on American history and government for teachers who do not have the background knowledge or the time to assemble it. States are mandating more classes in government and, at least in some cases, devising more rigorous standards in history. Thanks to a genuinely bipartisan effort among scholars and educators, "Educating for American Democracy," a new "roadmap"—not, to be sure, a curriculum—is available to schools that want to steer clear of red-blue mayhem. Among the most intriguing of recent school reforms is the so-called "classical school," a model based on the study of great books and the conscious molding of character. Classical schools constitute a throwback to an earlier age, or perhaps an imagined era, of verities—the good and the true—widely shared and unironically pursued. They are, not surprisingly, far more popular in red America than blue; yet they speak to a hunger for civic, moral, and intellectual coherence that may well transcend politics. It is that wish to escape the steel cage of our culture wars, to find our way to a deeper and less ideological connection to our history and ideals, that gives me some small, modest hope for our future.

I

Civics Without Knowledge

It is second period on a Friday morning in late September 2023 at Waubonsie Valley High School in Aurora, Illinois, forty miles west of Chicago. Kristan Crawford and Alyssa Battaglia are teaching a tenth-grade class called "Society," which combines American history and literature. The students are reading the Declaration of Independence. Moving around the class, I can see that many of them find the archaic language tough sledding. Though they took a U.S. History class in eighth grade, none of them can recall having seen the text or learning anything about it. The work of literature they are reading concurrently is Arthur Miller's *Crucible*, though it is set in the early Colonial rather than Revolutionary era. While the kids are silently reading, I ask Miss Crawford whether she's worried that the students will lose track of chronology if they have to switch back and forth between eras. She arches an eyebrow; Miss Crawford is a history teacher with a master's degree in the subject. "Our Social Studies chair," she says, "wants it to be more thematic-based than chronology-based." Unlike history, social studies is, by design, organized thematically rather than chronologically. The department chair, Adam Dyche, later explained to me that he thought a thematic rather than chronological approach "may increase the relevance for the kids."

Miss Battaglia, the English teacher, comes over, and we talk about *The Crucible*. The kids find it easier than the Declaration, but they balk at reading a whole novel. Even English classes are supposed to assign excerpts rather than full texts. I'm now getting mildly concerned that the kids are on their own, but their teachers have a burden to unload to this stranger in their midst. Miss Crawford says, "History has been pushed to the side within Social Studies because there's too much reading and writing. That creates too much stress, and it makes the kids feel bad about themselves, and then the parents get upset and the school hears about it. It's just devastated me." She is suddenly holding back tears. World History, she says, has given way to a class called Human Geography, which requires far less reading and writing. Miss Battaglia says, "Teachers are just counting the years to retirement."

This is not at all what I have come to Waubonsie Valley to hear. The school is part of Illinois's "Democracy Network," high schools that use innovative programs to fulfill the state's Civics requirement. Waubonsie Valley has earned that distinction. Later that morning I visited a science teacher, Carl Armstrong, who had instituted a program called "Prairie Restoration" drawing on the school's Botany and Environmental Science classes. Armstrong had students grow plants from seed and then transplant them into the fields that ran behind the school and on either side of the Waubonsie Creek. The greenhouse behind his office was now empty, but soon it would be filled with up to four thousand plants. Over the past twenty years, he and his students had transformed the local environment. Beavers, bald eagles, and soft-shell turtles have returned to the creek; tall grasses trap the fertilizer that had previously polluted the waterway; and thanks to the butterflies that now feed there, the Waubonsie Creek has been incorporated into the Fox Valley Monarch Center. "The kids," Armstrong said to me, "have a sense of contributing to something that's been around longer than they've been alive." Armstrong was so passionate about environmental science that he had written and self-published a novel set five hundred years in the future in which the earth had been saved by forcibly returning places like Aurora to their natural state.

That was why I had come to DuPage County in suburban Illinois. Mary Ellen Daneels, a former Social Studies teacher in nearby West Chicago High School, had established the Democracy Network to encourage schools to think about civics in the broadest possible sense, to incorporate it across the curriculum, in student government and after-school activities. "Prairie Restoration" was precisely the kind of participatory exercise she hoped to foster. Thanks in part to a $3 million grant from the Chicago-based McCormick Foundation, Daneels had been able to expand the network so that it covered one-sixth of the state's high school students; she was planning to install the program in middle and elementary schools. Daneels had become a kind of Johnny Appleseed of civics education, traveling to deeply conservative rural districts in southern Illinois to spread the idea of participatory civics. In something called the Civics Language Perceptions Project, Daneels had learned how to use "consensus" words, such as "we the people," rather than "trigger" words, such as "civics action," which in the Fox News universe was understood as "left-wing social engineering." The goal of civics, as she understood it, was to establish a vocabulary of "we the people" to bridge our deepening divisions.

The Democracy Network sounded like just the place I needed to visit. But when I mentioned my plans to Amber Northern, a senior researcher at the Fordham Institute, which among other things rates state academic standards, she said, "Why would you want to go to Illinois? We gave them an F in History."[1] That was news to me. Only once I had spent time in the schools did I recognize that none of the special attention, training, or money that had been lavished on civics had been extended as well to history. More than that: while the schools I visited in DuPage County embraced the idea that a healthy democracy depended on a kind of civic awareness and engagement that schools could teach, they seemed scarcely conscious of the air of lassitude that reigned in many classrooms.

Waubonsie Valley is the kind of big, diverse, middle-to-upper-middle-class high school you could find all over the United States. Of the 2,500-odd students, 39 percent are white, 25 percent Asian, 19 percent Hispanic, and 11 percent Black. Only 23 percent of the students are poor enough to qualify for a free or reduced lunch. It's no surprise, given the overwhelming correlation between academic performance and socioeconomic background, that Waubonsie students significantly outperform the state average on standardized tests; the school has earned a "Commendable" rating, the second highest of five categories. The halls are clean and the kids are calm and well behaved. Waubonsie Valley offers a course, or at least a club, for almost every possible student interest. When I first drove up and tried to figure out which of the innumerable portals of the massive building actually constituted the entrance, I saw a sign that said, "Planetarium." Adam Dyche, the Social Studies chair who served as my host, explained that, yes, Waubonsie Valley had its very own planetarium for Astronomy class, not to mention an Aquatic Center with diving pool and Mr. Armstrong's big greenhouse.

I spent first period in Chris Wolak's twelfth-grade Government class. The walls were plastered with historic campaign posters; in the center of the room Mr. Wolak had put a battered "soapbox" to be used for holding forth. The subject of the day was "political socialization"—how people come to hold the views they do. The kids broke into groups to decide how to rank the various influences—family, economic status, race, and so forth. Mr. Wolak explained that they would soon begin a semester-long project in which they would track their own civic engagement—"my voice, my beliefs, my activities." Mr. Wolak was extolling the virtues of civic engagement when the giant TV screen at the front of the class—and of every classroom—suddenly lit up. It was time for "Warrior Update," a weekly show. A student read the Pledge of Allegiance and delivered the daily announcements. "Are you interested in traveling to Italy, Switzerland, or France?" You could. Another presenter delivered congratulations to the golf team and the math team for recent victories. The scene switched to a classroom, where a student expertly interviewed a new teacher. "For Warrior Update, I'm Mackenzie Green." It was all very polished, but Mr. Wolak had run out of time.

Waubonsie Valley knew how to cater to its clientele. That, of course, was part of the bitter plaint I would hear next period from Miss Crawford and Miss Battaglia. They asked whether I knew about the surveys that had been distributed to both teachers and students in the Indian Prairie School District, which included Waubonsie Valley, to ask what social studies electives they'd like to see. This was, at least for old-guard teachers like them, the last word in educational consumerism. The survey listed eleven possible courses. Among students, the big winners were "Street Law" and "History of Hollywood." The big losers were AP

African American Studies and Latin American History—despite the sizable numbers of Black and Latino students, who, it was widely believed, were eager to learn about their own history and culture. Teachers, more politically conscious, voted in larger numbers for AP African American, but the big winners were "History of Hollywood" and "Sports in Society." World History, which had been supplanted in the curriculum by Human Geography, scored in the middle of the pack, though far ahead of Latin American History. (Mr. Dyche later told me that the school planned to offer Street Law, and to restore World History, in 2025.)

Miss Crawford brought me to meet her colleague Kelly Rose, a twenty-eight-year veteran and star teacher. Miss Rose was a small ball of fire with short gray hair and rectangular glasses. We sat in her empty classroom. It was true, she said, as I had heard, that teachers were discouraged from getting advanced degrees in their subject matter rather than in pedagogy. She had master's degrees in both theology and Asian history. "Our administration is not really intellectual," she said. "People like us"—she included Miss Crawford—"would never get hired today." She mourned the demise of World History, for which, she said, one student too few had signed up. "You're not going to be tolerant of Muslims if you don't know that the Abbasids once ran the show," as she put it. When she talked about the 1979 hostage crisis in U.S. History, she told the kids about Iranian history, including the American role in the overthrow of Prime Minister Mohammad Mossadegh in 1953. Miss Rose took an extremely dim view of some of the shibboleths of progressive pedagogy that had been incorporated into Illinois's state standards for history and civics instruction. She regarded "inquiry-based learning" as a euphemism for kids studying whatever interested them—street law or the history of Hollywood. "Inquiry-based learning is not going to help me when I'm in the voting booth," she said. "It's not going to help me choose someone based on their policies." For that, she thought, you needed knowledge.

I sat in on Miss Rose's AP European History class. It was an enthralling experience that reminded me very much of my own AP European class in eleventh grade, possibly the first class I had ever loved. The subject of the day was the age of exploration. The blackboards and whiteboards around the class were filled with information. Miss Rose had listed aspects of "the Medieval Mind and Worldview," and then a series of events that "start to SHATTER the stability of world order." The diminutive teacher raced around the classroom popping questions. "Does the Renaissance cause the age of exploration? Does the age of exploration spread the Renaissance? Why do we need a centralized nation-state before we can explore? Why do you need free peasants" rather than serfs?

The students lobbed possible answers: You have to be able to focus the nation's resources; you need an effective military. Miss Rose talked about capital and markets, and then dropped her voice to a conspiratorial whisper: "You can't use these words until the eighteenth century; economics won't be *invented* until then." Miss Rose then posed the big question: Which countries would enjoy a short-term advantage in exploration, and which a long-term one? Spain and Portugal had seaports, a centralized state, religious uniformity, access to slaves. (Miss Rose corrected herself. "I need to change my vocabulary—*enslaved people*.") That was great in the short term; they got the gold. "Who had to be innovative to get the gold?" France did; the French developed a merchant class that cornered the market in beaver furs. So, too, England and Holland. So they won out long-term. In fifty minutes, Miss Rose had almost delivered a miniature version of Max Weber's *The Protestant Ethic and the Spirit of Capitalism.* I went up to thank her, and Miss Rose said, "Thank *you*. I can't tell you how much you lifted the morale of this building." Apparently word of our conversation had spread fast, at least among the old guard.

Miss Rose was an exceptional teacher who was able to pitch her class to the academic level of the best students at a school with a well-to-do population. But she and Miss Crawford and Miss Battaglia and others—the ones among whom, I suppose, word of our conversation had spread—believed strongly that every child would benefit from a rigorous curriculum and high expectations. They were disappointed in their school in that regard; but my experience elsewhere in DuPage County led me to conclude that Waubonsie was neither better nor worse than its peers. At nearby Metea Valley High School, I attended another "Society" class in which narrative history had been largely eliminated in favor of a thematic focus. The class was organized according to four grand themes, including "Leadership" and "Freedom and Justice." When I asked one of the teachers whether she was worried that the kids would wind up with a muddled sense of American history, she reassured me that they already had a solid background from classes in fourth and eighth grades. Given what I had seen at Waubonsie Valley, that didn't seem likely.

A few periods later, in Ben Lundy's U.S. History class for sophomores and juniors who had chosen not to take "Society," the kids drew a blank at the question, "What new political system came along as a result of the American Revolution?" Mr. Lundy poked and prodded. "Am I the only one paying attention here?," he asked plaintively. Finally a student piped up: "Democracy?" "Democracy, thank you," the relieved teacher responded. The question of the day was: "How did the Constitution strengthen the government as compared to the Articles of Confederation?" The kids didn't seem familiar with the Articles or, for that matter, with the United States Congress. They were stumped when Mr. Lundy asked them to explain the difference between the two houses. One boy launched a trial balloon: "They get elected for life?" It wasn't clear which house he was thinking of.

The academic expectations dropped precipitously in a school further down the socioeconomic ladder. At West Chicago High School, where the student body is 70 percent Hispanic, the AP classes are a mix of white, Asian, and Latino kids while the regular classes consist almost entirely of lower-scoring Latino students. Many of the students in Joe Zeman's eleventh-grade U.S. History class were reading far below grade level. The official subject of the day's class was the differing points of view held by patriots and loyalists in the years just before the American Revolution broke out. The actual subject, however, was more basic: How can you tell, from reading a document, what the point of view of the author was? The same was true in Nick Caltagirone's class later that day, where the students were comparing rival accounts of the Boston Massacre to find cues that would tell them which side the author was taking. What do you learn from the title of the essay or the identity of the author? What words showed "slant"? Mr. Caltagirone couldn't get a response. He told me later that the kids didn't have the vocabulary to make sense of the passages. He provided them with definitions and paraphrases, but it was still hard going. Both teachers responded to even the smallest spark, but neither was able to kindle the occasional one-word response into the flame of discussion. Both classes were almost entirely silent.

Neither Waubonsie, nor Metea Valley, nor West Chicago was a "failing school." Yet so many of the classes I sat in on were painfully silent. Save at the very highest levels, the students had very little substantive knowledge, and the teachers had learned to adjust themselves, often very unhappily, to those vast blank spaces. How could it be that in member schools of the select Democracy Network, students seemed to know so little? One reason, plainly, is the one that Amber Northern of the Fordham Institute had mentioned to me—the vacuity of the state's history and civics standards.

Illinois's standards are built around skills mastery rather than content knowledge; actual content is to be determined locally. Thus the history standards for all of high school take up a quarter of a page; requirements include "evaluate how historical developments were shaped by time and place as well as broader historical contexts" and "analyze key historical events and contributions of individuals through a variety of perspectives, including those of historically underrepresented groups." The civics standards are equally vague.[2] The evaluators at Fordham, who share Kelly Rose's aversion to much of progressive pedagogy, gave an F to the civics as well as the history standards. They observed that the "disciplinary concepts" around which the standards were structured "are so vague as to be useless to teachers, students, parents, curriculum planners, and assessment designers."[3] Fordham gave Illinois high marks for the articulation of skill development but noted tartly that the civics standards, covering thirteen years of school, included a total of four proper nouns: "Illinois," "United States," "Illinois Constitution," and "U.S. Constitution."

The really remarkable thing about the Illinois standards is that they represented the best thinking of the social studies profession at the time they were adopted. Shawn Healy, formerly a program officer at the McCormick Foundation, the chief funder of the Democracy Network, had played a key role in persuading Illinois to adopt a law making civics instruction mandatory in 2015 and then in writing the state standards. When I asked Healy how the standards had come about, he said that the vagueness had been intentional. First, he said, the authors felt that they should yield decisions about content to districts and teachers. Second, he said, they feared that "if we put a bunch of content in we were going to be part of the culture wars; it's a very fraught endeavor." And finally, they followed the lead of "The College, Career and Civic Life (C3) Framework for Social Studies State Standards," which they regarded as the state of the art.

The C3 Framework, published in 2013, was the product of a three-year collaboration among the National Council of Social Studies and the major professional bodies in geography, history, economics, and civic education, among others. The C3 Framework was itself a response to the proposed state standards for all major subjects known as the Common Core, devised in 2010, which also laid out a sequence of skills that students were to master over time. The framework was written in order to guide state officials in writing standards to implement the Common Core. That guidance, the authors wrote, "takes form in an Inquiry Arc," which in turn is based on "four Dimensions of informed inquiry in social studies." The first of these dimensions is the development, by both teachers and students, of "compelling" questions meant to structure inquiry, such as "Was the American Revolution revolutionary?" or "Was the Civil Rights Movement of the 1960s a success?" With these compelling and "supporting" questions in hand, "teachers and students determine the kind of content they need in order to develop their inquiries." That's Dimension 2. Dimension 3 is "Evaluating sources and using evidence," while Dimension 4 is "Communicating conclusions and taking informed action."[14]

State standards have only an indirect bearing on actual teaching. Some states with rigorous standards have very poor academic outcomes. Nevertheless, standards reflect shared beliefs about curriculum and pedagogy, and to some extent shape them. The kinds of progressive nostrums that Kelly Rose and Kristan Crawford deplore are embedded in Illinois's standards. That includes, above all, the faith that "content" will emerge from the experience of inquiry. A teacher with deep knowledge of her field will, indeed, be able to determine the right primary or secondary texts needed to answer a well-framed "compelling question."

A teacher without that knowledge may be at sea. And of course the very premise of the C3 Framework and the Illinois standards is that the entire realm of domain-specific knowledge, whether of history or geography or economics, is a dependent variable of the mastery of domain-neutral skills such as "evaluating sources and using evidence."

It is striking to compare the implicit pedagogy of the C3 Framework or of the state standards in Illinois and many other states with that of the kind of Advanced Placement class that Kelly Rose was teaching. The College Board's AP U.S. History curriculum consists of four hundred pages of chronologically organized subject-matter knowledge and sources—followed by ten pages of "Historical Thinking Skills" that students are to master as a result of their studies. The skills in question, including "identify and explain historical developments and processes" and "analyze arguments in primary and secondary sources," are not different in nature from the kinds of skills stipulated in documents such as the C3 Framework; rather, they are understood to emerge from a deep immersion in historical material.[5] Thus, students are to learn how to compare arguments by reading the U.S. Supreme Court justices' interpretations of the Fourteenth Amendment in *Plessy v. Ferguson*. That is what Kelly Rose was doing. The authors of the AP curriculum do not regard pedagogy as the teaching of factual material in the absence of skills development; rather, they seem to have a distinctive view about the relationship between them.

Shawn Healy, who is now senior director at iCivics, one of the nation's leading providers of instructional materials in history and civics, is not disposed to defend either the standards or his own role in formulating them. He no longer subscribes to the consensus they represented; he regards the C3 Framework as a "relic" of a time when skills mastery was all the rage. The state standards document based on it, he says, "is just terrible; it borders on the ridiculous." Yet Illinois itself doesn't seem to have gotten the message. The standards were revisited in 2022—but without adding any proper nouns. The most substantive changes were political rather than pedagogical. "The marginalization of multiple groups" was added to a standard on the rights and responsibilities of citizens, while "the impact disenfranchisement has" was added to one on voting access. The state legislature has also mandated in recent years that the history curriculum include units on Black History, Asian American History, Native American History, Media Literacy, and Holocaust/Genocide Education. In 2021, Illinois also adopted "Culturally Responsive Teaching and Leading Standards," admonishing teachers to "Understand and value the notion that multiple lived experiences exist, that there is often not one 'correct' way of doing or understanding something, and that what is seen as 'correct' is most often based on our lived experiences."[6] Here was a genuine pedagogical change, but one that seemed likely to further undermine the schools' sense of intellectual authority.

The idea that successful learning entails the mastery of content-neutral skills also infuses the teaching profession. That was why Kelly Rose thought that people like her, with advanced subject-matter degrees, had become an anachronism. Almost all of her colleagues with master's degrees had received them from education schools, which focus on imparting pedagogical skills rather than substantive knowledge. Shawn Healy told me that the education school at Illinois State University, the local "teacher factory," was "just too light on content." But that approach shapes the mentality, as well as the capacities, of graduates. Prospective teachers imbibe the skills-mastery doctrine that still dominates the profession. Don Pankuch, the head of the Social Studies department at Metea Valley, was the one who first told me about the district-wide policy to discourage academic degrees. Unlike Rose, however, Pankuch accepted the underlying premise. "The most important thing is to know how to reach a student," he said. "What does it matter if you know your subject matter well if your kids aren't learning it? You often find that the best teachers are the ones who struggled with their subject in school, because they get it when the kids have trouble." That was, to say the least, a counterintuitive thought.

Long before she was head of the Democracy Network and the Illinois Civics Hub, Mary Ellen Daneels was a social studies teacher at West Chicago. In 1993 she and a colleague invented a kind of model congress in which students in a Government class spent a semester writing and voting on legislation and meeting with local and state officials who explained to them how the mechanisms of government actually worked. A decade later, Shawn Healy arrived at West Chicago as a rookie teacher and began teaching the Legislative Simulation, as it was called, with Daneels. The exercise felt completely different from the conventional classes Healy otherwise taught. "It was student-centered, and so authentic," Healy recalls. "It was the pinnacle of my teaching career. I thought, 'Why doesn't every kid in Illinois have this experience?'" He, and Daneels, and others, then set about to spread the opportunity for civic learning throughout the state.

They were hardly alone; scholars, educators, and state and national political leaders had begun to call for a national commitment to civic education. President George W. Bush convened two White House meetings on the subject; organizations such as the National Conference of State Legislatures issued calls for state-level programs of civic learning. Foundations had come to regard civic education as an important new funding area. In 2001, the Carnegie Corporation, a force for educational reform since its founding in 1911, teamed up with the Center for Information and Research on Civic Learning and Engagement at Tufts University to make a comprehensive study of the subject. Their 2003 report, "The Civic Mission of Schools," proved highly influential, including in Illinois. The authors lamented a general civic disengagement that extended from involvement with churches and community organizations to voting and learning about political issues. (Today's crisis of polarization was still far over the horizon.) Though the phenomenon had many sources, chief among them, the report stated, was a drastic decline in civic instruction in the schools that had begun in the 1960s, when "the risks of encouraging in-class political discussion began to rise." Schools also focused increasing attention on standardized tests, which typically covered skills-based subjects such as reading and math rather than history or literature.

The authors made a point of distinguishing the programs they advocated from conventional civics classes that featured "a teacher instructing students on the minutiae of federal legislative procedures or election law." The goal of reviving civic engagement was not chiefly academic. "Some of the most important outcomes of civic education," the authors noted, "are attitudes and skills." The goal of civic education, therefore, should be to produce citizens who not only are "informed and thoughtful" but also "participate in their communities," "act politically," and "have moral and civic virtues." The "promising approaches" that the report detailed were instructive. The first was "formal instruction in U.S. government, history or democracy." The others, however, were "discussion of current issues," "service learning," extracurricular activities focused on civics, "student voice in school governance," and "simulations"—that is, what West Chicago had been doing for years. Knowledge matters, but attitudes and skills mattered more.

Carnegie then funded the "Campaign for the Civic Mission of Schools" to help local organizations implement the report. In 2006, a Chicago-based organization used a very modest grant to set up the Democracy Schools Initiative to identify schools already committed to civic education and to help them expand their programs. West Chicago was one of the four original members. In 2010, Shawn Healy moved from the school to the McCormick Foundation, which funded and took over the fledgling network. Other grantees produced the "Illinois Civic Blueprint," which called for a statewide commitment to civics. At that time, Illinois was one of only ten states that did not require a civics or government class for high school graduation. In 2015, the state passed a law including that requirement, as well as a requirement for service learning, as the "Civic Mission" report had proposed, and training and professional development for teachers. The law also called for the revisions to the state's social studies standards that would be made the following year. Illinois thus committed itself to civic education at the same moment that the state was drafting its content-free standards. The emphasis in civics education on service learning, on the cultivation of dispositions such as tolerance, and the relative de-emphasis on direct instruction made it a natural fit for the pedagogy of skills mastery.[7]

The members of the Democracy Network had implemented the kinds of programs suggested by the Civic Blueprint or already had such programs in effect. Yet in my visits to those schools, I was sometimes more impressed by the unofficial and uncoordinated activities of individual teachers and students than I was by the formal civics exercises embedded in the curriculum. Indeed, one of the virtues of the modern, all-of-the-above high school is that it offers space to both students and teachers to pursue ends that interest them, including civic ones. I was struck by several episodes at Metea Valley, a giant school, like Waubonsie, encircled by parking lots and divided into subunits designated by letters A through H. In the morning I went to Orchestra practice—one of Metea Valley's seven organized bands or orchestras. When I told the teacher, Mark Liu, about my project, he was immediately seized with the subject. "Should school teach citizenship?," he asked. "Should it just be subject-matter mastery? Or should every subject also have lessons in civility, tolerance and so forth?" Before he had a chance to finish his thought, the PA system blared with Metea's own version of moral exhortation: "You belong here, you are loved here, you are accepted here. And remember—go Mustangs!"

Dr. Liu then turned to his orchestra, and I quickly understood that he knew the answer to his own question. The group had students of many different ability levels working together; parents of members were invited to bring their instruments as well. The orchestra aimed for excellence—but not only. Dr. Liu addressed the whole group. Though he wore shorts and a T-shirt, he spoke with great seriousness. "You are a family unit," he said. "If everyone takes care of each other, you can become a harmonious community." He offered one final admonition as everyone began to rehearse: "I want to remind you to take care of the person next to you. If you have conflict, it's like you're displaying your argument in front of the whole world."

After school I attended the opening meeting of Metea's Ethics Club. Don Pankuch had told me that, though it was overwhelmingly middle-class, the school's solid test scores were due mostly to its large contingent of Asian students, who make up a third of the population. Sure enough, all four of the returning veterans of last year's Ethics Club were South Asian. At least a dozen students, ethnically mixed, had come to hear about the club's activities. One of the vets explained that the goal was to discuss ethical issues, and, not incidentally, to prepare for the National High School Ethics Bowl. The year before, they had placed second in the regional finals. He asked the others to read a case study about Amazon's "gift exchange" program, which allows users to instruct Amazon to convert an unwanted gift into a gift card, which the beneficiary could use to purchase a preferred gift.

The ethical question to be considered was, Does this denigrate gift-giving? The kids batted the question around. One of the club officers asked, "Does the intent of the gift-giver outweigh the value of the gift itself?" Another suggested, "Maybe we should focus on: What is the idea of gift-giving?" This provoked yet more discussion, including from students who had initially been silent. One asked, "If the real purpose of giving a gift is to make the receiver happy, then the giver should be happy if you exchange it for something you want more." Others thought him naive. I talked to a kid in a hoodie who told me that the Romans had practiced gift-giving at feasts for the gods, which he felt "debased" the holidays. The issue, he said, wasn't moral but cultural: "it undermines social bonds." The conversation continued for more than an hour.

The Ethics Club seemed to have tapped a vein of moral seriousness that the school otherwise barely addressed. I felt the same way about Dr. Liu's impromptu homily, quiet and deeply felt in contrast to the ritual sentiments blared over the PA system. Both reflected personal choice rather than a systematic commitment by the school. Perhaps that was too much to ask of the common school in the early twenty-first century.

Nevertheless, West Chicago High School has placed its civic commitment at the core of its mission. At the time Mary Ellen Daneels had begun teaching there, the neighborhood the school drew from was largely white and middle-class. Now it is largely Hispanic and less well-to-do, though hardly impoverished; 40 percent of the students qualify for a free or reduced lunch. The teachers I talked to there worry about whether their kids will graduate, but also whether they will leave high school with a sense of what it means to be an American citizen. They worry, that is, about what used to be called "Americanization" in an earlier era when Jewish and Catholic immigrants from eastern and southern Europe poured into a largely Protestant, northern European country. A century ago, both our major institutions and the immigrants themselves embraced the model of assimilation known as "the melting pot," in which foreign identities were purged in the furnace of school, work, leisure, military service. We still look to school to furnish a civic identity to newcomers, but neither school nor all immigrants subscribe to the model of shedding inherited identities. "Americanization" is now deeply contested terrain. In *No Citizen Left Behind*, Meira Levinson, a professor at the Harvard Graduate School of Education, writes that students are now acutely conscious of, and protective toward, their racial and ethnic identities; helping them fully develop those identities will increase their civic engagement. She suggests that schools teach "code-switching" so that students can move fluidly between their ethnoracial and their civic identities.[8] The idea that schools can overcome the resistance of non-white, non-middle-class students by reinforcing their sense of identity also lies at the heart of "culturally relevant" pedagogy.

I never heard anyone at West Chicago use the language of racial particularism; I never encountered talk about culturally relevant anything. In fact, for all the explicitly identitarian language of the new standards and state mandates, I never heard any preaching of any kind from any teacher at West Chicago, Waubonsie Valley, or Metea. Their professional ethos overrode whatever personal politics they had. John Chisholm, a Government teacher at West Chicago High, told me that he always recounted for students his bitter memory of getting a C– on his first paper in a college Government class when his liberal teacher objected to his defense of the 2001 Patriot Act. That, he said, is why he and his colleagues never reveal their own party allegiance. "I tell the students that I hope they can come to know their own viewpoint and the views of others," said Chisholm. "That would put them way ahead of me at their age."

I would often find, in the coming months, that while the skies over America's schools are torn with strife, the classrooms themselves are fairly doctrine-free. Progressive teaching is not the same thing as progressive politics. West Chicago organized its social studies curriculum around what the C3 Framework had called an essential question, one that frames debate and leads to more specific "compelling" questions: "What is an effective citizen in a global community?" The compelling question for eleventh-grade U.S. History was, "What does it mean to be an American?" Though formulated in the language of progressive pedagogy, these are precisely the kind of old-fashioned questions that conservative culture warriors imagine that schools no longer pose. It was the goal of Mr. Zeman, Mr. Caltagirone, and the other history teachers to prod and cajole their largely immigrant classroom to think about citizenship and American identity; the obstacle was not ideological, but cognitive.

What was distinctive about West Chicago was a democratic ethos that struggled with the stratification imposed by the very different ability levels of its very different populations. For many years the staff declined to track students or to teach AP classes, for all that they might have enjoyed doing so. The school was so sharply divided between the large fraction of Hispanic students who did poorly and the quarter of the school that was white and Asian and largely middle class, who mostly did well, that offering honors and Advanced Placement would have separated out the student body into two schools. John Chisholm told me that the school came under pressure from the district superintendent and in 2011 began offering honors and AP classes. Now virtually all classes are tracked, with the sole exception of twelfth-grade Government, which all students at whatever level must take. The teachers insisted that the class's very premise of shared citizenship and equality would have been destroyed by hierarchy.

Candy Fikis's senior Government class *looked* different from the other classes I had attended at West Chicago, because it included a representative mix of Hispanic, white, and Asian kids. The class was designed, as the state standards required, to expose students to the founding documents and to the core aspects of American government, but also to promote debate on controversial topics and to offer an exercise in simulation. The day before I arrived, the students had held a debate on a hypothetical state law that would subject minors who had committed a serious felony to adult time. Miss Fikis had had them read the Fourth, Fifth, Sixth, Seventh, and Eighth Amendments in the Bill of Rights and explain how they bore on the question and also read an article on the issue and list pros and cons. Each had to write a statement to be used during debate. Now, like the students in Chris Wolak's class at Waubonsie, they were working on a "civic engagement self-survey." The definition of "civic" was extremely broad: doing your homework on time counted as civic responsibility. Possible goals included speaking up in class every day. If school is a student's community, then perhaps handing in work on time, like submitting to jury duty in the adult world, counts as discharging your civic obligations. Still, it's a low bar.

As it happened, I had arrived at the very outset of the legislative simulation that Mary Ellen Daneels had invented thirty years before and which had been going strong ever since. Already students in all Government classes—the whole senior class—had been assigned to learn about the distinction between liberals and conservatives and to draw up a "Political Profile" that would declare where they belonged on the political spectrum and explain why. Miss Fikis had also instructed them to describe their own views of limited government and federalism. There were 194 self-professed Democrats and 45 Republicans, with most clustering somewhat left of center. (Miss Fikis told me that when she had been a student at West Chicago, when the area was far whiter, the figures would have been exactly flipped.) Now they would begin electing officers to the model congress—legislative assistants, caucus leaders, floor leaders, a speaker of the house. Candidates would campaign and stand for election in their party. Students would vote for the issues that most concerned them. Groups consisting of five students would choose one of those issues. Each member would then assume a specific responsibility—research, polling, lobbying, and the like.

Once students had written and advocated for their bills, legislative committees consisting of about twenty students would convene in November to decide whether or not to report them out for consideration by the full house. In early December, the house would convene to deliberate and vote. I promised to return then. West Chicago, and the other schools I had visited, seemed unable to address or even to fully acknowledge the academic shortcomings that undermined their professed civic goals. Yet precisely because civic education was not an academic domain but rather a kind of hybrid of knowledge and practice, the Legislative Simulation might provide a different kind of answer to the problem of teaching civics.

2

How History Became Social Studies, and Meat Became Meatloaf

In 1892, in the wake of a series of muckraking articles that exposed a shady subculture of machine politicians handing out teaching jobs to loyal hacks, a new professional organization called the National Education Association convened a group of eminent scholars to suggest reforms to the public school curriculum. The Committee of Ten, as the group came to be known, was mandated to select the most important academic subjects and propose the best methods of instruction and assessment, the proper age at which to begin, and the ideal frequency of instruction.[1] This august body, headed by Harvard president Charles Eliot, the most celebrated educator of the day, in turn appointed subcommittees for each of the nine selected subjects. The group selected to oversee "American History, Civil Government and Political Economy" included Woodrow Wilson, then a professor of government at Princeton, as well as other scholars and educators; the renowned historian Frederick Jackson Turner served as a consultant.

At the time, the typical high school taught English and American history, while somewhat less than half taught classical history, and a smaller fraction taught European history or a sort of mishmash called "General History."[2] Late-nineteenth-century primers offered a highly romanticized version of the past: "myths and legends of ancient Greece, heroes of the American Revolution, the discovery of the New World, and other stories designed to inspire patriotism and moral certitude," as a modern historian sardonically puts it.[3] In the widely used McGuffey readers, the Founders were "assigned the stature of biblical heroes" while "the events of American history were portrayed as developments in a holy design."[4] Children who made it as far as high school were thus learning American history and government, but often from unqualified teachers who were using academically dubious material.

The history subcommittee unexceptionally concluded that students of the public schools didn't know enough history and should be studying it in a more coherent fashion. In its final report, the subcommittee recommended that history instruction begin in fifth grade with biography and mythology, progress to American history and "civil government," then to classical, French, English, and, finally, American history again before a final intensive study of one period or topic in twelfth grade. What is more surprising is the report's democratic spirit, for at a time when less than 10 percent of Americans graduated from high school, these mandarins insisted that all American students, and not just the tiny fraction that were college-bound, both could master such subjects and needed to do so to become effective citizens.

No less important, these solons openly and even mockingly criticized the joylessness of the typical course of study. "Learning disconnected facts," they wrote in their final report, "as is often true of history textbooks, is as useless as recalling what one has had for dinner for the last thirty years." Recitation by rote from texts, they declared, should give way to discussion. Students in high school should be given the chance to read outside reference books and to bring in examples of literature. And in the new subject of "civil government" they recommended a program of study that included forms of learning altogether independent from texts and even classrooms—debates and mock town meetings, visits to local courts and municipal government.[5]

The impaneling of the Committee of Ten was itself a sign that a new age was dawning in American public schools. New Englanders had first established and promulgated public schools in order to instill Protestant virtue in students. Bible study formed a central part of the curriculum.

That had begun to change with reformers such as Horace Mann, a devout Christian who nevertheless believed that scripture had little or no place in the classroom. By the late nineteenth century, forty-one of the nation's forty-six states had passed laws prohibiting sectarian instruction in public schools. It was this more secular spirit that encouraged scholars to engage in large-scale intellectual reform. But schools continued to be understood as the national hatchery of personal and civic virtue. The state of Washington's 1897 law banning religious teaching was typical in this regard. "It shall be the duty of all teachers," the statute read, "to endeavor to impress on the minds of their pupils the principles of morality, truth, justice, temperance, humanity and patriotism. . . . and to train them to the true comprehension of the rights, duties and dignities of American citizens."[6]

The movement for academic reform gathered pace. In 1897, another new organization, the American Historical Association, appointed its own group, known as the Committee of Seven, to study the teaching of history in the public schools. This equally eminent body included Albert Bushnell Hart, Harvard's one-man American History department, and Herbert Baxter Adams, a professor at Johns Hopkins who had been among the founders of the AHA. The Committee of Seven went about its work much more systematically than the NEA group had done, sending out questionnaires to three hundred representative high schools. The results left its members more optimistic about the state of affairs than the Committee of Ten had been. Whether because of the effect of the earlier report or, more likely, because of the more careful survey, they found that three-quarters of respondents required at least four hundred classroom hours of history—the equivalent of two full years. Half said that all of their teachers had specialized in the subject. They found as well that "the old rote system"—which the Committee of Ten had deplored—"is going by the board."[7]

Apparently recognizing that readers might not share their conviction that the study of history was central to the educational experience, the authors of the Committee of Seven's report devoted a chapter to "The Value of History." The student who had learned "to look at matters historically," they wrote, "has some mental equipment for the comprehension of the political and social problems that will confront him in every day life." Studying civil government—that is, current institutions—would not be enough; the student "should know of nations that have risen and fallen; he should see tyranny, vulgarity, greed, benevolence, patriotism, self-sacrifice, brought out in the lives and works of men." This almost constituted a paraphrase of Jefferson's dictum that students should learn to recognize "ambition in all its shapes." The scholars added that teaching history effectively would jolt young people out of their complacency: "They should be led to see that society is in movement, that what one sees about him is not the eternal but the transient." Finally, the study of history helps students see the relation between cause and effect, helps them learn how to systematically arrange facts, instills "the scientific habit of mind and thought," and allows the pupil to acquire "a knowledge of facts that is to him a source of pleasure and gratification in his after life."[8] It is not easy to improve on this list of moral, civic, cognitive, and cultural virtues of the study of history.

The Committee of Seven then offered an early version of what we would call "history standards." The committee's report proposed a four-year chronological program of study, proceeding from ancient to medieval and modern to English to American history, and stipulated what topics most merited study within each domain. Its authors suggested, just as the Committee of Ten had, that teachers supplement a textbook with vivid material drawn from the school library, including letters, journals, and travel accounts. They also proposed that students visit museums and historical monuments and study lithographs and pictures as well as books. The authors were men (and one woman) who had devoted their lives to history, knew its joys, and wanted to ensure that children had the opportunity to feel something of that spark. The teacher, they wrote, "needs to have a living sympathy with the tale he tells. . . . He must have had his own imagination fired and his enthusiasm kindled."[9] The Committee of Seven report proved highly influential. Subsequent studies found that many schools had copied almost verbatim the proposals made by the committee and by a similar report on the teaching of history in the elementary schools.

The reports of 1892 and 1897 had been shaped by the new spirit of intellectual reform within the confines of a traditional curriculum. But by the first years of the new century, the immense convulsions of industrial life had drastically altered both the schools and the world of pedagogical thinking. Progressivism, which today we think of chiefly as the political effort spearheaded by Teddy Roosevelt and others, was in fact a movement of moral, cultural, and educational renewal that sought, above all, to improve the health and well-being of ordinary Americans, and especially of the millions of immigrants flooding into the nation's cities. The wish to create healthier conditions of individual development made education a central progressive concern. The new generation of reformers shared the horror of enlightened educators at the deadening routine that dominated so much of school life, but they offered a far more systematic critique that traced the failure of schools to the reactionary spirit of the society at large.

The prophet of educational progressivism was the philosopher John Dewey. The essence of life, Dewey wrote in his 1898 *Democracy and Education*, was growth; the child was not a box to be filled with knowledge but a developing organism whose intrinsic desire to learn had to be encouraged. "Education is not an affair of telling and being told," Dewey wrote, "but an active and constructive process." Progressives were animated by a deeply Rousseauean faith in the natural capacities of the child and thus by a corresponding fear of the corrosive effect of social institutions, very much including schools. G. Stanley Hall, a psychologist at Johns Hopkins and a mentor of the young Dewey, wrote that the child's guardians "should strive above all to keep out of nature's way. . . . They should feel profoundly that childhood, as it comes fresh from the hands of God, is not corrupt, but illustrates the survival of the most consummate thing in the world . . . the body and soul of the growing child."[10]

Dewey never questioned that children needed to be guided by institutions, including school, but he took a very dim view of the routines and structure of conventional schooling. Though he would later change his views, the young Dewey regarded the whole traditional corpus of school learning—the very subject of the Committees of Ten and Seven—as a kind of dead weight anchoring the classroom and the child to the past. A backward-looking curriculum destroyed the vital link between knowledge and actual life. Traditional subject-matter pedagogy constituted "a building into the mind from without" rather than a development from within. The good teacher, by contrast, identifies the student's interest—a key Deweyan word—and adapts the material to it.[11]

The idea that the school might serve as an instrument of social change, rather than as a means to transmit the wisdom and values of the past, appealed deeply to the idealistic, forward-looking men and women who had chosen a career as teachers. At the same time, larger changes in society almost impelled the schools into such a role. The arrival of twenty million newcomers from eastern and southern Europe between 1883 and 1920 had filled the schools of America's great cities with children who had no prior experience of American life. While nineteenth-century educators had taught pupils the rudiments of "civil government," school officials now used a new term—"civics"—to describe the more all-encompassing ambition to introduce foreigners to the meaning of American citizenship. Society now demanded that schools serve as the forge on which great masses of new Americans would be hammered out—a very different role from the more scholarly one that Woodrow Wilson or Albert Bushnell Hart had envisioned.

In 1915, the U.S. Bureau of Education issued a pamphlet titled "The Teaching of Community Civics." Rather than beginning by circumscribing a field of study, as the Committee of Seven had done with history, the (unnamed) author or authors began by asking, "Who is the good citizen?" The answer: the person who cares about the welfare of his or her community. In the nineteenth century this might have entailed little more than being a good neighbor; in a rapidly urbanizing and industrializing nation, however, the good citizen had to learn about available "social agencies," a term that included both physical resources such as schools and parks and the burgeoning world of government bodies and programs such as pure-food laws that the progressives had brought into being. Civic education ultimately meant helping the child understand how he fit into his local, regional, and national community and how those communities served the public good. That education included—for the older students—familiar academic subjects such as history and economics, but also learning about the world around you, whether the postman and the policeman or the jobs people did or the "social agencies" and their operation.[12]

The field to which civics belonged was something new called "social studies." In 1912, the NEA had established a Committee on Social Studies in order to firmly establish this new field in the school curriculum. The term was used to refer collectively to the social sciences, including both established fields such as economics, geography, government, and of course history, as well as relatively new fields of study such as psychology and anthropology. In some schools, social studies was taught as an amalgam blending these fields together—into a meaningless "stew," critics charged. In others, each was treated as a separate subject. In all cases, however, social studies was understood as the study of "problems"—the social and economic and cultural problems that modern industrial society presented to citizens. Social studies was interested in the past insofar as it threw light on the present. Its goal was to clarify the student's own world. "Community civics" was thus central to this new field.

In 1916, the NEA's Commission on the Reorganization of Secondary Education published a "Report of the Committee on Social Studies." What united the various topics of this new field, the authors explained, was that all related "directly to the organization and development of human society, and to man as a member of social groups." Their ultimate goal was "the cultivation of good citizenship." The report, which was compiled by educational professionals rather than by scholars, struck a far more practical and pragmatic note than the Committee of Seven had. While the Committee of Seven had not even included patriotism in its long list of the virtues of the study of history, here the authors wrote bluntly that students learned history "to develop a vivid concept of American nationality, a strong and intelligent patriotism, and a keen sense of the responsibility of every citizen for national efficiency." The value of the past was instrumental. "Children live in the present and not in the past," the authors wrote—as if adults read history because *they* lived in the past. History mattered insofar as it touched on "the present life interests of the pupil."[13]

In the language and thinking of the report, a soaring and distinctively Deweyan idealism mingled strangely with the industrial-age spirit of the assembly line. The authors repeatedly cited Dewey himself to the effect that school must adapt itself to the child and his interests rather than demanding that the child adapt to the demands and routines of school. They proposed an entirely new twelfth-grade class that they called "Problems of Democracy" in which the student would bring to bear all she had learned about the social studies in order to make sense of the modern condition. Yet Dewey abhorred the language of "national efficiency" with which the report was rife. Dewey understood education as a lifelong process of growth and self-creation, while the authors treated schools as a kind of factory for the production of loyal, intelligent citizens. A good citizen was not one endowed with the judgment to make wise choices but rather "the thoroughly efficient member" of the collective body known as society.

Tellingly, the Committee on Social Studies recommended a differentiated curriculum in which only the college-bound would pursue academic subjects through graduation, while others would take more explicitly vocational and practical classes. The mandarins of the Committees of Seven and Ten appeared to have more faith in the average citizen than did the progressive educators of the Committee on Social Studies. Put otherwise, the demands of national efficiency meant that students needed to be prepared for the place they would occupy in an increasingly complex and differentiated economy. The pragmatic and anti-intellectual spirit of the report can hardly be understood without taking into account the colossal changes overtaking the schools. In 1910, the national high school graduation still stood at about 10 percent; by the mid-1930s, it had reached 50 percent.[14] In a single generation, schools had been transformed into giant factories.

Though the authors urged schools to teach history every year in middle and high school, the lasting legacy of the report was to formalize social studies and incorporate history within it, and thus treat chronological study as an indirect, and often ineffective, means of illuminating the problems of the present. Students were to learn civics before history so that they could understand why history was worth learning at all. The authors shared Dewey's skepticism of the formal curriculum, describing at length the program of an elementary and middle school in

Missouri that dispensed with subject-matter domains in favor of a curriculum of "problems." Sixth-graders might spend eight weeks learning about "transportation" and then return to a study of the history of transportation the following year. As it was torn between idealistic aspiration and the demands of social efficiency, so the report seemed unable to resolve the tension between mastering a corpus of knowledge and deferring to the student's interests.

John Dewey began having second thoughts almost as soon as literal-minded teachers began offering what they regarded as progressive pedagogy. "It is the danger of the 'new education,'" he wrote in 1902, "that it regards the child's present power and interests as something finally significant in themselves" rather than as material upon which the wise teacher can build.[15] Toward the end of his life, in a 1938 lecture titled "Experience and Education," Dewey first reaffirmed the principles that had guided his thought from the outset, criticizing traditional education as a breeding ground for "docility" and asserting that "there is an intimate and necessary relation between the processes of actual experience"—the child's lived experience—"and education." But he then complained that progressive education had reacted to the traditionalists' unquestioning acceptance of the wisdom of the past by dismissing the past altogether. In order to find the proper balance, he wrote, we must ask, "how shall the young become acquainted with the past in such a way that the acquaintance is a potential agent in appreciation of the living present?"[16] Dewey wanted children to reach for the stars, but the educators of the day wanted them to be fitted for their station.

Progressivism had, in fact, taken the school world by storm. By the 1930s, Deweyan thinking had attained a virtually consensual status in education schools, in the work of leading scholars, and among major funding organizations such as the Carnegie Foundation. Professional educators were equally committed to the social studies. Yet by most accounts, schoolrooms largely felt as they had a generation or two earlier—neither child-centered nor fired with the "living sympathy" for the subject that the Committee of Seven had regarded as the prerequisite for effective teaching. Though some acolytes had taken Dewey's theories to extremes the philosopher himself had never imagined, most

American schools had dressed up the traditional classroom with a few progressive flourishes. Here was an early illustration of a general principle: education theory is highly ideological, and thus subject to drastic change, while schools themselves are driven by pragmatic calculations that make them resistant to change. Schools change much more slowly than school doctrine does.[17]

The early- and mid-twentieth century was, by most accounts, the high point of civic education. Starting in 1917, the year after the NEA report, virtually all states passed laws requiring civic education. In the burst of patriotism that followed the Allied victory in World War I, states also began to require instruction in the Constitution; by 1931, forty-three of the forty-eight states had done so.[18] Civics classes modeled on the NEA recommendations became widespread and were generally taught in eighth or ninth grade; in their senior year, students typically took either a class in government, which entailed the study of political institutions and Constitutional principles, or Problems of Democracy, the class proposed in the NEA report.[19]

But schools were only the most ubiquitous of the many institutions that taught Americans about their history and government. In 1924, the original copies of the Constitution and the Declaration of Independence were removed from State Department vaults and put on exhibition at the Library of Congress. Six years later, the god-like faces of the presidents began to appear on Mount Rushmore–the "Shrine of Democracy," as supporters called it. In their daily lives, Americans became accustomed to flag-raising celebrations, the Pledge of Allegiance, and Memorial Day commemorations (and in the South, to saccharine recollections of The Lost Cause and the old plantation culture). Organizations with a specifically civic or democratic sense of purpose blossomed. These included patriotic advocacy groups such as the American Legion, good-government organizations such as the League of Women Voters, and youth bodies such as the Boy Scouts and Girl Scouts. And local newspapers abounded. Household penetration of newspapers would peak in

1950 at 124 percent, meaning that the average household received more than one newspaper. Schools prepared children for life, but virtually every other institution and organization shaped the graduates according to the same principles.

American democracy at midcentury looked invincible and unshakable; yet this was also the first moment when cultural mandarins began to publicly worry that Americans knew too little of their own history. The entry into World War II gave impetus to those fears. In 1942, the celebrated historian Allan Nevins took to the *New York Times* to complain that students arrived in college woefully ignorant of history. Nevins complained that only twenty-six states required students to take classes in American history. In much of the country, he observed, "a little American history is interjected into a course of 'social studies.'" Students were "given a few days to build model wigwams and log cabins" rather than a rigorous course of chronological study. This may be the earliest known attack on the replacement of chronological history by thematic social studies.

The typical student, Nevins wrote, had heard of the Stamp Act, but not the Molasses Act; Harriet Beecher Stowe, but not Hinton R. Helper.[20] It is possible that in 1942, Helper, a Southern abolitionist writer, was far better known than he is today, but Nevins's dudgeon at this lacuna of historical knowledge may have struck even readers of his own day as hyperbolic. To our own ears the complaint may imply preposterously high expectations. Nevertheless, the following year the *Times* commissioned Nevins and a colleague to conduct a survey of seven thousand college freshmen, which found that few could name prominent businessmen, labor officials, or railroad barons. The *Times* disclosed to presumably shocked readers that most students didn't know that the Homestead Act had been passed in 1882 or that beforehand federal land had been sold for $1.25 an acre.[21]

Some of Nevins's colleagues dismissed him as a reactionary. Historian William B. Heseltine lampooned Nevins's campaign as "the Committee to Defend America by Memorizing the Presidents."[22] Nevertheless, the American Historical Association agreed to undertake a national survey of history teaching. That survey, released in 1944, concluded that Nevins had been wrong. "The evidence is overwhelming," the report stated, "that American history is taught in the vast majority of schools in three cycles"—typically the fifth, eighth, and eleventh grades. The authors of the report found that while in 1899, only 45 percent of surveyed high schools taught American history, the figure had reached 95 percent by 1916 and had stayed there since then. Social studies, though a convenient scapegoat, was not guilty as charged. The subject was typically being taught not as a farrago, as Nevins and the other critics alleged, but as separate classes in geography, economics, and civics; and while more class time was being devoted to the subject, history continued to be taught within the various social sciences.[23]

The authors did something that no one appears to have attempted before: they administered a history test. The test, consisting of sixty-five multiple-choice questions, was given to 1,322 representative high school students and to social studies teachers, soldiers, Americans who appeared in *Who's Who*, and representative adults. The students averaged twenty-two correct answers while their teachers had forty-five. The report concluded that "if knowing American history means knowing facts, dates and events," the answer was no; but if it meant "understanding of trends and movements, appreciation of past events and persons," the answer was yes. That might seem like a generous conclusion, but the questions had been set at a Nevins-like level of difficulty. One question so relatively easy that a majority of students got the right answer was: "At the close of the Spanish-American War, American opposition to the annexation of the Philippine Islands was based chiefly on which of these?" The available answers were (A) fear of antagonizing Japan, (B) the belief that colonial possessions were out of keeping with democratic values, (C) fear of competition with the domestic sugar industry, and (D) the cost in lives and money of subjugating the islands. (The right answer was B.) One of the tougher questions asked, "Which of these best accounts for the sharp decline in the market price of grain during the second quarter of the nineteenth century?" Students at midcentury really did seem to have more historical knowledge than Professor Nevins thought, even if less than he wished.

Those administering the survey did, however, discover something dismaying: students who had taken a history class did only slightly better than those who hadn't, and high-achieving students did only slightly better than average ones. The authors concluded that factual knowledge doesn't readily stick because "the human being learns slowly and forgets quickly." Put otherwise, students seem to lose their grasp of "facts, dates, and events" while retaining a broader, if vaguer, understanding of "trends and movements." The study also found that the representative adult cohort had done significantly better than any group of students. Americans were learning their history not just from school but from newspapers, the radio, movies, novels, and elsewhere. That is, the rich civic culture of midcentury America served as an ongoing form of education in history and government.

Nevins's critique reemerged in the 1950s, a period notorious for mocking thinkers as "eggheads" or "longhairs." Now, for the first time, scholars openly aligned themselves against a pervasive progressive ethos that deprecated the acquisition of knowledge. The critics included some of the nation's best-known educators: Robert Maynard Hutchins, president and chancellor of the University of Chicago, as well as historians Albert Lynd and Arthur Bestor. Lynd, who gained actual experience of his subject as a member of his local school board, identified a relatively new problem: the hegemony of professional education schools over the credentialing and the conduct of teachers. The "new pedagogy," Lynd wrote, was based on skills and social utility rather than knowledge; the education schools who supplied teachers' formal credentials were training them through innumerable courses in pedagogy, which struck Lynd as "unadulterated pap," rather than subject-matter expertise.[24]

Bestor, a more eminent figure, wrote a highly influential jeremiad titled *Educational Wastelands*. Bestor shared Lynd's disgust with the stranglehold of the education profession, recalling a young scholar he knew who had been warned off a career in the schools by the professor of education in charge of assigning teachers because her excellent grades proved that she loved literature too much. "We don't teach subject-matter," her Deweyan professor had said; "we teach children." Bestor did not blame Dewey, a great philosopher with the highest aspirations for children, but rather a kind of debased and anti-intellectual version of progressivism.

The reductio ad absurdum of this bastard Deweyanism, Bestor wrote, was the new craze for programs in "Life Adjustment," whose advocates—including in the exalted progressive precincts of Teachers College at Columbia University—argued that the many students not destined for college should instead focus their efforts on "the basic problems and situations of everyday living in our democracy." This was essentially what the 1916 NEA report had proposed. Bestor took a very different view of the demands of democracy. He insisted, as the Committees of Seven and Ten had, that in a democracy every student should have a liberal education, by which he meant "the deliberate cultivation of the power to think." Bestor wrote that he didn't know whether education was better or worse than it used to be—only that it was not nearly as good as it needed to be.[25]

Bestor blamed social studies; but social studies almost seems to have become shorthand for the vocationalization of schools, the proliferation of a kind of folk-Deweyan pedagogy, the growing power of the ed school. In the 1950s, social studies did begin to supplant history, but it did so as part of a larger movement away from academic courses and toward a more vocational and practical curriculum—a movement that had begun a generation earlier when schools had begun preparing all students, rather than a chosen few, for high school graduation. In 1910, 83 percent of high school students took a foreign language; by 1955, the figure had dropped to 20 percent. The differentiation first advocated in the NEA report had given rise to the practice of "tracking" students into either academic or nonacademic programs. While Dewey's high ideals had not been able to survive the transition to mass education, what one education historian calls "administrative progressivism"—the ethos of "social efficiency" that led to students being sorted according to their projected future role in society—had come to govern the schools. "The administrative progressives," this scholar concludes, "were responsible for turning the meat of academic subjects into meatloaf."[26]

The 1960s hit the stodgy world of public schooling like a torpedo amidships. The seigneurial posture of figures such as Bestor and Hutchins, their faith in "the best that is thought and said," came to seem risible to radical critics who regarded school as the chief tool of oppression of an intolerant, paternalistic society. Both the call for academic rigor and the uplifting language of civic education disappeared almost entirely from critiques of schooling. Some of the polemical works of the time, including *Death at an Early Age,* Jonathan Kozol's deeply moving account of the brutality and casual racism of the Boston public schools, influenced public opinion as effectively as anything that had been written about education over the previous generation.[27] These exposés forced readers to confront the failure of inner-city public schools and the vacuity of schooling in general. But unlike Dewey and the earlier progressives, many of these critics didn't really believe in school at all, and thus dismissed the central role of public education in fortifying democracy. Both Jonathan Holt, author of *How Children Learn*, and Ivan Ilich, author of *Deschooling Society*, insisted that children learn best when guided by their own interests rather than the demands of adults in school, and thus advocated returning the child to the home environment.

In the most thoughtful and nuanced of these broadsides, *Crisis in the Classroom,* Charles Silberman vividly evoked the tyranny of the lesson plan, the period, the clock, and the hall pass, and raged against the low expectations that doomed ghetto youth to failure. It need not be so, Silberman argued: "public school *can* be organized to facilitate joy in learning and esthetic expression and to develop character." Silberman did not accept that schools had to choose between "rigor" and "joy." Education "can be simultaneously child-centered and subject- or knowledge-centered," he wrote. The schools Silberman admired gave students great freedom in shaping their own course of study while also, or so he claimed, making serious intellectual demands.[28] The tenor of the educational reform of the sixties—indeed, of the politics of the time in general—was profoundly democratic but also deeply hostile to patriotism in any form. So systematically unjust a society had little call on the loyalty of citizens.

Schools reacted; schools *always* react to changes in their social and intellectual environment, even if they almost always do so in ways that dilute or corrupt the new doctrines they seek to incorporate. There was a mania for Silberman-style "open schools" where students planned their own course of study and teachers served as advisors. At Scarsdale High School, which I attended from 1968 to 1972, the kids who wanted to smoke dope and think deep thoughts went to our own open school in a separate annex and did no one knew what. The rest of us laughed at the endless invocation of "relevance" the way Arthur Bestor said that he and his high school friends had mocked "social studies" half a century before. In the summer after my freshman year, the *New York Times* scandalized readers with a front-page article about Scarsdale's summer school class in guerrilla warfare, including a mock skirmish in the forest, taught by our deeply right-on young Social Studies teacher. The program's administration explained that the class was "totally relevant to today's world."[29] Civic education, at the height of the Vietnam War, circa 1970, was revolutionary.

Just as the "Reconstructionists" of the 1930s had taught students to be skeptical of the blandly patriotic accounts in traditional textbooks, so practitioners of what was known as "the new Social Studies" called for "inquiry-based learning" as well as a "structural" approach to the major disciplines that would call conventional narratives into question. But the new Social Studies, like classes in guerrilla warfare, proved to be a flash in the pan. One advocate noted that the structural focus required a level of subject-matter mastery that few teachers attained.[30] It proved far easier for schools to adapt to the clamor for relevance than to actually transform the environment of learning as critics such as Silberman called on them to do. Elective courses catering to student interest exploded. One study of a big California high school found that students were taking classes in "Girl Talk," "What's Happening?" and "Man To Man." The school was giving class credit for yearbook, band, glee club.[31] Instead of asking more of themselves, schools asked less of children. Tracking increased drastically; the fraction of students in the "general" rather than the academic track increased from 12 percent in the late sixties to 42 percent a decade later.[32] The net effect of the 1960s reforms was not to make learning more joyous, but to make it easier.

In 1984, John Goodlad, a leading scholar of education, published *A Place Called School*, the results of a massive study of schools by a team of academics. Goodlad concluded that schools remained every bit as dreary and as mindless as Silberman had found them fifteen years before. Despite a rhetorical commitment to "creativity" and individual instruction, in the average classroom teachers meted out facts and students pretended to listen. Students perfected an attitude that Goodlad called "affective neutrality," equally devoid of hostility and of enthusiasm. What students actually enjoyed were taking field trips, building things, interviewing people; what they got was text-based learning. "For most students," Goodlad concluded, "academic learning is too abstract." Students "need to smell and touch what they read and write about." The subjects they reported enjoying most were gym and art; their least favorite subject was Social Studies. Teachers talked about encouraging inquiry and reasoning, he observed. "But something strange seems to have happened to them on their way to the classroom. The topics of study become removed from their intrinsically human character, reduced to the dates and places readers will recall memorizing for tests." Like Silberman, Goodlad concluded that school must become more experiential, more humane, and more respectful of the capacity of young people to direct their own lives.

The long-standing fear that American schools had lost their sense of purpose, and that children were emerging from high school half-educated, had been almost entirely anecdotal; critics such as Bestor and Lynd had cited inane ed school course catalogs and disgruntled business leaders as proof of the low estate. As teaching in America was locally determined, so, too, was testing. But the growing popularity, starting in the 1950s, of the SAT tests and of the College Board's subject-specific Achievement Tests began to provide both a form of absolute measurement of academic performance and a baseline from which to measure growth or regression. The establishment in 1969 of the National Assessment of Education Progress, administered annually to students in the fourth, eighth, and twelfth grades, offered a far more fine-grained assay of school learning in the major subject areas. Critics interpreted the data according to their preconceptions: progressive critics found the schools empty and joyless, while a new generation of more conservative thinkers concluded that the schools had lost their commitment to rigor.

The traditionalist concerns were fused into a kind of nuclear warhead in "A Nation at Risk," a 1983 report commissioned by President Ronald Reagan's secretary of education. In an updated version of the old argument from "national efficiency," the authors luridly declared that "if an unfriendly foreign power had attempted to impose on America the mediocre educational performance that exists today, we might well have viewed it as an act of war."[33] This almost hysterical national security framing had the unfortunate effect of obscuring the real evidence of failure that the report furnished and encouraging progressive critics to view the entire exercise as an assault on humanistic ideals. The authors reported that SAT scores had fallen forty to fifty points from 1963 to 1980 (though the pool of test-takers had widened at the same time). Performance on Achievement Tests had tumbled since the mid-1950s. American students were falling behind on international comparisons. The causes were not hard to find: American students took less rigorous courses, and did far less homework, than students abroad; a "cafeteria-style curriculum" allowed students to choose entertaining rather than difficult courses; many teachers had been drawn from the bottom of graduating classes and trained in "educational methods" rather than subject-matter knowledge. Now it seemed that the era whose anti-intellectualism Arthur Bestor and others had lamented had in fact been America's Athenian age; what had counted as lax then constituted rigor a generation later.

The NAEP exam supplied alarming news about subject-matter ignorance. In *What Do Our 17-Year-Olds Know?*, Diane Ravitch and Chester Finn, then an official in Reagan's Department of Education, closely scrutinized the results of the 1985 NAEP survey of knowledge of history and literature. They found that only one-third of students could place the Civil War between 1850 and 1900 or could explain what the Emancipation Proclamation did. Only 21.4 percent knew what Reconstruction was. No more than 40 percent could identify the Renaissance, the Reformation, or the Magna Carta. Ravitch and Finn pronounced the results "shameful."[34] Allan Nevins may have set impossible standards in 1942, but the students of his day looked like wizards in comparison with this cohort. It was all but unimaginable that the students of 1980 could have correctly answered a third of the questions on the 1944 history exam. How many would even have known what the Spanish-American War was? Nor could one conclude that these students displayed an "understanding of trends and movements"—unless you believed, as some progressives seemed to do, that historical understanding had nothing at all to do with historical knowledge.

Yet 78 percent of the cohort in the NAEP study were taking a U.S. History class at the time of the test. Perhaps that simply proved, as the authors of the 1944 study had argued, that factual knowledge did not stick. But that commonsense answer had fallen out of what was becoming an increasingly polarized debate. For Goodlad, Silberman, and other progressive critics, the poor outcome only proved that Social Studies had become a dead zone of recitation and memorization. Traditionalists did not dispute the point. Ravitch and Finn opposed this lifeless form of pedagogy just as Woodrow Wilson and his colleagues had a century earlier, warning against a tedious regimen of "disconnected facts." But their answer was not more field trips and less reading, more relevant electives and fewer Founders and Framers. Instead, they admonished schools to make history come alive through the reading of journals, biographies, and autobiography. They also recommended that students take history starting in the upper elementary grades, and that their teachers be educated in the subject. The answer, in short, lay in a rich and rewarding immersion in the material of history.

Almost a century had passed since the Committee of Ten had recommended that all students—that is, all future citizens—receive just such an immersive education. They had believed, as the Founders had and then Horace Mann after them, that good citizenship required a solid understanding of American history and government. Perhaps that goal had never been fully achieved; in any case, it had receded over time. By the 1980s, the tide was running the other way: a mastery of subject matter had come to be associated with rote memorization and lifeless texts. "Rigor" had come to be seen as a euphemism for a call to arms to win the global education contest. Yet all this came at a time when Americans had not learned to fear and hate members of the other political party or to pry apart the restraints that hold a liberal democracy together. How much more dangerous would the national ignorance become in a more fragile time!

3

Beautiful Content

THE MODEL OF THE CLASSICAL SCHOOL

I arrived at Founders Classical Academy of Lewisville, Texas, on September 11, 2023. In Texas (though not in New York, where the catastrophe occurred), 9/11 is designated Patriot Day and is observed in schools with commemoration and oratory. Bewilderingly, or at least anachronistically, I was greeted by cheering cowgirls with pom poms and ten-gallon hats. I later learned that they had been deployed as part of an annual fund-raiser; Founders is a charter school that depends on donations to supplement the funds that, like all public schools, it receives from the state. I parked my car and found my way to the gym of the lower school, where the K–5 kids gather every morning. Usually the students from one grade recite a poem they've memorized. Today, for Patriot Day, the fourth-graders recited the Preamble to the Constitution: "We the people of the United States . . ." all the way down to ". . . ordain and establish this Constitution for the United States of America." I was sitting on the bleachers with the third-graders, and we all applauded. Then the kids formed up by grades and, on the way out to begin the day, shook hands with their teachers and the school's headmaster, Jason Caros.

Established in 2012, Founders is the oldest of a network of twenty-three "classical" schools, chiefly in Texas and Arkansas. The Founders network is one constellation in an expanding galaxy of about 275 classical charter schools; if you add in private Catholic and Protestant schools that call themselves "classical," about 250,000 students now attend such schools. If you live anywhere outside the Sunbelt, you may never have heard of this movement, though it is one of the fastest-growing school reforms in the country. Classical education is largely a red-state phenomenon. To liberal critics, these schools represent the thin edge of the wedge of cultural warfare. One report describes the terms "classical" and "traditional" as "dog whistles to attract conservative families with Christian nationalist identities anxious to place their children in schools that reflect early and mid-20th century values, pedagogy, and curriculum."[1] Caros and his staff would repudiate the "Christian nationalism" allegation while arguing that there is much to be said for those traditional values, pedagogy, and curriculum.

A fifty-five-year-old former social studies teacher deeply grounded in classical learning, Caros regularly composes erudite bulletins for the school's parents. A month earlier, just before the start of the school year, he had used the school's crest as a means of explicating its values. The crest featured a bald eagle protected by a shield with red and white stripes and stars on a blue field; one talon clutched three arrows, the other a key. The eagle was, of course, the symbol of America, and thus imbued with both patriotism and the sacred principle of liberty. The arrows, Caros wrote, "signify the universals upon which everything we do is rooted—truth, goodness, and beauty." The key "represents the acquisition of wisdom." At the base was the school's motto: *Scientia Virtus et Libertas*, or "Knowledge, Virtue, and Liberty." The motto expressed a premise dear to the Founding Fathers. As Caros put it: "If we want to maintain our individual liberties, our societal freedoms and flourish as a people, we must have a well-educated and virtuous citizenry."

You can tell a lot about a school from design choices, both intentional and inadvertent. After the morning meeting had ended, I followed Caros to the lower-school building, which, like Founders' middle- and high-school buildings, is a strictly functional brick rectangle. The interior was equally plain. Most elementary schools are filled with adorable pictures drawn by the kids, taped-up samples of student work, bright colors, and encouraging slogans. At Founders, one hallway had posters of the Constitution, the Declaration of Independence, and Mount Rushmore—and nothing else; another had the Founding Fathers; a third featured Cleopatra and other images of ancient Egypt. We walked past a class of third-graders who were standing up, reciting a poem. I noticed that all the desks were facing forward. "That's intentional," Caros said. "In a lot of public schools, the kids are in a circle or they're facing each other. Our view is that children should be facing the teacher. The goal is instruction, not socialization." The risers of the high school's main staircase bear the names of the great texts that students will read, more or less in ascending chronological order: *The Iliad* of Homer, Herodotus's *Histories*, Sophocles's *Antigone*, Plato's *The Republic*, and on up to *Paradise Lost*, *A Tale of Two Cities*, *Two Treatises of Government*.

Very few public schools in America, and mostly those in small towns, run from kindergarten through twelfth grade. Classical schools are the exception. Their ethos of truth, goodness, and beauty requires a steady cultivation of childrens' habits, values, and capacities from an early age. Caros and his faculty are engaged in what they regard as a countercultural project, working against the grain of a progressive, utilitarian culture that they believe offers too little to children and demands too little of them. Students shaped by that culture through the age of fourteen would bridle at Founders' strictures and might not be able to meet its expectations. Those expectations, in turn, are embedded in an explicit, and traditional, curriculum.

Early grades at Founders feature a good deal of repetition and recitation. The children were working on phonics the morning I arrived in Arianna King's second-grade class. The word of the day was "ninth." King said the word three times, slowly. She pronounced each sound, and asked the children to repeat it together. Phonics instruction, which begins by breaking down words to their constituent sounds, involves far more tedious repetition than the "whole language" or "balanced literacy" pedagogies that took the world of schooling by storm a generation ago, when "joy" was the great watchword; but phonics has been found to be far more effective for many children who do not take naturally to reading. Yet this second-grade classroom showed that a focused and "teacher-centered" pedagogy did not drain the joy from schoolwork. King was no martinet, and the class atmosphere was more playful than stern. She wound through the classroom inspecting notebooks and singing, "She'll be coming 'round the classroom when she comes." The next day King read them "The Emperor's New Clothes" and discussed the constituent elements of fairy tales. "It must begin, 'Once upon a time,' and end, 'Happily ever after.'" There has to be magic. King asked what "the lesson" of the story was. One girl threw up her arm: "Don't let other people make clothes for you!" Then everyone made crayon drawings of the story.

As I moved up the grade hierarchy, I found little evidence of the alleged stifling effects of an old-fashioned curriculum and pedagogy. In Daniel Bishop's sixth-grade English class, the students were reading a *Children's Homer* compiled by the great Irish poet and novelist Padraic Colum. (They would have already encountered a more elementary version of the story in third grade and would read the great Fagles translation in ninth; a student I met at lunch quoted his ninth-grade teacher as saying that they encountered Homer first as baby food and finally, when they were ready, as adult nourishment.) The students didn't know they were reading a classic; they treated *The Iliad* like a superhero story—which of course it is. One boy raised his hand with a complaint: "You said that Iris is the messenger of Hera, but in the book it says she's the messenger of Zeus." Another boy asked if, after death, Achilles would join the other heroes. He would go to the Underworld, Bishop said. The student, plainly upset, rejoined, "The book says that if he died with honor, he would go to where the heroes are." Bishop gently explained that for the Greeks, the Underworld was not Hell. Next up after Homer was the Book of Genesis.

The elementary and middle school program at Founders is largely, though not wholly, based on the Core Knowledge curriculum. Its author, E. D. Hirsch, a retired professor of English Literature at the University of Virginia, enjoys a standing in classical education almost equal to Aristotle. In his 1987 book, *Cultural Literacy*, Hirsch attributed the declining scores on standardized tests to the influence of Dewey and other progressives. Schools had moved away from a traditional emphasis on content toward the mastery of content-neutral skills. (Hirsch regards the shift from history to social studies as a symptom of that larger change.) Hirsch asserted that students learn to understand texts not by mastering general and transferable skills such as "finding the main idea," but rather by gaining a broad vocabulary and stock of knowledge. Hirsch and colleagues then developed a curriculum in the main school subjects that featured narrative history; vocabulary; names, dates, and places; and an upward spiral from fairy tales to classical children's literature to adult novels.

Core Knowledge initially met with ferocious opposition from the reading profession and educational progressives generally, both because it challenged the consensus view about skill acquisition and because Hirsch chose, perhaps foolishly, to append to his book a list of five thousand words and expressions that "literate Americans know." He was instantly stereotyped as a culture warrior standing at the ramparts of white male European culture, like Allan Bloom, though Hirsch was a political liberal who was also a pedagogical traditionalist. In fact, many subsequent studies have confirmed Hirsch's views about how children learn. Most famously, a 1988 study found that, when shown a passage about baseball, poor readers who knew a lot about baseball did better than more competent readers who knew less; familiarity with words and concepts trumped general decoding skills. A recent comparison of seven hundred students who applied for admission, by lottery, to Core Knowledge schools and were accepted, with sixteen hundred who were not, found, remarkably, that the Core Knowledge schools had eliminated completely the typical socioeconomic achievement gap in reading.[2]

Jason Caros had encountered *Cultural Literacy* as a social studies teacher in the early 1990s. Hirsch's account of the findings of cognitive psychology offered scientific vindication of Caros's belief that a child needs to be conscientiously trained rather than allowed to learn according to his own impulses. He became a Hirschian. In one of his letters to parents, Caros offered an excellent summary of Hirsch's conclusions refracted through a classical lens. He recalled that in the opening line of *The Odyssey*, "Sing to me of the man, Muse, the man of twists and turns," Homer invokes Mnemosyne, the muse of memory and the mother of all the muses. That exalted status, Caros wrote, signified that for the Greeks, "it is precisely memory that leads to knowledge, and knowledge gives birth to thinking and creativity." What we commit to memory enters the "storehouse of previously learned knowledge" known as "long-term memory." Thinking, Caros went on, requires that we draw on that storehouse to make sense of new information.

How, then, do we build that storehouse of knowledge? Through practice, which is to say learning, repeating, memorizing. "While some modern educators refer to drilling in school as 'drill and kill,'" Caros wrote, "drill done well, with passion and expertise by the instructor, and in small quantities over time, should never be kill." Caros had an answer to the problem of factual knowledge sticking. It was true, he wrote, that students won't recall a mass of disconnected facts. "But if they think about what they are thinking about more deeply," he concluded, "and especially if they get to the meaning of what they are thinking about, the likelihood that the information moves into long-term memory increases." In short, the Deweyan idea that students will only learn well in a pedagogy that is "child-centered" rather than "subject-matter centered" is wrong. But so, too, is the view that requiring students to learn particular things amounts to the kind of drudgery that any free-spirited child will repudiate—that children won't learn what they can't "smell or taste." Traditional learning will motivate children if it is offered with passion and expertise; if memorization is required in small quantities over time; if objects of knowledge are made real through the search for meaning. That is, of course, a great deal to ask.

The elementary school teachers at Founders do not talk about Homer or Aristotle. Quite a few of them are moms who sent a child there and then caught the bug. Karen Buchanan had homeschooled her three daughters before hearing that the local school offered a content-rich curriculum. First they went to Founders—her youngest, Lily, was the current school council president—then she applied for a job. Kimberly Drechsler, a second-grade teacher, taught at a private Christian academy before finding out about Founders, which struck her as a Christian academy minus the Bible verses. Many of these women attend the same evangelical church, the Villages, in nearby Flower Mound, which one of them described to me as having "a Southern Baptist flavor." I came to think of the elementary school faculty as both the bearer and the enforcer of the Founders code of rectitude. When Mrs. Buchanan herded her third-graders back in the building after art class in an annex, she scrutinized them closely. "Is your shirt tucked in? Is your collar buttoned all the way up?" Only when everything was squared away did she open the door to allow the children to file in, one at a time.

Middle school is the blurry terrain of no-longer-and-not-yet. Students have built intellectual foundations but are not yet ready to form ideas of their own; they're no longer obedient but not yet self-governing. Even at Founders, teenagers sometimes act like teenagers. One day I heard Miss Rogers begin her seventh-grade Logic class—after the kids all rose and said, "Good afternoon, Miss Rogers!"—by complaining of a "serious disruption" the day before. The kids had been dropping water bottles on the floor. This was pretty tame seventh-grade behavior, but Miss Rogers read them the riot act: any more fooling around and water bottles would be banned. The mania for hydration has made the water bottle a fixture of the modern classroom. A student asked plaintively, "What will we do if we're thirsty?" Miss Rogers snapped, "You'll have to go fifty minutes without a drink." That was the only disciplinary moment I witnessed in my week at Founders.

But Founders makes no concession to adolescent unruliness. Once the kids had been duly admonished, Miss Rogers began a lesson on "fallacies of relevance" by discussing what she called the "sub-sub-category of abusive and circumstantial ad hominem attacks." Included in this group was what the Romans call *tu quoque* and we, Miss Rogers explained, call "whataboutism." She was teaching them not simply to recognize falsehoods but to understand the particular perversions of logic that lie behind them—a very advanced version of the kind of civic instruction that often comes under the heading of "media literacy." That said, Miss Rogers made no reference to an American president who had perfected the art of the abusive ad hominem attack, circumstantial as well as direct. The civics lesson remained classical.

Middle school at Founders is not too early to direct the attention of students to the beautiful, the true, and the good. One morning, Jason Caros suggested I go to a seventh-grade Math class taught by Kevin

Gillett, a new teacher, fresh out of college, where he had studied classics and the Church Fathers. Gillett, who also had a minor in math, had volunteered to take over the pre-algebra class once a month to talk about why math was worth caring about. In his first class, on math and beauty, he had, he told me later, been delighted to find that when he asked about beautiful structures made possible by math, the kids had come up with the Taj Mahal, the Louvre, and Versailles. His subject today was the meaning and history of rational numbers, those whose exact value can be worked out (unlike, say, the square root of two). "What are rational numbers good for?," Gillett asked. For different jobs, the kids said. Like what? Architecture or cooking. Gillett explained that decimals could be rational numbers. "Why do we use decimals?" "It's easy to add or subtract," said one kid. "Why?" That was harder—there was a common denominator of 100.

Gillett, a young man with a thin beard and mustache on a round, merry face, bounced eagerly around the room. He had no text; he was talking math. The very subject, he pointed out, had been developed three thousand years ago, before the use of paper. What did mathematicians use? The kids were stumped. Fingers! This produced an uproar. Thus, Gillett explained, the near-universality of base 10. But since the Babylonians had used base 60, we divide hours and minutes into sixty units. The kids were, so far as I could tell, rapt. Gillett closed with a bizarre story about the Pythagoreans, who so deeply objected in principle to the idea of irrational numbers that when a sailor tried to prove their existence, they threw him overboard.

Caros considered a class on the beauty of mathematics to be central to the mission of *scientia virtus et libertas*—to civic education, as the classical school understands it. So, too, did Gillett. When I went to see him the next day, he said that he did not understand why classical schools were coded as "conservative" and could not see why they couldn't flourish in blue states. "Most people," he said, "want to live a good life." That was the line of work he thought he was in. An education in beauty and truth, Aristotle said, shaped a virtuous person. Who wouldn't want that? Yet Gillett recognized that classical schools were built on an epistemology very different from that of progressive education. He had given this question serious thought. Starting with Rousseau's *Emile*, and then continuing through Kant and Hegel, Gillett argued, the goal of education had become "to free the student from the supposed bonds of society." The "interior self" was real; everything else was "superstructure." Education liberates the self by demolishing the structures. Whereas, said Gillett, "a classicist would say, 'Well no, you don't get to choose who you are in certain ways. There's capital T truth, there's capital G good.'" Gillett felt that he and the students were engaged in a collective effort to understand the true and the good.

Improbable though it sounds, I routinely fell into discussions at this level of intellectual seriousness at Founders—though only with the high school faculty (of which Gillet was otherwise a member). The subject we kept circling around was the difference between the classical and the "progressive" ethos. I was struck that almost everyone regarded progressivism as their doctrinal antithesis. They did not use the word in its conventional political sense. No one ever spoke the words "critical race theory" or "woke" or even "Joe Biden." No doubt they thought about those things in their private lives, but as classical teachers their concerns lay elsewhere. They objected, rather, to the orientation of conventional schooling, which they used interchangeably with "progressivism," toward the market and toward "college readiness." Jonathan Rogers, a tall, thin, scholarly teacher of ancient and medieval history, told me that progressivism as he understood it "has more of a utilitarian focus; there's an immediate social purpose that's rooted in the time and place of our own day. That's why you teach social studies instead of history." Caros recounted for me with real horror a story he had recently heard about a school where teachers in each grade met weekly to review student test data and then draw up individualized plans. That would, in fact, count as state-of-the-art pedagogy in many schools. Caros's reaction had been: "You can't have a school like that and teach beautiful content."

This is a strange, but telling, misunderstanding. Dewey and the founding progressives were deeply anti-utilitarian; Dewey regarded the vocational orientation of education as profoundly antidemocratic, because it limited real intellectual development to the college-going elite.[3] Nor would it be fair to say that the teachers I met at Waubonsie or Metea

Valley regard their job as preparing children for the workforce. Yet Caros and his faculty were pointing to something real: the bastardized Deweyan thinking of "administrative progressivism" and "life adjustment"; the obsession of most schools with "meeting standards," irrespective of the value of those standards; the blithe acceptance in conventional schools of the values of the surrounding world and of the child's peer culture. Waubonsie polled students about what new electives the school should offer. Classical schools do not have to conduct polls to know what is worth teaching and learning: Founders Classical Academy of Lewisville puts it on the risers.

What really makes classical education fundamentally different is what Gillett described as capital letters. Classical education has a *telos*, a goal of human development. Aristotle called that supreme good *eudaimonia*, a word typically translated as "happiness" or "human flourishing." The good life is the life lived in accord with virtue. Education is ultimately a form of training—above all, in reason—that makes the good life possible. This is what Caros and Rogers and others meant when they disparaged the utilitarian goals of typical education. In *Politics*, Aristotle wrote, "There is a certain kind of education that children must be given not because it is useful or necessary, but because it is noble and suitable for a free person.[4]

Secular liberals do not believe in capital letters. Education begins with the child and her interests and developing faculties, not with the subject matter and its intrinsic nature. The liberal ideal is individual development: education allows each of us to become, not the ideal citizen, but whomever we wish to be. It helps us with the central work of throwing off the superstructures. School, like society itself, is not teleological, but rather consciously agnostic about ultimate goods. That posture is both liberating and limiting. In *The Death of Character: Moral Education in an Age Without Good or Evil*, sociologist James Davison Hunter argues that the moral education that once suffused American public schools depended on a shared Christian ethos. First secularism, then progressivism, knocked away that prop; what was left behind was a thin tissue of therapeutic language that was, Hunter writes, "oriented towards the end of personal well-being."[5] Hunter observes that the progressive model of the teacher as "the guide on the side" rather than "the sage on the stage" is a reflection of the principle that the truth lies within children rather than in some external body of principle, and thus that the teacher's goal is to help each child discover his own truth.

Classical schools, as Kevin Gillett puts it, do not enthrone the "interior self" and thus do not regard individual autonomy as the supreme good. They believe in a good external to the student. They do not—or at least Lewisville does not—expressly stipulate the content of that good, but rather insist on the existence of external categories such as the beautiful, the true, and the good. They are not ambivalent about the formation of character and do not distinguish—any more than Aristotle would—between "character education" and "civic education." Founders does not regard students as near-peers whose autonomy needs to be fully respected, but as minors who need to be directed in order that they may fully flourish. Students wear a uniform: hunter-green polo shirt with school crest, though high school students may also wear a light-blue button-down or long-sleeved Oxford shirt with school crest. No colored undershirt. Belts in black or brown only. Girls' skirts should fall to the knee. Boys must be clean-shaven with trimmed sideburns and hair short enough not to touch the collar when standing; girls must eschew dangling earrings, visible body piercings, nose rings. And rules don't just cover physical appearance. Cell phones must be stowed in lockers. Even minor forms of plagiarism, such as copying a sentence without citation, are subject to severe punishment. The rules impose a striking uniformity: students at Founders look much more like each other, and behave much more like each other, than they do at the typical public school.

That uniformity, however, is the mark of a pervasive ethos. A very high and thick wall separates Founders Classical from the surrounding world of peer culture. That wall is built out of values that are understood to be sacrosanct, if unspecified. Caros and his colleagues would say that it is possible to pursue supreme goods without stipulating their nature—without, for example, supplying an explicitly Christian gloss to truth or goodness. The evangelicals and Christian nationalists who advocate for private religious classical schools would say that it is not, that the ultimate end of schooling is the acceptance of revealed truth.[6] Is that the ground truth of classical education? That is, are there any grounds for the fear that classical schools are a

Trojan horse for Christian nationalism or at least for a form of religiosity at odds with the liberal commitment to a secular public space?

The impulse that first gave rise to classical schools was, in fact, religious. The first modern schools to call themselves "classical" were private Protestant academies; some Catholic schools, which felt uncomfortable with the pagan-sounding label, also followed a classical curriculum. Many conservative Christian parents in the home-school movement also began adopting classical instruction programs. Donald Howard, the founder of Responsive Ed, which oversees the Founders Classical Academies, also established Accelerated Christian Education, which offered "knowledge units" for Christian homeschoolers. Though Howard has left Responsive Ed, its current head, Charles Cook, worked for Howard designing the curriculum, which promoted creationism and a far-right-wing version of American history.[7]

Classical schools might have remained niche institutions that catered to conservative Christians had they not converged with a very different reform—the charter school movement. Charter schools are public schools that are governed not by the local school board but by a public agency, often a university, with which they sign a "charter" laying out their educational program. The charter is typically renewed if the school proves educationally effective and financially stable. Charter schools are an ideologically neutral reform: the idea was developed in the mid-1980s by a centrist policy thinker in Minnesota who wanted to give school reformers the leeway to try new things. Since that time almost every state in the country has passed laws permitting charters to operate; as of this writing, an estimated 3.7 million students attend eight thousand charter schools. Some are very traditional but others are highly progressive. Charters enroll a higher percentage of low-income and minority students than do public schools generally.[8]

Classical schools seized on the charter movement—and were changed by it. The founders of the Trinity schools in Phoenix, one of the first of the self-proclaimed classical Christian institutions, realized that they could turn Trinity into a public school by removing the religious affiliation and content. In 2003, Veritas Prep Academy was born as an Arizona charter school; Veritas spawned a network, called Great Hearts, that now has twenty-five thousand students in forty schools in Arizona and Texas. Responsive Ed started up in 1998 with a network of charter schools serving dropouts and students at risk of failure. In 2010, Hillsdale College, a conservative Christian school in Michigan, established the Barney Charter School Initiative to stand up classical charter schools; the very first school it opened was Founders Classical Academy of Lewisville. The role of Hillsdale highlights the political conservatism that continues to infuse elements of the classical school movement even as it has shed its sectarian origins. However, Responsive Ed ended its relationship with Hillsdale—amicably, it appears—in 2021.

Like most charter schools, Lewisville Founders chooses students by lottery. Nevertheless, the children who attend are the ones whose parents wanted them to go. What's more, Dallas is one of the most conservative big cities in America; the school draws from a church-going, conservative pool of families. But the kids aren't privileged. Demographically and economically, Lewisville is a fairly typical satellite town of a major Sunbelt metropolis. The median income is slightly below the American average of $74,000. Forty-five percent of the 935 kids at Founders are white; 22 percent are Asian, 20 percent are Hispanic; 7 percent are Black. Yet as the school's reputation has spread, immigrant families have applied in increasing numbers, so that the lower grades are much more diverse than the high school.

This reflects a larger trend: a 2023 study found that while enrollment in classical charter schools in Texas had grown sevenfold over the previous decade, growth among Asian American and Hispanic students had far outpaced growth among whites.[9] The traditionalism, rigor, and discipline of classical schools—the thick wall against peer and popular culture—appeals to many newcomers to the country. About 15 percent of students at Lewisville are classed as second-language learners, though I heard very few strong foreign accents. Only 20 percent of the kids come from poor enough backgrounds to qualify for a federally subsidized lunch. Because the Lewisville school system itself is only 37 percent white and has 30 percent of kids below the poverty line, Lewisville Founders continues to draw from a disproportionately white and middle-class parent body. This is also true of classical schools generally—though to a diminishing degree. The consequence is that Founders applies its strict rules to what is already a rule-abiding population and does not have to deal with issues of race and gender that beset so many other schools. There is no LGBTQ+ club, and I did not hear about or see any trans kids.

There probably aren't many kids at Founders who would dye their hair green if they were allowed to. "They're very compliant," as John Woods, who teaches twelfth-grade Western Civilization, mildly complains. "There's a kind of Stoical ethos that exists here, and that's both good and bad." Orderliness created the conditions for good teaching, but Woods said that he wished for a little more rambunctiousness. That confirmed my own impression. Every day for a week I sat at lunch with the high school kids and tried to find evidence of teenage rebellion or at least run-of-the-mill sarcasm. I can't say that I succeeded. No one complained about the no-cell-phone rule. A number of kids told me that they were proud to go to a school that was so much more rigorous than the ones their friends went to. Clover, a tenth-grader, told me that she really liked grammar class, with its minute classifications and arcane diagrams. When I asked if she found the school conservative, Clover said that she assumed that most of her teachers were, but none of them ever discussed their politics or their religion. "The other day Mr. Rogers brought up LGBTQ issues," she said delightedly. "Mr. Rogers?," I said. He *was*, he had told me, a conservative who had once worked for the National Right to Life Committee. "Yes," said Clover: "He told us that the Emperor Hadrian had a male student as a lover."

The high school faculty at Lewisville is overwhelmingly white, male, and scholarly. Most teachers wear khakis, a button-down shirt, a sport coat, and, often, a tie. Lewisville Founders looks, and often feels, like a New England prep school, circa 1966. Like so many successful institutions, Lewisville has taken shape around the character and temperament of its founder. Jason Caros was born into a Greek Orthodox family in Fort Lauderdale and grew up with heavy infusions of classical learning. After training at an Orthodox seminary to enter the priesthood, Caros found that he loved teaching and became a social studies teacher and administrator in Volusia County on Florida's Atlantic coast. He read deeply in classical literature, in history, and in the founding texts of cultural conservatism. His personal touchstone was Russell Kirk's 1974 *Roots of American Order*, an immensely ambitious work that advocated the "ordered liberty" of Cicero and the ancients, and the moral order of the New Testament, as against the contemporary American belief in liberty as freedom from all constraint.[10] Deeply attracted to the classical model, Caros had been hired to run the first school in the Founders network. A pedagogue by nature and calling, Caros continued to teach classes every year.

One day after school, I met with Caros in his office. He wore a baseball cap to cover his bald scalp; he was then receiving treatment for a rare form of cancer, thymic carcinoma. In his only concession to illness, besides the cap, Caros had decided not to teach a class that year. Otherwise he maintained a stoic equanimity. Caros explained to me his philosophy of hiring, which he considered central to Lewisville's success. First, he said, he tried to avoid candidates who had been to education school and who thus had an expertise in pedagogy rather than subject matter. This, alone, distinguishes his staff from that of the high schools in Illinois where, I had been told, teachers were discouraged from getting a subject-matter advanced degree. Caros believed that a thoughtful person could pick up classroom skills relatively quickly, whereas subject-matter mastery would take years. "When I look at new hires," he said, "I always consider three things, which correspond to Aristotelian categories." First was *logos*. "Do they know their subject?" Second was *pathos*. "Do they have passion for teaching and their subject?" And third was *ethos*. "Do they share the school's mission, which is building character?"

Caros could afford to set such high standards because a certain cadre of well-educated conservative young men were eager for the chance to teach beautiful content. The lure certainly wasn't financial. Charter schools are typically underfunded, and Caros can only promise that he will not pay worse than 10 percent below the salary scale in local public schools, which starts at $58,000 in high school. The appeal lay, rather, in the mission. Jonathan Rogers, the classical history teacher, had once worked in the antiabortion movement, but after years among doctrinal conservatives he had concluded that institutions only make progress with "an affirmative vision." Classical education embodied just such a vision. Some had tried the other side. John Woods got a PhD in history from Fordham and then taught very unhappily in a New York City high school that he found far too controlling of both student and teacher behavior. In 2018, he applied for a job at Founders, near where he had grown up. "There's more freedom than you'd have at most schools," he told me, "even though there's a conservative ethos. I don't ever feel there's something I can't say." He was free to teach beautiful content.

One morning in his Western Civilization class, Woods prepared the kids to talk about Marx's *Communist Manifesto* by retracing the evolution of political thought from Hobbes to Locke to Hegel and Kant. The students quietly scribbled in their spiral notebooks. No one spoke up. The next day was more interactive by design. The big question for the day, Woods explained, was whether we should think of Marx as a liberatory and egalitarian figure, as his admirers did, or as an authoritarian seeking to engineer human behavior. Ryan, sitting next to me, raised his hand to say something he and I had just talked about: "You can't take away human nature." The working class, Ryan said, would oppress people just as the bourgeoisie had. Jesse said that he found Marx condescending: "He uses big words to try to impress the working class with how educated he is." Woods tried to complicate matters. For all his vaunted atheism, he explained, Marx had adopted the eschatology—the end-time view—of the Old and New Testaments, but "he took Jesus out of the equation." That was a difficult thought and perhaps asked more of the kids than they could give. "He's an authoritarian," Ryan said in closing. "He wants power."

After lunch that day, I sat in on tenth-grade Paideia, a Greek word that sums up the ancient principle of education as training for life and which is deployed almost totemically in the world of classical education. The teacher, John Tutuska, was academic even by the standards of Founders, a thickly bearded, bespectacled figure with the shy, halting, and occasionally propulsive manner of a born philosopher. His subject that afternoon was the nature of humor. What makes something funny? Is it incongruity? "Take a minute," he said. He suggested they think about examples of something funny because incongruous. Both in Paideia and in Moral

Philosophy, which he taught to seniors, Tutuska was forever probing, pausing, seeking reflection while he drummed his fingers nervously on the lectern. He had fallen in love with philosophy at a Franciscan college where he encountered Aristotle's idea that a life of moral virtue meant not sacrifice but fulfillment. He was a man who seemed to live his subject. A few students responded to his prompts. Most, however, remained silent.

Lewisville does not have a class called "Civics," perhaps because civic ideals permeate the curriculum and the larger school culture. Nor does the school offer opportunities for the kind of civic experience that distinguishes the Democracy Network. Part of what it means to build, and to dwell behind, the thick walls of classical education is to trust to the power of classroom instruction—and thus of books—to shape the child. In tenth-grade Government, Brad Dietzen talked about *Federalist* no. 9 and no. 10. The class had already read St. Augustine and Aquinas, Hobbes and Locke. Dietzen did, however, celebrate Patriot Day by showing a video of George W. Bush at Ground Zero. This was the closest anyone came to partisanship. As a graduate of Hillsdale College and then an employee in the college's Washington office, Dietzen may have been a more confirmed culture warrior than his colleagues.

Dietzen's students had been silent as he delivered a lecture on what was, after all, extremely difficult material. I could not tell whether the academy's high school teachers had pegged their expectations too high or whether a compliant and rule-observing student body bit its collective tongue when a more voluble bunch, trained in the art of self-expression, would have spoken up. John Woods admitted that he wasn't quite sure. The combination of the school's very strong emphasis on order and the pervasive conservatism sometimes made the kids resist his efforts to push them out of their comfort zone. They dismissed Teddy Roosevelt, and even FDR, as progressives; perhaps that's what they had heard at home. "My goal," Woods said, "is to spur them to be a little more reflective than they were before."

Many of the kids may, in fact, have known more than they said. I later saw videos of oral presentations of three of the end-of-semester final projects required of all seniors. The projects required close reading of texts and were striking for their moral and spiritual seriousness. None of the kids had chosen sports, or pop culture, or sci-fi, or any of the subjects that appeal to typical eighteen-year-olds. One considered the relationship of man's nature to technology, one discussed the "sin" of narcissism in Oscar Wilde's *Picture of Dorian Gray*, and the third explored the themes of charity and forgiveness in *Les Misérables*, framed by the argument of C. S. Lewis—a great favorite in the classical world—that charity must be understood not as an emotion but an act of will, and thus a moral choice.

After a week in Lewisville, I felt that I could reach a few general conclusions. First, Founders' content-rich curriculum succeeded by the measurements the school world puts the most store by. Caros had always taken the view that a school with a strong curriculum and good teachers did not need to take time off for "test prep," as virtually all schools do. Nevertheless, in 2022, Founders as a whole scored a 95 on state achievement tests. This placed it at the top of the list both of schools in the Founders network and of district schools generally, though the district includes Flower Mound, one of America's wealthiest suburbs. In the spring of 2023, 97 percent of Lewisville Founders Classical Academy eighth-graders passed the state history exam; 82 percent of those "met standards," while 59 percent demonstrated "mastery." The corresponding statewide figures were 60, 31, and 15. In eleventh-grade history, Founders students were 100, 95, and 77, while the figures statewide were 95, 71, and 39. (Any exam for which 95 percent of students pass is way too easy.)

Second, Founders had not donned the veil of classical education to obscure an ideological or sectarian agenda. The school's commitments were cultural and pedagogical, not political. The kids in seventh-grade U.S. History read Joy Hakim's excellent series of texts, just as they do in good schools in liberal places. Caros had nothing to hide. I was an emissary of the blue world in the heart of Texas, yet Caros had granted me virtually complete freedom to wander around and talk to anyone, including students. I would soon discover that schools are deeply paranoid about journalists. I would not be permitted to visit many schools I had hoped to see; at others, I would be watched like a hawk. I can't entirely blame school administrators and building principals, given the perpetual storms that keep depositing new layers of dust and grime on the schoolhouse. But Caros trusted me to look with my own eyes. Neither teachers nor students seemed guarded in talking to me; everyone seemed to assume that a fair-minded visitor would admire what he saw. The expectation of virtuous behavior apparently extended even to me.

The atmosphere of Founders Classical Academy, starting from its very name, may be more overtly patriotic than that of the average blue-state public school, but it is not doctrinal. Liberal educators distinguish between the "reflective patriotism" that they wish schools to cultivate and the unthinking, intolerant variety that seems to have engulfed half the country. Though geographically in that dubious half, Lewisville opts for reflectiveness. In one of his notes home, Jason Caros wrote that "one of the things that makes this land worthy of praise" is the humility and hopefulness implicit in the Preamble to the Constitution (which I had heard the kids reciting my first morning): "We the people of the United States, in order to form a more perfect union . . ." We know, Caros went on, that "we are a work in progress, and strive for improvement." But we cannot make this effort, Caros told the parents, absent deep knowledge. "If you don't know about your country's past, good and bad, and if you do not understand the principles that undergird and propel it, you are likely to believe anything negative someone tells you about it, or you become an apathetic spectator within it." The reelection of Donald Trump implied an addendum: if you don't know your country's history, you are likely to believe anything crazy or mean-spirited about it.

The kids at Founders gave every appearance of being happy. "Happiness" is a very important word at Founders Classical, because Aristotle tells us that a life devoted to seeking virtues leads to *eudaimonia*. Happiness was thus central to Founders' conception of education for citizenship. The strict rules, and the stern academic demands, had not turned the kids into galley slaves—though it may have made them even more compliant than they had already been inclined to be. Founders had shaped certain "civic dispositions," though not the same ones being nurtured in Illinois's Democracy Network. Students do not experience school as a proto-democracy in which they practice the skills of active citizenship. They do not debate controversial issues. They live in the past far more than the present. They learn ideas from books, and they acquire a sense of the good life from the school's codes and its pervasive ethos. They come to think of "character" not as a set of personal choices leading to maximal self-realization, as James Davison Hunter puts it, but rather as the willed and reflective embrace of virtue.

The culture of Lewisville suited the culture of its community very well. But many of the kids I would meet in the coming year would not have put up with the rules and the overwhelming air of rectitude. A gay student, a trans student, even a mildly rebellious or slightly weird kid—anyone disinclined to be compliant—might have been unhappy there. Possibly a flaming liberal would have felt out of place. Their parents might have headed for the door as soon as they saw sixth-graders rising to sing out, "Good afternoon, Miss Rogers!" Expressive individualism is the default ethos of our secular liberal culture. The classical school, as embodied by Founders, is a powerful model; but the wild variety of American life can never be clamped down on the Procrustean bed of a single form of schooling.

Is Founders a powerful model—or just an extraordinary outlier? The waters of school reform are endlessly muddied by this question. Extraordinary schools typically have extraordinary leaders who are able to attract extraordinary teachers. They generally regress to the mean when a gifted, often a founding, head departs—at which point they can no longer be seen as embodying a generalizable model. Jason Caros is an extraordinary educational leader who has fashioned his school by his own lights. What would Lewisville be without him? The classical model is too new, at least in the world of public schools, to have been subjected to rigorous study. We don't know whether classically educated students have a deeper grasp of American history or government than do similarly situated students at nonclassical schools or, of course, whether they become better citizens. It's impossible to say for sure what elements of the approach at Founders Classical Academy either can be generalized or we should wish to be generalized to other schools. Yet one thing seems plainly true: good teachers want to teach beautiful content, and students will flourish if good teachers are given a chance to do so.

4

1619 v. 1776

THE WAR OVER THE AMERICAN PAST

On August 18, 2019, the *New York Times Magazine* devoted an entire issue to a single subject—the four hundredth anniversary of the first arrival of slaves on the shores of North America. The goal of the "1619 Project," as it was called, was to "reframe the country's history by placing the consequences of slavery and the contributions of Black Americans at the very center of our national narrative." The re-centering was a sweeping intellectual enterprise. The articles, written by scholars as well as journalists, argued that slavery, and its enduring legacy, accounted for the decision of the colonists to declare independence from England as well as many of the ugliest aspects of modern American life: "the brutality of modern capitalism," the absence of basic social supports such as universal health care, America's uniquely punitive criminal justice system, and the "destructive, sectarian style of politics with which we now live." The authors called on readers to recognize that it was not the noble ideals in whose name the country had been founded but the poison of slavery and racism that constituted the foundation of the American story.[1]

The "1619 Project" posed a profound challenge to the understanding of that story that has shaped our textbooks and our civic identity. Of course there never has been, and never can be, a single universally accepted American narrative. Yet there has been a rough consensus about our fundamental nature. When we express regret over the erosion of civic identity, we are in part mourning the loss of that shared narrative. The fragmentation of our politics both reflects and magnifies the fragmentation of the national narrative. Though almost wholly ignorant of American history, Donald Trump had run in 2016 (and would run again in 2020 and 2024) with the promise to restore an unspecified but glorious era in the past—to "make America great again." Trump never said, but perhaps did not need to say, that the America he would restore was the one ruled by white men like himself. Trump could not let the 1619 challenge to his narrative stand unopposed; in the fall of 2020, the White House ordered up a counterhistory, known as the "1776 Report," that minimized race, deprecated liberal reform, and placed the Founders on a lofty pedestal. These dueling narratives further polarized the teaching of American history and reduced hopes for a shared national history to a pipe dream.

Textbook wars are an old subject in America. As early as 1913, progressive Southern historian William Dodd concluded that "two distinct histories are being taught in the schools"—one Southern and pro-Confederate, one northern and antislavery. In 1919, Mildred Lewis Rutherford, historian-general of the United Daughters of the Confederacy, ordered Southern school administrators to reject any textbook that called the Civil War "a rebellion" or claimed that it had been fought to defend slavery rather than states' rights. Southerners successfully pressured Northern publishers to release separate, whitewashed versions of their history books or to bowdlerize classic texts such as David Saville Muzzey's *An American History.*[2] Critiques of capitalism were no more welcome in the North than critiques of slavery and Jim Crow were in the South. Charles and Mary Beard's 1921 *History of the United States*, which treated the defense of private property and market power as central to the Constitution and to American politics, was denounced as "treasonous" and banned in many school districts, as were other works by the so-called "new historians" of the era.

American textbooks in the middle of the twentieth century had as settled a view of race and civil rights as they did of the virtues of the marketplace. A leading historian of textbooks writes—in a book titled *Teaching White Supremacy*—that through the 1950s, most texts used in schools described slaves as content with their lot, radical abolitionists such as William Lloyd Garrison as dangerous extremists, the cause of the Civil War as Northern unwillingness to allow the South to pursue its distinctive culture, and Reconstruction as "rule by Northern carpetbaggers, Southern scalawags and illiterate Negroes."[3] Few challenged the so-called Dunning school—the view, associated with the immensely influential Columbia historian William Dunning, that after the Civil War, the North had made a futile and coercive effort to impose its values on the South. Historians thus converged around the view that slavery was terribly wrong but so, too, was Reconstruction.

The marginalization of slavery and race from American history was finally challenged by the great revisionist works of the 1950s, including C. Vann Woodward's *The Strange Career of Jim Crow* and Kenneth Stampp's *The Peculiar Institution*. Woodward put the lie to the Dunning school by demonstrating that Southern elites had cultivated the Black vote in the 1890s when they hoped to use it to restore their own position and only began to treat Black suffrage as an outrage against nature when they no longer faced pressure from the North to show compliance with civil rights laws. They had, in effect, accepted the need to "legislate morality" when it was in their interest to do so. The North had given those elites permission to institute the new racial laws out of what was seen as the higher good of sectional harmony. Woodward concluded that Blacks had become "the national scapegoat in the reconciliation and reunion of north and south."[4]

The revisionist view began to work its way into school texts with John Morton Blum's 1963 *The National Experience*. Most students continued to learn about scalawags and carpetbaggers, but by the 1980s, in the aftermath of the civil rights movement, a new generation of American history texts had incorporated the revisionist view. These texts represented a new and more progressive consensus about not only race but also the economic issues that Charles Beard had first raised a century before. Any such consensus is, by its nature, both entirely informal and open to innumerable differences of interpretation. Nevertheless, one can find the central themes repeated in almost any of the eighteen texts currently accepted for use in the AP American History course. Among the authors of these works are the leading scholars in the field, including Alan Brinkley, Eric Foner, H. W. Brands, David Blight, and Mary Beth Norton.[5]

Thus *A People and a Nation*, first published in 1984 and continually reissued since then, features on the cover of its sixth edition (published in 2011) Winslow Homer's 1865–66 painting *Near Andersonville* showing a freed Black woman gazing out at a transfigured world—an implicit statement about the centrality of slavery and race to American history.[6] The authors tell students about Beard's views of the Constitution without endorsing them and observe that the document "contained both direct and indirect protections for slavery" without placing those protections at the core of the convention's debates. The long chapter on slavery begins with a heart-rending description of the largest slave auction in Southern history and describes the antebellum South as "not just a society with slaves but a slave society," in which all values and political and economic practices were shaped, and warped, by slavery.[7]

The chapter on slavery concludes with a set of questions about the present: "Does slavery's heritage require permanent redistributive justice in our current society? And who or what is responsible for continuing disparities in the family stability of blacks and whites: history (the nation's policies) or individuals (personal behavior)?" Textbook authors often shield themselves from controversy by posing questions rather than making flat assertions. Nevertheless, the young reader of *A People and a Nation* would emerge with a deep respect for Abraham Lincoln's moral commitments and pragmatic decision-making, a recognition of the tragic failure of the hopes kindled by Reconstruction, and a high regard for the progressives' hope that "democracy could be reconciled with capitalism."[8] She would be inclined to see American history as a perpetual struggle to form "a more perfect union," placing even terrible failures along an arc of history that bent toward justice.

The "1619 Project" was hardly the first effort to shatter the civil rights–era liberal consensus. Many radical historians in the 1960s produced accounts that placed class struggle at the heart of American history. By far the most prominent was *A People's History of the United States*, written by Boston University professor Howard Zinn in 1969. Despite the title, Zinn's text was not classic social history that told a nation's story through the experience of ordinary people but rather a polemic that recast the American story as a permanent, Marxian struggle between "the people" and the powerful. Zinn described the American Revolution as a subterfuge designed to transfer power from one set of elites to another and the Civil War as a struggle between the economic barons of slavery and those of free labor. He characterized Reconstruction, progressivism, and the New Deal as conscious efforts to offer just enough reform to blunt the working class's revolutionary demands for radical reform. Zinn speculated that representative democracy itself served as a means to dilute the force of those demands.[9] Yet in many quarters, and widely on the left, *A People's History* was revered as an unmasking of the brute face of American power—a proof, as one scholar put it with retrospective dismay, "that everything I had learned in school was a sugar-coated fairy tale."[10] Zinn's text has sold more than two million copies and is widely assigned in high schools and colleges. That said, the book was typically paired with a mainstream work or even an openly conservative one in the history classes I attended.

What Zinn did for class, the "1619 Project" did for race, reorienting the American story around a gross injustice that liberal historians had allegedly treated as a sideshow. American history, as the authors understood it, was not a gratifying narrative of fitful progress but an ugly record of blind resistance. The opening essay, a compressed and highly personalized history of race relations by Nikole Hannah-Jones, the journalist who had organized the entire effort, contained the most explosive claims. "Conveniently left out of our founding mythology," she wrote, "is the fact that one of the primary reasons the colonists decided to declare their independence from Britain was because they wanted to protect the institution of slavery"—which, they feared, Britain was prepared to abolish. If that is so, she went on, "this nation was founded not as a democracy but as a slavocracy." And if *that* is so, of course, then the central mythos of a nation created in the name of universal ideals of liberty and equality is vacuous self-congratulation. As with the Revolution, so with the Civil War: Hannah-Jones described Lincoln as a white supremacist who blamed Black people for the war and expected freed slaves to butcher their masters. And so down to our own time: in the face of Jim Crow and racial oppression, Hannah-Jones wrote, "for the most part, black Americans fought back alone." The essay was as relentlessly monocausal as the *People's History*, though the cause was a different one.

Hannah-Jones was a journalist; her ultimate concern was thus with the present, not the past. The collective effect of the whole project, especially in the expanded book version that appeared two years later, was to force the reader to reckon with the racial origins of injustices that appeared to have nothing to do with race. It was the cotton plantation that gave birth to "the culture of acquiring wealth without work, growing at all costs and abusing the powerless." White legislators opposed free medical care because it would "breed dependence" in Blacks. The antidemocratic theories of John Calhoun, slavery's arch-defender, have gained a new life in "contemporary arguments against the expansion of democracy." All this—our American reality—was the fruit of a poisoned tree. That is why it was not only historically but morally correct to think of 1619, not 1776, as the year of America's birth. Here was a new form of the antipatriotic polemic of the 1960s: civic education in the light of the "1619 Project" would consist of tearing away the veils that have blinded us to systematic injustice.

The imprimatur of the *New York Times* ensured that the "1619 Project" would have an extraordinary impact. In 2020, the *Times* produced a podcast series based on the project and in 2023 a six-part television documentary. In 2021, Random House published the book-length version of the project as well as *Born on the Water,* a children's version, trumpeting both in a remarkable marketing campaign involving weekly full-page ads in the *Times* and the *New York Times Book Review. The 1619 Project* has sold more than 500,000 copies and *Born on the Water* more than 150,000. The National Educational Association distributed copies to educators and established a "1619 Project Resources Page." One of the central goals of the project from the outset had been to create curricular resources; the *Times* partnered with the Pulitzer Center for Crisis Reporting (no relation to the Pulitzer prizes) to do so. The center maintains a "1619 Project Education Network," which says that the material it publishes has reached

10,500 students. That's a modest number compared with the reach of the major instructional providers, but many informal school networks have begun to create material of their own based on the books and the magazine. Many teachers have been inspired to create their own lessons.

But once an idea enters the national bloodstream, the influence it enjoys goes far beyond its immediate effects. The "1619 Project" reflected a growing consensus on the left; the report was published the same week as Ibram X. Kendi's *How to Be an Antiracist*, whose central claim was that racism was so deeply embedded in American society that even neutrality on questions such as reparations or affirmative action reinforced racist structures. Robin DiAngelo's *White Fragility*, with its kindred view of the universality of racism, had appeared the year before. The killing of George Floyd nine months after the publication of the "1619 Project" appeared to confirm the claim that the lives of Black people did not, in fact, matter. It is fruitless to try to separate out the influence of these documents and events. What is clear is that after 2019, the climate of thought in educational circles changed. In 2020, as I will discuss, educators in Virginia called on the state to change teaching and curriculum in order to establish "an anti-racist school culture and climate." The following year, Minnesota adopted new state standards in history, government, and Ethnic Studies that reflected the 1619 view. So, two years later, did Rhode Island. The idea that racial domination was the ground truth of the American story had become conventional in progressive circles, much as the centrality of the class struggle had been in 1969.

But was it true? The liberal historians who had written the mainstream textbooks—many of whom had devoted much of their careers to studying slavery, the Civil War, and Reconstruction—did not think so. They feared that the next generation of students would be taught to think of America as a wicked country defined by white supremacy. A revisionist campaign soon began. The first blow came from Sean Wilentz, a prominent historian at Princeton University, who argued in a speech in November 2019 that abolitionism had in fact arisen in the colonies before spreading to England, where it remained a fringe view; the ideologies of slavery and antislavery had struggled for supremacy from the Revolution to the Civil War.

Only the blinders of our own time, Wilentz observed, keep us from understanding what an astonishing breach the abolitionists had made with the immemorial history of enslavement; equally, how the Declaration's assertion of universal equality broke with the hierarchical organization even of colonial society, not to mention the aristocratic structures of England. Insisting that the fact of slavery blots out all such ideals, Wilentz wrote, "can leave our understanding of American history susceptible to moralizing distortions that seem compelling simply because they defy reassuring versions of the past"—because, that is, they tell us that everything we learned in school was a sugar-coated fairy tale.[11] Wilentz was not claiming that slavery and its legacy mattered *less* than Hannah-Jones and her colleagues thought, but rather that the role it played was more nuanced than they believed.

Other leading figures, including James McPherson and Gordon Wood—among the last survivors of the sixties generation of American historians who had established the liberal consensus—gave interviews in which they castigated the "slavocracy" theory. Wood noted that, because the founding generation believed that slavery was dying out—which it appeared to be until the invention of the cotton gin—winning agreement at the Constitutional Convention to abolish the Atlantic slave trade in twenty years, far from a trivial concession by the South, as Hannah-Jones treated it, seemed to "set slavery on the road to extinction." Like Wilentz, Wood argued, as he had in many of his books, that "the Revolution unleashed anti-slavery sentiments that led to the first abolition movements in the history of the world."[12] Others noted that, for all the racism with which he had been born and raised, Abraham Lincoln regarded the Declaration's proclamation that "all men are created equal" as the great American commandment; and that Frederick Douglass, once a stern critic, had come to regard Lincoln as the tragic hero of the Civil War.

These figures spoke as historians criticizing what they regarded as faulty history. In a letter to the *New York Times Magazine* at the end of 2019, Wilentz, Wood, McPherson, James Oakes of the City University of New York, and Virginia Bynum, emerita professor at Texas State University, wrote that though they welcomed the "profound, unsettling questions about slavery and the nation's past and present" that the "1619

Project" had raised, they were "dismayed" by factual errors that "suggest a displacement of historical understanding by ideology." What made the factual errors so grave was the ideological current running beneath them—the insistence that America was irredeemably racist. As Oakes said in an interview of his own, "the worst thing about it is that it leads to political paralysis. It's always been there. There's nothing we can do to get out of it."[13] Oakes and the other signatories believed that, even at its worst moments, America has within it the capacity for self-renewal; the authors of the "1619 Project" seemed to believe that self-renewal could come about only after an act of self-abasement or self-abnegation.

In his response to the letter, *New York Times Magazine* editor Jake Silverstein defended Hannah-Jones's claims about the Revolution and about Lincoln, but then made an additional assertion with which most or all of the five historians would have agreed: "The very premise of The 1619 Project, in fact, is that many of the inequalities that continue to afflict the nation are a direct result of the unhealed wound created by 250 years of slavery and an additional century of second-class citizenship and white-supremacist terrorism inflicted on black people." Something like that view has been at the heart of the liberal response to Black poverty and disadvantage since 1965, when Lyndon Johnson promulgated his Great Society legislation.[14] The "1619 Project" included new scholarship—also highly disputed, to be sure—that showed the tendrils of slavery and racism reached yet deeper into current American society than had been previously understood. Some liberal historians had declined to sign the letter because they had no wish to align themselves against what felt like a just and timely indictment of contemporary American society. Yet it nevertheless remained true that in order to advance this claim, the authors, or certainly the lead author, had wrenched American history from its moorings. This was the fallacy that historians call "presentism"—reinterpreting the past in order to explain the present.

The liberal critics of the "1619 Project" were conflicted; conservatives, and enemies of all things woke, were gleeful. The Black pundit and linguistics scholar John McWhorter condemned the enterprise as "performance art" offering "attitude" rather than facts—"a call for dumbing ourselves down in the name of a moral crusade."[15] Robert Woodson, a leading Black conservative, organized a patriotic project called "1776 Unites," which offered a countercurriculum to 1619. Planned lessons celebrated figures such as Booker T. Washington, who prized work and self-reliance over the struggle for rights and higher education, as well as "largely unknown, heroic African-American figures from the past and present who triumphed over adverse conditions."[16] By 2020, the first of several book-length attacks, *1620: A Critical Response to The 1619 Project*, had appeared. The author, Peter W. Woods, was the president of the National Association of Scholars, an organization of conservative academics. Woods collected and conscientiously explained all of the intellectually serious criticisms of the project, whether from left, center, or right. He was plain about his own view: "The 1619 Project," he wrote, "aligns with the views of those on the progressive left who hate America and would like to transform it radically" in a way that would "endanger our hard-won liberty, our self-government and our virtues as a people." Woods proposed that we trace America's origins instead to the arrival of the *Mayflower*, whose passengers signed the Mayflower Compact, in which they vowed to "covenant and combine ourselves together into a civil body politic." America grew, not from slavery, but from a social contract among equals.[17]

On May 25, 2020, George Floyd was killed by a policeman who kneeled on his neck for more than eight minutes; the video of that terrible event unleashed a whirlwind. Protests against police violence, racism, and racial injustice exploded across the country. In a nation already profoundly polarized, the protests instantly deepened the split between the Left and Right. While the young people in the street and their many sympathizers saw George Floyd's death as a latter-day lynching, conservatives were less upset by the evidence of police brutality than by the protests against it. On September 1, President Trump, then running for reelection against Joe Biden, visited Kenosha, Wisconsin, where a white policeman had shot a Black protestor and then two days later a teenage white counterprotestor had shot three demonstrators. Far from condemning the shootings, Trump blamed "violent mobs" inspired by "reckless far-left politicians" for the destruction of property. Asked whether he accepted the 1619 thesis of structural racism, Trump said, "I don't believe that at all."[18]

On Constitution Day, September 17, Trump convened a White House Conference on American History. There he called for a new history, or counterhistory, of race relations. "Critical race theory, the 1619 project, and the crusade against American history," the president declared, "is toxic propaganda, ideological poison that if not removed will dissolve the civic bonds that tie us together." (Two weeks earlier, Christopher Rufo of the conservative Manhattan Institute had used an appearance on Fox's *Tucker Carlson Show* to declare that "critical race theory" had become "the default ideology of the federal bureaucracy and is being weaponized against the American people."[19]) Trump had, of course, become president by pitting the American people against one another with reckless audacity; now he proposed to somehow reknit those frayed civic bonds by impaneling a 1776 Commission that would promote "patriotic education."[20]

On November 2, the day before the election, Trump issued an executive order establishing the commission, which was authorized to publish a report on "the core principles of the American founding" and to work with other branches of the federal government "with regard to their efforts to ensure patriotic education."[21] As chairman of the commission, the Trump White House chose Larry Arnn, president of Hillsdale College; the executive director, Matthew Spalding, was dean of Hillsdale's Washington, D.C., campus.

This was a public acknowledgment of Hillsdale's unique standing in the conservative world. Though it does not use the word, Hillsdale is a "classical" college in the same way that the Founders schools in Texas are classical charter schools. Students read great works of philosophy, theology, literature, history; their attention is directed to the eternal principles of the good, the true, and the beautiful. The campus's conservatism is cultural rather than political; one liberal journalist noted that the "ardently pro-Trump contingent" among students and faculty "appears to be small."[22] Yet Hillsdale is much more than a college campus. From the time he took over Hillsdale in 2000, Arnn aspired to turn his school into a hub of the conservative intellectual world. He endorsed Trump in early 2016, a highly unusual act of overt partisanship for a college president.

Many of Hillsdale's graduates worked for Trump and hard-right politicians such as Senator Ted Cruz of Texas and Representative Jim Jordan of Ohio. Governor Ron DeSantis of Florida, conducting his own "war on woke," asked Hillsdale scholars in 2019 to help rewrite the state's civics standards in a more overtly patriotic vein. Arnn and Spalding had deep connections with the central nodes of the conservative network, including the Heritage Foundation and the Federalist Society. Hillsdale had, in effect, used the intellectual credibility of its classical campus to become a political powerhouse. Press accounts would later implicate several Hillsdale officials in efforts to overturn the 2020 presidential election results in Michigan. (Hillsdale disputed some of the claims and stated that the officials had acted in their "personal capacity.")[23]

Matthew Spalding says that the White House approached him well before the formal announcement of the commission, and that he agreed to temporarily step down from his Hillsdale position in order to run the new body and write the report. He points to the broad mandate laid out in the executive order to insist, contrary to Trump's own words, that the intention was never simply to counter 1619 with 1776. Spalding had written a biography of George Washington and had long taught a graduate course tracing the origins of the American founding from the English Civil War. "I try to understand history as it was understood by those who were there," he said. This was a pointed, if indirect, shot at those, like the authors of the "1619 Project," who look to history to vindicate present-day views and, Spalding would say, are quick to judge historical figures by present-day standards.

Spalding hoped to pose, and answer, the big pedagogical questions as well as the political ones: "Is civic education mainly a project to educate students about history and content that has some substantive meaning in terms of their role as citizens, or is it more about getting students involved in action, in participation?" But then Joe Biden won the presidency and the whole effort was orphaned; Biden would cancel Trump's executive order almost the moment he took office. (Spalding says, somewhat improbably, that he was fully prepared to continue under President Biden.) The only thing the commission produced was the report on the founding—1776 v. 1619.

Hillsdale's signature was legible even in Trump's executive order, which declared that "the American founding envisioned a political order in harmony with the design of 'the Laws of nature and of Nature's God,' seeing the rights to life, liberty and the pursuit of happiness as embodied in and sanctioned by natural law and its traditions." Cultural conservatives, many of whom trace their intellectual roots to the philosopher and historian Leo Strauss, look backward, like Strauss, to a time when truths were understood to be grounded not in contingent human experience but in a permanent natural order. For the Hillsdale conservatives in particular, the crucial pivot in Western history is the shift at the outset of the twentieth century from natural law to "relativism" and from a language of universal rights to one of socially determined group rights. (Mainstream intellectual historians typically argue that the widespread acceptance of the doctrine of evolution put an end to faith in changeless and universal laws inhering in "nature.") The executive order did not name the "1619 Project," but the target was unmistakable: "in recent years, a series of polemics grounded in poor scholarship has vilified our Founders and our founding." Lest the point somehow be missed, the order went on to note that many of these polemics "have highlighted America's history related to race." The new report would put race in its proper place in American history.

The "1776 Report," as the document mandated by the commission was called, appeared the day before Joe Biden was sworn in, and thus two days before the commission itself was dissolved. No historical narrative as one-sided as "1776" could have attracted a bipartisan following; it was, however, ideally positioned to serve as a right-wing counter-mythos. The central theme of the "1776 Report" was that America is an exceptional nation founded on noble ideals. Though Americans, like all people, are flawed, the authors wrote, the wrongs they have committed "have always met resistance from the principles of the nation, and therefore our history is far more one of self-sacrifice, courage and nobility." Those principles, above all the "natural equality" of all men and thus the right of all to life, liberty, and the pursuit of happiness, "are found in nature and not created by man or government; rather, men create government to secure natural rights." Those principles were then embedded in the governing structure laid out in the Constitution, which, the report emphasized, carefully limited government to explicitly enumerated powers. The Bill of Rights secured what the authors called "the first freedom"—not freedom of speech and assembly, but religious liberty. The only other right the authors singled out was the right to bear arms, which, they argued, "is required by the fundamental natural right to life"—a claim that even the defenders of gun rights on the U.S. Supreme Court have not chosen to make. At this point an impartial reader might have wondered about the authors' insistence that "the facts of our founding are not partisan."[24]

Slavery is, of course, a serious problem for the argument that "natural equality" constitutes America's foundation. The report discussed slavery under the heading "Challenges to America's principles." The very first point the authors made is that while many Americans regard slavery as a "uniquely American evil," it has been "more the rule than the exception throughout human history." This is absolutely true, and both Sean Wilentz and Gordon Wood had cited that fact in the face of the "1619 Project" condemnation of the Founders. But to elevate the issue of ubiquity over the special horrors of American chattel slavery—on which the report was silent—and to insist on the abolitionist bona fides even of the slaveholding Founders, implies a greater sense of outrage over criticism of the founding demigods than over the cruelty of the practice itself. In fact, most forms of slavery in the past, from ancient Rome to the Barbary pirates, were imposed by victors over the vanquished, did not carry the badge of biological inferiority, and could be escaped through various means, including the purchase of liberty. The fact that American slavery was uniquely brutalizing and degrading does not obviate the truth that our slaveholding ancestors wrote emancipatory documents, and meant every word of them; but the grudging admission, or nonadmission, of that history absolves Americans of responsibility both for past and present injustice.

The "1776 Report" then takes a very odd turn, for the next "challenge to America's principles" is progressivism. Adherents of this view were said to have rejected the Declaration's premise that people are "endowed with unchanging rights" in favor of a credo that "there were only group rights that are constantly redefined and change with the times." This assertion would have outraged leading progressives such as John Dewey, Herbert Croly, or Louis Brandeis and would raise a laugh from the authors of *A Nation and Its People*, who write that the progressives extended an American tradition of attack on "unfair privilege" that stretches back to Andrew Jackson.

Though the progressives have long been criticized for their deference to experts and their suspicion of popular democracy, the report hyperbolically describes early efforts at economic regulation as an antidemocratic program intended to make the state "operate independent of the people." The suggestion that progressives were proto-totalitarians is made explicit in the report's discussion of the ensuing challenge to founding principles—Fascism and Communism, ideologies that share the progressives' "utter disdain for natural rights." Like the progressives, the authors note, Benito Mussolini "sought to centralize power under the management of so-called experts." This startling diatribe was presented as part of an allegedly nonpartisan effort to clarify America's founding principles.

The final challenge to the narrative of American exceptionalism is "Racism and Identity Politics." The authors celebrate the civil rights movement and the ringing faith of Martin Luther King, Jr., in American promise. By contrast, they lament the turn to programs such as affirmative action "that run counter to the lofty ideals of the founders," though they are otherwise silent on the racial disparities that remain glaring in the United States. (The race-transcending view of King, though much cherished on the right, ignores King's own politics, which included a call for a "broad-based and gigantic" plan of reparations that he compared to the GI Bill.[25]) In a passage that feels like an almost mischievous response to the "1619 Project," the authors trace the alleged progressive doctrine of "group rights" to the argument of John Calhoun, the arch-defender of slavery, that rights belong to "groups or races according to historical evolution." The intellectual roots of today's identity politics thus lie in white supremacy. I was so dumbstruck by this suggestion that I asked Spalding if he really believed it; he said that he did. "Having destroyed the foundation of rights in human nature," Spalding said, it was all too natural to embrace "a rights-based argument about groups."

The "1776 Report" concludes with a call for "national renewal" through patriotic education, echoing Trump's own language (which perhaps had actually been Hillsdale's). This would entail recognizing the centrality of the family, reforming higher education to end the "deliberately destructive scholarship" that served as "the intellectual force behind so much of the violence in our cities" and teaching schoolchildren a love of "America's true heritage." States and school districts, the report admonished without the slightest hint of irony, "should reject any curriculum that promotes one-sided partisan opinions, activist propaganda or factional ideologies"—at least ones that "demean America's heritage."

The Trump administration's patriotic history was thus even more tendentious than the *New York Times'* antipatriotic one. Both treated profoundly arguable propositions as incontestable, though the "1776 Report" was even more self-righteous in its claims of nonpartisanship. Neither, at bottom, was really a history. Both were polemical accounts of contemporary life that furnished a reading of our past to account for our present. At least half the country would have found either version utterly unpalatable. Both were instruments for further polarization in our polarized time, as if we aspired to reproduce the period after the Civil War when the two halves of the country read mutually incompatible accounts of our history. And both were highly influential.

The two stories spread by different means. The "1619 Project" had the immense power of the *New York Times* and a major national publisher behind it. The "1776 Report," though enjoying no such cultural standing, had Hillsdale College. The college offers online classes which, it says, reach three million viewers, and publishes a newsletter, *Imprimis*, that it says reaches six million readers. (One issue of *Imprimis*, adapted from a lecture delivered at Hillsdale by Roger Kimball, editor and publisher of the *New Criterion*, described the January 6 insurrection as "a hoax."[26]) And while it would be stretching a point to say that Hillsdale has the status in conservative culture that the *New York Times* enjoys among liberals, Hillsdale's authorship raised the standing of both itself and the report. Conservative governors, including Glenn Youngkin in Virginia and Ron DeSantis in Florida, invited Hillsdale scholars to help rewrite their state standards. The "1776 Report" became a canonical document in right-wing circles. In the very first interview I conducted with a classical educator, I noticed that Casey Churchill, principal of the Liberty Common School in Fort Collins, Colorado, had positioned two books in front of his laptop camera: E. D. Hirsch's *Cultural Literacy* and *The 1776 Report*. They were, he said, his touchstones.

Yet not every conservative either endorsed the "1776 Report" or shared the view that traditional pedagogy was inextricable from conservative politics. David Bobb taught political science at Hillsdale and was founding director of its Washington branch before leaving in 2013 to establish the Bill of Rights Institute, a curriculum provider. His conservative bona fides are beyond cavil. Yet Bobb came to view the war against progressive instruction as a catastrophic misstep. "The 'I'll-see-your-Howard Zinn-and-raise-you approach is stoking rather than solving the problem," he said to me. "The long-standing arms race over social studies has suggested that we need a progressive version of history and civics and a conservative version of history and civics. I think that's wrong. I think we need not just a meta-narrative but the kind of rigorous thinking that comes from studying primary-source documents and reaching students and touching their hearts." That entails engaging in activities as well as acquiring knowledge.

Perhaps most important for the propagation of Hillsdale's version of American history is the network of classical schools grouped under its Barney Charter School Initiative. The very first such school was Founders Classical Academy of Lewisville, which broke away from Hillsdale in 2021. At first these schools used various pieces of Hillsdale-approved curriculum, but in 2021 the college produced its own lesson plans; those for history and civics are known as "the 1776 curriculum," and very closely track the "1776 Report." As of mid-2024, the Barney Initiative had twenty-five schools in its network; Hillsdale says that another fifty license its curriculum.

The 1776 curriculum is identifiably "classical." Students are expected to gain a fluency with major names, places, dates, and events and are tested on all of them. Teachers are expected to immerse themselves in historical knowledge. The two first books on the list of teacher resources for the middle school unit on the Civil War are classics that happen to have been written by liberal critics of the "1619 Project"—*No Property in Man*, by Sean Wilentz, and *Battle Cry of Freedom*, by James McPherson. The student text is the young reader's version of *Land of Hope*, by Wilfred McClay, a Hillsdale faculty member. The default American history text in the world of conservative and classical education, *Land of Hope* is patriotic, conservative, antiprogressive—and reflective, erudite, and conscientious. Students are expected to read major speeches by Abraham Lincoln, portions of Frederick Douglass's autobiography, and the Reconstruction amendments. Those are not the kind of expectations you typically see in middle school, at least nonclassical ones.

Yet Hillsdale's middle school American history curriculum is hardly an ideology-free zone. Among the "enduring ideas" students are expected to gain from the unit is that slavery was immoral and dehumanizing, "as are any ways in which one person or group of people is favored over another due to the color of their skin." In other words, a line runs straight from slavery to affirmative action. If some teachers at Lewisville regard this as an enduring idea, they certainly don't say so in class. Hillsdale's civics curriculum is yet more overtly patriotic, pious, reverent. Thus Unit 4 of the high school civics curriculum, "Equality in America," begins with a reminder to teachers that the American commitment to equality has "resulted in the greatest degrees of freedom, prosperity and security for most peoples in human history," and that even the terrible fact of slavery must be balanced against the willingness of most Americans to fight and die for "equality and freedom for all." (Few historians would argue that Union soldiers thought they were fighting to end slavery.) Teachers are also reminded that "slavery and the slave trade were practiced almost everywhere, including by Arab and European slave traders and even among Africans themselves."

The unit on "Progressivism and the State," Hillsdale's great idée fixe, barely pretends to objectivity. One of the "keys to the lesson" involves progressive politicians: "Their purpose, once elected, was not actually to govern or to represent the will of the people per se, but rather to lead the people to desire and demand certain policy outcomes." The mania of the unit's author collides with the formally nondirective ethos of the lesson plan in an almost comical pretense of deference: teachers are to "review with students," "walk students through," and "help students understand" how the progressives subverted the meaning of the founding documents, undermined democracy, turned the state into a leviathan. The New Deal and the Great Society—phases 2 and 3 of progressivism—come in for similar treatment.

Dr. Spalding regards himself as an educator and scholar rather than a culture warrior. He did not, he said, have the impression that most teachers are secret propagandists for left-wing politics. "I find that most teachers want to teach," he said, though perhaps they've been unconsciously shaped by progressive teacher training. The big problem, he thought, was lack of solid content. The 1776 curriculum really does address that problem, as is true in general of classical schools and those that follow the Core Knowledge program. Yet it also encourages teachers to actively proselytize in ways that would be unthinkable in mainstream textbooks or curricula. "Encourage" is probably too gentle a word; the curriculum tells them what all right-thinking Americans believe and entrusts them with the sacred task of infusing that wisdom into schoolchildren. No doubt this is what Plato had in mind in *The Republic*; but Plato did not believe in democracy.

Hillsdale had offered to let me speak to Dr. Spalding's colleagues in Washington, to Wilfred McClay and Katie O'Donnell, head of the Barney Initiative, and perhaps to visit a Hillsdale classical school, but the offer vanished after my interview with Dr. Spalding. Perhaps I shouldn't have asked him if he really believed that John Calhoun was the fountainhead of modern identity politics. (Emily Davis, Hillsdale's head of communication, later confirmed that the offer had been withdrawn after the interview "wasn't as productive as hoped.") I had positioned myself as a political liberal but a pedagogical traditionalist. That was not good enough: Hillsdale does not appear to distinguish between politics and pedagogy.

The Left and the Right share the illusion that America's public schools have been seized by the other side. Conservatives imagine the typical classroom as a kind of witches' coven of critical race theory. Progressives generally trust teachers, who largely share their worldview, but think that right-wing governors and their henchpersons in school administration are plucking books from libraries and terrorizing independent-minded teachers. There is some truth to the latter view, but as I've shown in earlier chapters, most teachers are deeply committed to keeping partisan politics, including their own, out of the classroom. So the air war between 1619 and 1776 has not obliterated the classroom, even if a certain amount of shrapnel has rained down on teachers and students.

Yet the distribution of power between those two polar understandings of America is about to shift radically. While the administration of President Joe Biden made only small and insignificant gestures of support for 1619, the Trump administration regards 1776 as gospel—and, what is more important, regards the inculcation of a "correct" view of history as central to the larger war over the culture. Early in his term, President Trump issued an executive order titled "Ending Radical Indoctrination in K-12 Schooling." One section reestablishes the 1776 Commission. The commission is charged with "promoting patriotic education" through facilitating public lectures, giving awards to students, and advising national parks, museums, and other sites that seek to explain American history. It is also supposed to support "Task Force 250," a body established by the president to celebrate the Semiquincentennial. Hillsdale College may thus become, in effect, the White House office for the propagation of American history.

The air war will be greatly intensified. But what will change schools fundamentally is the Trump administration's view that what goes on inside the classroom is a matter of national politics rather than local control. The heart of Trump's executive order is the "ending indoctrination strategy." The order directs federal agencies, including but not limited to the Department of Education, to eliminate federal funding for schools that teach a range of what will now be officially prohibited views, above all "discriminatory equity ideology," which "treats individuals as members of preferred or disfavored groups, rather than as individuals," claims that some people are "inherently racist, sexist or oppressive, whether consciously or unconsciously," or that some "should feel guilt, anguish or other forms of psychological distress . . . because of actions committed in the past by other members of the same race."

It doesn't matter that very few teachers propagate such views; local activists, or parents, or opportunistic politicians will claim that they do. Some schools, possibly including some discussed in this book, will be threatened with losing federal funding that now pays for reduced or free lunches or for services to disabled students. Other schools will take note. Soon enough the new order may prove self-enforcing. Schools will wipe out even the faintest traces of "1619" instruction. Some no doubt will fall in line with the new codes of patriotism; many more, perhaps, will default to banalities that offend no one, and teach no one.

5

Hamilton on the Stage and in the Classroom

In late October 2023, I attended a matinee performance of the musical *Hamilton* with thirteen hundred ecstatic New York City public high school students. Along with other invited guests, I sat in a box upstairs at the splendidly baroque Richard Rodgers Theater on West 46th Street; the orchestra below us was filled with kids who could hardly believe their good fortune in missing a day of school in order to go to a hip-hop musical. Many of them had never seen a Broadway show, and they were in no way restrained by the rules of decorum. At the end of every song, a shout rose up and then tapered off as the kids settled in for more. They yelped at the first appearance of George Washington, who was played by Tamar Greene, a burly Black guy. They cried out in dismay when Hamilton gave way to the seductress who would later blackmail him. They recoiled in horror when Hamilton's son Philip died in a duel not long before Hamilton himself would. At intermission, one of the other guests came back from the ladies room and reported that she had found two girls crying.

This was an audience that had experienced the play with a totality of absorption almost unknown to the experienced theater-goer. Afterward, several of the cast members and techs came back on stage for a Q & A. The kids were flabbergasted, like the credulous patrons of a magic show, when a slight young man announced that he had been the mincing, prancing, scornful King George III. They asked "What's your favorite song?," and "Is it hard to play a character that you might consider racist or sexist?," and, of course, "How can I get into acting?"

I had seen *Hamilton* before, but not, of course, through those eyes. What the play seemed to be saying to *them* was that American history belonged to, and could be claimed by, all Americans; that a rank outsider with nothing to his name could nevertheless rise to dizzying heights through talent and ambition; that through art the remote past could come fully alive; that even the most abstruse issues, such as the chartering of a national bank, could furnish the material for a song or a speech; that popular and familiar art forms, such as hip-hop, fully belonged in the intimidating world of the Broadway theater; and that there had been a time when patriotism had been a cause worth dying for. Underneath it all, *Hamilton* conveyed the idea that complexity was good; the fact that Hamilton was a complex man enveloped in a complex story made his story stronger, not weaker. It was as if the most moving and sophisticated lesson in history and civics had been illuminated in a lightning flash.

The performance I had seen was the centerpiece, and payoff, of the Hamilton Education Project. Six times a year, the producers of the show set aside all tickets, at a bargain basement $70, for high school juniors who have been studying the founding era. (The schools pay, not the kids.) The arrangement dates to the spring of 2015, when Lin-Manuel Miranda, the creative genius behind the play, and Jeffrey Seller, the producer, paid a visit to James Basker, the executive director of the Gilder Lehrman Institute of American History, which functions both as a repository of rare American documents and as a provider of instructional resources and professional development in history and civics. Miranda wanted to use the play to reach out to high school kids; Ron Chernow, who had written the biography on which the play was based, had suggested he speak to Basker, who doubles as a professor of literary history at Barnard College. Basker agreed to develop curricular materials around the play; Seller agreed to offer the cut-rate tickets. Gilder Lehrman's education team had a brilliant inspiration, or at least one very much in keeping with the spirit of *Hamilton*: students would qualify for a ticket not by taking a class or writing a paper but by staging a performance—skit, song, dance, as they saw fit—based in Hamilton's world. They would do, in miniature, what Miranda himself had done. By the fall of 2023, two hundred thousand students had performed their way to an afternoon at the Richard Rodgers Theater.

Seeing *Hamilton* through the students' eyes made me realize that I had to learn more about Eduham, as the program is informally known. I had already spent a day at the Academy of American Studies, a high school in Queens that Gilder Lehrman had helped establish in the late 1990s. Students at the academy have to take two years of global history and three years of American history, as well as a year of "Participation in Government and Law" and a semester of Economics. The school also offers what appears to be every Advanced Placement course in history and government created by the College Board. The academy seemed like the right place to watch the development of the Hamilton project.

The Academy of American Studies is the kind of school you see on TV shows about the urban kaleidoscope. The student body is 36 percent Hispanic, 35 percent white, and 24 percent Asian (and only 3 percent Black). But those numbers hardly capture the experience of sitting in a classroom. Like most New Yorkers, I try to figure out the ethnic box in which fellow citizens belong. So dizzying was the demographic blend at the academy that I was almost always wrong. Hispanic? No; Maghreb. Filipino? No; Nepalese. Here was the contemporary urban school par excellence. That said, I never heard a classroom discussion about identity, the subject that children of color are said to be obsessed with. The students spent a lot of their time learning about the remote past, if not quite as much as those in classical schools do.

On my earlier visit, I had sat in on a ninth-grade World History class. The students had separated into groups on either side of the classroom to prepare for a debate they would be holding the next day: "Alexander of Macedon: Hero or Villain?" A few weeks earlier, they had held the same debate over India's classical-era emperor, Ashoka. The "hero" team had won, though only after fully acknowledging Ashoka's brutality prior to his conversion to Buddhism. Their teacher, who I will call Mrs. Lopez, wanted to first make sure that everyone agreed on terms. "What makes you a hero or a villain?," she asked. The Villains said, "Because you're egotistical and narcissistic." The kids had read up on Alexander's life. He thought he was a god. He murdered twenty-five hundred innocent people only because they resisted his conquest. Mrs. Lopez gently remonstrated. "This is war. This isn't 2023."

"But mass genocide still isn't okay," said one of the Villains. Fair point—though Alexander may have been guilty of a "mass atrocity" rather than genocide.

The Heroes, meanwhile, began quietly readying their ammunition. Say what you will, but Alexander spread the Hellenistic cult, rebuilt palaces that he destroyed, expressed remorse for that notorious slaughter. The students worked with one another quietly while Mrs. Lopez circulated, listening and offering tips. She had distributed a worksheet that asked the students not only to write down evidence for their view but to reflect on the work of their team and on their own contribution to the team. I asked one of the Villains what he had learned from losing the Ashoka debate. He admitted that he hadn't been ready when the Heroes challenged one of his claims. "You have to have your evidence right in front of you," he said ruefully. This time he'd be loaded for bear.

Though a regular old New York City public school—not a charter school—the academy was born with several advantages. First, it was one of two high schools established through a collaborative effort between the city's Board of Education and Gilder Lehrman. It had a purpose from the outset; and while other New York high schools have vocational themes such as medical technology, the academy's theme is academic and civic. The students seem to take their civic responsibilities seriously. The school's current and founding principal, William Bassell, told me that when, in 2016, he began seeking a new building, the students decided to form a New Building Committee, agitating for the new home at every borough-wide and citywide Department of Education meeting—even though the plan would come to fruition only after they themselves had moved on. The city finally gave in, and the new building opened in early 2022 in what had been a parking lot. Nor does it seem coincidental that

Bassell, though a lifer in the New York City public schools, is an opera nut who every year teaches an Opera Appreciation elective that involves several trips to the Metropolitan Opera. One morning I went with Bassell and the kids to the Met to see a rehearsal of Daniel Catán's surrealistic contemporary opera, *Florencia in the Amazon*.

The academy also occupies a special New York City niche of semi-selectivity. The school takes half of its students from those among the applicants who have scored high on a seventh-grade test of reading and math proficiency. The other half must be drawn equally from the top, middle, and bottom third of that distribution. The average student is thus better prepared and slightly more well-to-do than average. While 72 percent of New York students are eligible for free and reduced lunch, 58 percent of the academy's students are, which is to say that it's a working-class rather than a high-poverty school. The academy appeals to immigrants, perhaps because of the commitment to the kind of traditional curriculum that also draws such families to classical schools. The school's outcomes are impressive. The graduation rate is 96 percent. Virtually all graduates go to college immediately after high school. Not surprisingly, the students score about ten points above the city average on the U.S. and world history tests. At its best moments, the academy seemed to be dedicated to bringing the academic virtues of another era to the infinitely varied student population of today.

Gilder Lehrman is a leading player in a distinctively American solution to the problem of civic education. Because the formal education system has failed both to effectively teach history and civics and to prepare teachers to do so—and because, in any case, the United States has no national system of instruction—a network of public-spirited private actors has sought to fill the vacuum. The sense of alarm over civics that began with the 2003 Carnegie report on "The Civic Mission of Schools" prompted both educators and funders to set up nonprofit providers of curricular material and professional development. Today that field is crowded with organizations such as Gilder Lehrman, iCivics, the Bill of Rights Institute, the National Constitution Center, the Jack Miller Center, and the like. Collectively, they constitute a vast library from which any teacher from grade K to 12 is free to choose material on topics both recondite and grand.

Gilder Lehrman, for example, offers students online courses on topics in American history taught by some of the nation's leading scholars. The course on the Vietnam War is taught by Harvard's Fredrik Logevall, a leading historian of the war; the course titled "The 1960s in Historical Perspective" is taught by Georgetown historian Michael Kazin. Each consists of twenty-odd lectures with links to additional sources and quizzes. For teachers of all grades, the institute offers dozens of lesson plans on topics in American history. For a high-school-level class on "Andrew Jackson and the Bank War," a subject that may be covered only fleetingly in whatever material a history teacher otherwise has available, the lesson plan offers a general introduction with textual sources and then suggests that the students be divided into groups to briefly study and report back on six topics, including the Panic of 1819 and the first and second banks of the United States. The lesson plan supplies brief readings on each. Then the teacher is to choose six panelists to argue for and against the second bank as well as a moderator who is to prepare questions for both sides.[1]

Perhaps the best known of the nonprofit providers is iCivics, which bills itself as "the nation's premier non-profit civic education provider of high-quality, non-partisan, engaging, and free resources." The organization has a progressive reputation, though it was founded in 2009 by Justice Sandra Day O'Connor. iCivics goes to great lengths to engage students who might be turned off by academic vocabulary and classroom routine. Its vast catalog of lesson plans favors a jokey vernacular that is presumably meant to be relatable to teenage users. The one-page introduction to the classical origins of democracy for junior-high-level students features short paragraphs with snappy titles such as "Athens: Leader of the Pack" and "Gotta Get This Down on Papyrus."

iCivics' high-school-level lessons feature longer paragraphs with plenty of graphics and somewhat reductionist summations of great thinkers (from the unit on the Enlightenment: "Machiavelli was saying, 'Get real!'").[2] Each unit is followed by quizzes that, for example, ask the student to match a quotation to its author. As part of its commitment to softening the harsh edges of classroom life, iCivics offers a wide array of games designed to reinforce learning. Thus "Brief The Chief" invites students to interact with a video of cartoon versions of the presidents and various statesmen in order to gain the knowledge needed to, say, advise President Lincoln on how he should follow up the Emancipation Proclamation.[3] There is a thin line, which the iCivics material may cross, between meeting-them-where-they-are and outright condescension.

One of the most heartening aspects of the world of civic resources is how little one hears the mighty thunder of 1619 v. 1776. Even providers thought of as "conservative" make a real effort to keep a thumb off the scale. The lessons offered by the Bill of Rights Institute, founded by former Hillsdale professor (and now apostate) David Bobb, are free of polemics or propaganda, though they reflect the belief of the classical school world that virtue should be directly taught. A lesson about Aaron Burr asks students to consider the difference between "self-serving" and "noble" ambition. Many of the classes are organized as debates, at times over questions that most liberals regard as settled, such as "Did the New Deal End the Great Depression?" and "Was the Great Society successful?"[4] But historians take both of these questions very seriously, and the institute's material pits serious scholars against one another. Bobb told me that in one recent exercise, he had included excerpts from both Nikole Hannah-Jones of 1619 fame and Robert Woodson of the party of 1776.

The students at the Academy of American Studies were slated to attend a *Hamilton* matinee in early February. One of the Government classes had been chosen to work up performances and then go to the show. I sat in on the class in December. The students had chosen their subject by reading through the Hamilton Education Project's website, which includes primary documents and secondary material on twelve major events and forty-three prominent figures from the founding period (some of whom, like Phyllis Wheatley, the formerly enslaved poet, had no direct connection to Hamilton). There were skits about *Marbury v. Madison*, raps about Thomas Paine's *Common Sense*, a debate over the national bank. Sarah, who wore a black headscarf, along with two non-Muslim friends, read a rap poem on the Whiskey Rebellion, though they were too prim to come down hard on the rhymes the way the *Hamilton* actors do. "By 1794, the farmers were still filled with rage / Because the unfair taxation affected their wage. . . . The protests continued, becoming extremely violent / The people of Western Pennsylvania would not remain silent."

Two boys imagined a debate between a republican Hamilton and a more democratic Madison as they met to write the *Federalist Papers*.

> HAMILTON: We need to make sure that what is built now is built on a foundation of intellect and proper structure. This cannot be done by the common man. Madison, don't be coy. We both know this.
>
> MADISON: I too hope to build this nation on a strong central government. But . . . we cannot simply say that the common man is not capable of rational thought. Are you trying to make an enemy out of the American people?

At the end of the skit, the ghost of Hamilton's father arrived and expressed shame for his abandonment of the boy. "Be a better man than I ever was and never falter," he intoned.

Then two kids, whom I'll call Luis and Fernanda, got up to deliver a dialogue between Hamilton and his wife Eliza set at the moment when Hamilton was setting off for the Constitutional Convention. Neither seemed to be a native speaker of English. Luis, in a stocking cap, gazed moodily at the black electrical cables that ran outside the classroom window.

> HAMILTON: Most of my ideas for government are far different from the ideas that the many others have. . . . I believe that representatives of states should be appointed for the duration of their life, though I think they should have a special name for themselves, and there should be one higher power that elects them.

Elizabeth: Surely other delegates will see this as an overstepping of power for the federal government.

Hamilton conceded that this was so and said that he had been studying the world's governing systems. Eliza suggested that he draw on the Magna Carta. Hamilton, shedding his funk, said that he planned to do just that. "Thank you, Eliza," he concluded. "I am nervous yet hopeful for the future of our great nation. And don't worry about me, I won't be eaten alive." Wild applause.

Though some of the kids were plainly not AP students, I was struck by how much actual research had gone into the projects. Several students told me that they had drawn on knowledge from the history classes they had taken in prior years. A few weeks after class, I was allowed to meet with half a dozen of them. I asked Sarah, whose parents had emigrated from Morocco when she was a baby, where she had gone to learn about the Whiskey Rebellion. "I wanted to find reliable sources," she said, "so I looked at websites that ended in 'org.' And then I asked my teacher if I could trust them." Sumerin, a Nepalese student who had come to America in eighth grade, said that he had found the archaic language of some of the primary documents too difficult, though he had read letters between Washington and Hamilton. Josh, who had played Madison in the dialogue with Hamilton, had found letters between the two in the local public library. He had noticed that Hamilton hated small talk, so he wrote Hamilton as "all business" and Madison as "more cautious." I asked if anyone had looked at a book. No dice.

I wondered if the experience had changed their view of America or American history. That was perhaps expecting too much self-conscious reflection on a very recent event. Nevertheless, Miguel—the ghost of James Hamilton—said, "I didn't really understand how American government works. I just thought that if something was good, the government should just do it. I've learned that the government is a complex system. People want different things, and there's going to be a conflict of interests." Things are more complicated than he thought: That was the kind of lesson that makes teachers feel they've actually accomplished something.

The academy had been assigned to the second and third rows of the orchestra for the February 7 matinee. I was sitting with the girls. (The students had spontaneously segregated themselves by sex.) One of them told me that she had put on *Hamilton* in fourth grade, and she knew every song by heart; in the course of the show, I would see her silently mouthing the words. Another showed me her phone so I could read the script of her Boston Massacre rap. The curtain rose and everyone cheered. We were about fifteen feet from the actor Trey Curtis when he bounded on stage and introduced himself to the world: "Alexander Hamilton!" Everyone around me screamed at once. The girls giggled at Thomas Jefferson, whom Miranda, with the consummate unfairness of a true artist at work, had reduced to a preening dandy—absurd, yes, but a perfect foil for his main character. They groaned, and I think maybe hissed, when the endlessly appetitive Hamilton surrendered to Maria, the seductress. They were raptly silent when they weren't giving vent to their feelings. And of course they cheered insanely when the curtain went down. I had been very struck, this time, by Hamilton's overwhelming and often brutal ambition. ("I'm not giving away my shot.") I asked the girl next to me whether she thought Hamilton was a good guy or a bad guy. "Maybe he wasn't such a good person," she said. "It made me think that Burr was a better person than I thought."

Hamilton, and the Hamilton Education Project, is a wonderful thing. We should wish that all students could participate in the project and see the show. Of course they can't; only about twenty-five thousand a year could at the peak. (Now it's down to about half that.) So the question, as with all wonderful things in schooling, is, what about it is generalizable? What lessons about civic education should we draw from Eduham? First, Eduham is not actually "civic" in the usual understanding of that word. Unlike West Chicago High School's Legislative Simulation, and unlike innumerable programs that send students to meet local government officials, the Hamilton program does not expose students to the workings of government. It does not teach students how to civilly disagree with one another; perhaps it does not encourage any of the main civic "dispositions." But students can have a deeply civic experience that does not involve their immediate world—in this case, by allowing them to engage actively with the American founding.

One of the distinguishing features of Eduham is that it is rooted in an academic discipline. Waubonsie's "Prairie Restoration" project was based on botany, a field with a remote connection to democracy, but it still allowed students to connect their studies to acts of citizenship; it linked intellectual understanding to civic experience. Eduham is rooted in American history; the students at the Academy of American Studies had, in effect, prepared for it through their unusually intensive study of government and history. Because the subject of *Hamilton* was the founding, that was the period of history the project drew on, but it would have been just as rich had the subject been the Civil War, or the Depression, or the civil rights movement. Mrs. Lopez had made a game of ancient history. If the Metropolitan Opera had been showing a work on Alexander the Great (or rather, "of Macedon," because his greatness is no longer to be conceded), Mr. Bassell could have incorporated that into a very rewarding experience.

Eduham requires students to engage in serious research in order to both prepare a creative performance of their own and go out in the world to enjoy a great work of art. This collapses the distinction that Matthew Spalding of Hillsdale College had made between textual knowledge and participatory experience. Conservatives such as Spalding believe strongly in the former and are inclined to deprecate the latter. So, too, are classical educators. Government class in Lewisville consists of reading the great texts. On the other end of the spectrum, a strain of progressive thinking treats student-initiated activities as "authentic" and close study of the great achievements of long-dead white males as a burden that today's diverse and deeply politicized students are bound to shuck off. "We are often taught about democracy and politics in boring civics lessons focused on the founding documents," writes Scott Warren, the founder of the "action civics" group Generation Civics. Warren would replace text-based learning with political action.[5] The one side would lock students in the classroom, the other would lock them out. Yet Eduham shows, or at least indicates, that one can design an experience in which the opportunity for personal engagement leads to a deeper relationship to texts.

Another intriguing aspect of Eduham is the relationship between personal creativity and scholarship, both at the level of the individual student and of the artwork in question. *Hamilton* is extraordinarily dense with historical fact, and even at times with arcane debate. Many scholars of the era fault the play as history: the real Hamilton was far more seigneurial, and less democratic, than the fictional one. Nevertheless, Lin-Manuel Miranda absorbed immense amounts of history, ran it through the centrifuge of his imagination, and decanted a wildly exuberant work of theater. That is a lesson in itself. Students are expected to reproduce that process in miniature by turning their research into a song or a skit. School does not always reinforce the idea that creativity depends on prior knowledge and can be a spur to knowledge. The students in that Government class might have read those letters and speeches had they been assigned for a mandatory paper, but what made the documents come alive was the chance to incorporate them in a performance of their own. Here, again, the alleged dichotomy between "knowing" and "doing" is too facile.

Finally, complexity—"Burr was a better person than I thought." In a world increasingly paralyzed by passionate certitudes, there may be no more powerful civic lesson than, "It's more complicated than you think." It turns out that everyone has, or believes they have, a good reason for believing what they believe. Sincerity is not to be confused with truth. What's more, experience shows us that even people regarded as heroes suffer from the same terrible flaws we mortals have. Alexander Hamilton was arrogant and reckless. Of course that recognition must not become a pretext for passivity: we don't want students to feel that there is no point in getting involved in democratic life because "it's so complicated." We want civic projects to draw on students' idealistic wish to make their world better, as many of them do. *Hamilton* makes political action feel thrilling even as we see that the hero is shaped by fierce ambition as much as by the passion for improvement.

What about the Academy of American Studies? What, if anything, is generalizable about *its* program? I was so beguiled by a curriculum devoted to American history and government that at first I envisioned the academy as a progressive alternative to classical education, a living proof that inner-city students could sit in a circle and debate current affairs and read contemporary books and nevertheless dedicate themselves to mastering difficult ideas. Unlike many other New York City public high schools, the Academy of American Studies makes no pretense of vocational education; if it purports to prepare students for anything in particular, it would be critical inquiry into the social sciences. Teachers trusted students to work among themselves; the students seemed to reward that trust by collaborating well among themselves. Mrs. Lopez had enough faith in her ninth-graders to let them prepare for debate with only a light touch of supervision.

In the period previous to Mrs. Lopez's class, I had visited Alisa Dorfman's senior AP Government class. The subject of the day was how representation works in a democratic system; students were to learn the difference between the "trusteeship" doctrine that sees the elected representative as guided above all by personal conscience and the "delegation" doctrine that envisions the representative as the direct agent of the will of constituents. They had already read three brief accounts of political dramas meant to illustrate these contrasting views. Using the guidance contained in her AP lesson plan, Mrs. Dorfman told the kids to form "Harkness Discussion Circles," student-led conversations designed to bring out the full complexity of issues under discussion. The group I sat in had read a passage about the dramatic resignation of Senator Alben Barkley of Kentucky as majority leader in 1944 after FDR had vetoed a revenue bill that Barkley had pushed through. One girl—my circle was all girls—observed, "It said that he was crying when he gave the speech." Why was that? "Maybe people cared more about party loyalty then," another hazarded. There was extensive debate about Barkley's motivation. Had he resigned out of pique or principle? Was he acting as a "trustee" or a "partisan"? Our leader made sure that the one quiet girl spoke up. Then she said, "I have a question: Would you want him to be your senator if he was still alive?" That was, really, the pith of the matter. All agreed that they would; Barkley seemed far more principled than politicians today.

The amount of material the students had been expected to master had been relatively scanty: they had watched a "sixty-second civics lesson" on the two models and read a one-page handout on a historical event. AP Government seemed to involve less reading than AP U.S. History. But they had also engaged in a thoughtful discussion in which all were included. They had, as the AP lesson plan directed, reflected on "the ethical responsibilities of a democratically elected representative."

Another thing struck me both in Mrs. Dorfman's class and others: though I was in Long Island City, Queens, New York, the heart of progressive territory, much of the class discussion would not have been out of place in, say, Indiana. When Mrs. Dorfman asked why people ran for Congress, the kids said, "They're all passionate about an issue," or, "You have to spend a lot of time reading newspapers." Apparently they hadn't gotten the message that people run for Congress to further their class interest. The students in ninth-grade U.S. History reflected on how the marriage between Pocahantas and John Rolfe promoted social peace—and not on the unequal power relationship between them. What's more, the decor was all wrong. Mrs. Morgenbesser, who taught twelfth-grade Government, decorated the front of the class with pictures of Black heroes–Muhammad Ali, Barack Obama, Martin Luther King, Jr.—but on either side of the smartboard had taped up images of Presidents Cleveland, McKinley, Teddy Roosevelt, and Wilson. Another Government teacher flanked his smartboard with posters of a Democratic donkey and a Republican elephant and chose as his inspirational figures Voltaire, Lincoln, and Du Bois. The teachers seem not to have gotten the message either. I would guess that the immigrant parents who sent their children to the school would be gratified at this immersion in Americana.

And yet . . . the academy never quite ascended to the station I had assigned it in my mind. Perhaps because it was an ordinary public school rather than a charter school, the academy hadn't escaped the gravitational pull of the larger public school system in the way that, for example,

Founders Classical Academy had. Few of the teachers seemed to have postgraduate degrees in history (though Bassell had one in English Literature). Rather than build their own curriculum, they used the city's own "Passport to Social Studies," a "scope and sequence" based on state standards as well as the Common Core Learning Standards. This turned out to be a pet peeve of James Basker of Gilder Lehrman. While New York City private schools typically hired teachers with subject-matter knowledge, he told me, almost all the public school teachers the organization worked with had emerged from ed school with specialized pedagogical skills but little to no subject-matter mastery. Gilder Lehrmann tried to fill that void, as similar groups did, by offering summer school programs of professional development for history teachers. That was a Band-Aid, not a cure.

I had also been dismayed by the academy's almost paranoid reaction to my request to visit. Though I knew that years of sensationalized press coverage had made many schools and school districts extremely gun-shy before journalists, in this case I had come recommended by Basker, effectively the school's founder. Nevertheless, Elizabeth Dudley, the head of Social Studies, seemed to have done her best to keep me at bay. I had to ask the press secretary of the New York City Department of Education to intervene, at which point it was agreed that I would be permitted to visit the school a maximum of three times. During those visits, Dudley trailed me from class to class, always smiling and helpful but rarely letting me out of her sight. I was not allowed to sit in the student cafeteria, as I had at Founders Classical. I was not to speak to a student at all without express written permission from a parent. Nor was I permitted to identify a teacher without consent. Alisa Dorfman was the only one who allowed me to use her name; all the other names I have used here are pseudonyms. I did not conclude from all this hugger-mugger that the school had something terrible to hide; rather, I thought that any institution this risk-averse was likely to stay within conventional limits.

It is possible that had I been able to stay longer and delve deeper, I would have had the kind of probing conversations with teachers that I had had at Founders or seen a class as inspiring as European AP with Kelly Rose at Waubonsie Valley. I had been delighted by some of the classes I sat in on, but in others instruction seemed mechanical. I sat in on a history class where the teacher mostly recited from a text and the kids obediently copied the notes she made on the whiteboard. In another class, students whirled rapidly through poems and artworks from the Harlem Renaissance. They seem to have had neither the time nor the guidance to make much sense of what they were seeing, and the observations they offered at the end of class were generally lame; but the teacher enthusiastically agreed even with obvious misunderstandings, as if the goal were encouragement rather than understanding. This was precisely the disconnect between knowing and feeling that Eduham sought to repair.

Eduham was a great program. If civic education could be reduced to a program, or a project, or a body of instructional material, we could insert it into the school like a laboratory technician inserting a modified string of DNA into a sick patient. But if education for democratic citizenship is not a discrete thing, like Physics or Gym, but something more like a culture, an orientation, an act of shaping—the DNA rather than a splice of it—then we must think more fundamentally about how and what we teach.

6

The History Wars in a Purple State

In the summer of 2022, officials from Virginia's Department of Education presented a draft of new standards in history and social studies to the state's Board of Education. Christonya Brown, the department's history and social science coordinator, described for the nine board members an extraordinarily exacting process of consultation and revision that had required eighteen months and included historians and economists, teachers and curriculum experts, historical museums, parents and students. The group had done extensive research on "inquiry-based practices" and thus focused the new document on "skills development" rather than "just memorizing a list of facts."[1] In the normal course of things, the board would have accepted the draft for "first review" and then solicited public comment at meetings around the state. But this was not a normal moment in Virginia. The standards had been prepared under Governor Ralph Northam, a Democrat, but in 2021 Glenn Youngkin, a Republican, had been elected governor, thanks in no small part to inveighing against liberal control of the schools. After Republicans had blocked Northam's late-term appointments to the board, Youngkin had gained a five-person majority.

"The Youngkin people," as one of his appointees later said, "wanted their own standards."

Administration officials found—and apparently leaked—a few telltale signs of wokeness in the four-hundred-page draft. A local news station reported that the new standards no longer described George Washington as "the father of our country" or James Madison as "the father of the Constitution," a moniker traditionally used in Virginia. Youngkin jumped on this omission to declare that the standards "still need significant work." His school superintendent, Jillian Balow, persuaded the school board to "pause" the proceedings. She and a group of conservative consultants and scholars then secretly devised a new version of the standards and sprang it on an unsuspecting board.

The ensuing donnybrook would recapitulate virtually every element of the increasingly ferocious state-by-state war over school standards—red versus blue historical accounts, progressive versus traditional pedagogy, "parental control" versus expert opinion, politicians versus educators. The debate would not end until eight months had passed, four drafts had been written, several central figures had been fired, and virtually everyone had become heartily sick of the whole affair. Owing to some combination of exhaustion and actual reservoirs of good will, Virginia improbably ended with a set of standards that at least minimally satisfied all parties.

While arguments over the content of textbooks or over the competing merits of history and social studies have been with us for a century or more, the debate over state standards, now such a fixed part of our educational landscape, stretches back just a few decades. Only with the shocking evidence of failure exposed in the 1983 "A Nation at Risk" report, and by ensuing studies such as *What Do Our 17-Year-Olds Know?*, did most states even begin to draw up standards in the chief subjects. Schools, and school districts, had long been left to themselves to teach as they saw fit; suddenly, it became all too clear that most of them were not up to the job. They needed to be held accountable to specified goals. In 1991, President George H. W. Bush announced an initiative called America 2000; he hoped to oversee the establishment of "world-class" national standards in the major subjects.[2]

The effort to create national standards collapsed by 1995. Governors were thus left on their own to devise state standards. In the rush to demonstrate accountability to suddenly worried voters, virtually every state had adopted standards in the major subjects by the late 1990s. Those standards varied enormously from state to state; some resembled curricula, with highly specified subject matter, while others provided teachers only a vague framework of study. Nevertheless, the very fact of publicly stipulating what children should learn, and how they should learn, turned parents and educators into partisans in ways they hadn't been before—above all, on standards for history and social studies.

One of the first states to adopt standards was Virginia, which did so pursuant to a legislative order in 1981. The standards were revised under a Democratic governor in 1988. In 1994, Republican George Allen became governor after promising, among other things, to go "back to the basics" on education. Early the following year, Allen's Department of Education presented a 179-page document laying out standards in social studies, English, math, and science. Allen called for phonics and traditional math, as many Republicans had. But he did something else that was quite new at the time: he proposed to completely rewrite the state's social studies curriculum along traditionalist lines. The new standards were highly detailed, and the detail itself carried a point: students must learn particular things. Third-graders would "identify major events in the history of England from 1215 to 1688 that contributed to the development of parliamentary democracy." So, too, with the other grades. Allen's traditionalism edged just deeply enough into cultural conservatism, for example by requiring elementary school students to learn stories from the Bible but not from other faiths, that his pedagogical ambitions looked very much like a war on liberal orthodoxy.[3]

Allen got that war. At the packed auditorium of Loudon County High School in early April 1994, parents, teachers, and school officials lambasted the standards as educational medievalism; one teacher who had gone to the Virginia public schools in the 1920s said that the curriculum very much resembled her own. At a subsequent hearing, one mother said, "I want my children to learn that not all exceptional authors are British, American, white or male." Several teachers argued that the standards asked too much of young children. Allen's staunchest public defender was Lynne Cheney, former secretary of the U.S. Department of Education and a prominent cultural conservative, who in a *Washington Post* op-ed piece assailed "the new conventional wisdom" that children "shouldn't be required to gain a command of facts." Allen ultimately lost moderate Republican legislators, several of whom called for a new panel to draw up new standards. After two months of polemical fury unheard of in school circles at the time, the Virginia Department of Education withdrew the proposed standards and agreed to try again.[4]

In the aftermath of Allen's failure, the budding culture war moved elsewhere; educational professionals were largely left to adopt state standards, good and (mostly) bad. That era of comity came to an end with the rise of Donald Trump and the "war on woke" on the one side, and Black Lives Matter, the "1619 Project," and *How to Be an Antiracist* on the other. On matters of culture and identity, the Right moved further right and the Left moved further left. Liberal states such as Minnesota began to adopt more progressive standards in history and civics, while conservative states such as Texas and Florida were reinforcing the patriotic content of civics curricula and rooting out "divisive concepts" such as critical race theory (CRT)—the doctrine that racism should be understood not simply as individual bias against Black people but as a set of practices baked into the deep structures of American society. The closure of schools during the pandemic confused, frustrated, and finally infuriated many parents. Governor Ron DeSantis of Florida and Governor Greg Abbott of Texas made "restoring parental control" shorthand for taking back the schools from woke educators intent on cramming CRT and LGBTQ+ ideology down the throats of unsuspecting children.

While the school world had long been a default progressive one, a whole substratum of conservative providers of instructional material, lobbyists, and polemicists had begun to form during the Trump years. Many of them regarded the burgeoning debates over schooling as the central battle of our time. The conservative activist Andrew Breitbart had famously written, "Politics is downstream from culture," a phrase that vividly captured the idea that cultural debate ultimately shapes political debate rather than the other way around. The path to victory over liberalism thus lay in seizing the high ground of culture. Hillsdale was one node in this new network; another was the Civics Alliance, a coalition of conservative organizations formed in March 2021 by the National Association of Scholars, a rival to mainstream academic bodies such as the American Historical Association. (It was the president of the NAS, Peter W. Woods, who had written the *1620* counterblast to the "1619 Project.") The Civics Alliance brought together antiprogressive activists such as Christopher Rufo, who had almost single-handedly weaponized CRT; Trump-adjacent thinkers such as Michael Anton of the Claremont Institute; conservative elders such as Roger Kimball of the *New Criterion* and Harvard's Harvey Mansfield; and leading figures in the classical schools movement and officials from obscure right-wing think tanks.

In its opening declaration, "Why We Need a Civics Alliance," the organizers explained that the alliance had come into being in order to counter "the New Civics," which "threatens to replace traditional civics education with neo-Marxist 'social justice' propaganda, vocational training for left-wing activism, and Alinsky-style community organizing techniques adapted for use in the classroom." Under the neutral-sounding guise of "service learning" and "civic engagement," the New Civics would "obliterate from our children's memory the America worth loving and defending and will create a cadre of trained activists dedicated to replacing the American republic with a neo-Marxist 'social justice' regime."[5] The letter cited as one example of this danger Illinois's law requiring schools to incorporate participatory activities into civics curricula. The authors did not specify whether they regarded replanting a local creek or holding a model congress as species of neo-Marxist social justice propaganda.

In early 2021, Stanley Kurtz, a leading figure in the Civics Alliance and a one-man army against all things woke, authored a model statute that he called the Partisanship Out of Civics Act. The bill stipulated that no teacher could be "compelled to address current events," that those who do so "shall explore such issues from diverse and contending perspectives," that students would not get credit for "lobbying for legislation," and that no teacher shall tell students that "one race or sex is inherently superior to another race or sex" or assert "the systematic nature of racism"—that is, CRT. Kurtz's model legislation proved to be a foundational text for governors in Florida, Texas, and elsewhere who would ban the teaching of action civics and CRT.[6]

Kurtz seemed to regard the typical classroom as a fiendish laboratory of indoctrination. In a lengthy email exchange (Kurtz declined to be interviewed in person or over the phone), I noted that I had spent quite a bit of time in schools observing actual civics projects and had yet to encounter the kind of woke orthodoxy that he was describing as rampant. Kurtz directed me to several civics projects that he regarded as appalling examples of left-wing partisanship. Some really were pretty appalling: after encouraging students to join a protest over a local development project favored by then Mayor Lori Lightfoot, a number of Chicago teachers had insisted that such partisan activity constituted just the kind of "civic engagement" Illinois law required. This claim was considered so indefensible that the teachers had been disciplined.

Nevertheless, Kurtz wrote that he considered gross politicization an inevitable consequence of the state's commitment to action civics. Because "many of the strongest supporters of action civics practice far-left politics," he wrote, we should hardly be surprised that, whatever formal invocations of neutrality are embedded in state law or local rules, in practice students will become junior soldiers for the Left. Kurtz himself had never sat in on civics classes and suggested that I had gotten a skewed picture because "teachers inclined to be political" would keep their intentions under wraps when I visited.

Thanks to activists such as Kurtz and organizations such as the Civics Alliance, conservative forces soon registered a series of successes in red states. In the summer of 2021 a committee appointed by South Dakota's Department of Education delivered a draft of new social studies standards widely seen as a turn to the Right; news accounts noted that the group had stripped out many references to the state's Native American history and culture.[7] But in a philippic published in the *National Review*, Kurtz wrote that "hard-left activists" had hijacked the process. Education officials had contracted with a consultant who promised to integrate the C3 Framework into the standards. That would guarantee that South Dakota students would be subjected to action civics and exercises in social justice. Yet only a few months earlier, as Kurtz noted, South

Dakota's hard-right Republican governor, Kristi Noem, had become the first governor to sign a pledge prohibiting the teaching of CRT and action civics. Though the Noem administration issued a revision that deleted the action civics language, Kurtz insisted that the deeper problems would remain. "Noem can still be a hero," he wrote, if she scrapped the standards and started again with a new committee.[8]

Kurtz told me in an email that his piece had prompted Noem to do just that, and there's no reason to doubt the claim. In April 2022, Noem commissioned a new committee to draft new standards and appointed Will Morrisey, a retired professor of politics at Hillsdale College, as facilitator to the committee. South Dakota's history and civics standards already skewed rightward: the investigators from the Fordham Institute had complained that the standards paid "strikingly little attention to civil and voting rights" and declined to say that slavery had been the cause of the Civil War. The new standards, which the South Dakota Board of Education would approve in 2023, showcased Hillsdale's unalloyed reverence for the Founding Fathers and treated Booker T. Washington as a vastly more significant figure than W. E. B. Du Bois. Yet they also replaced a focus on the acquisition of skills with explicit dictates on content. One member of the commission explained that the new version had interred the "John Dewey progressive notion about skills" and what he claimed to be Dewey's ambition to "funnel students into jobs" rather than to prepare them for citizenship—an echo of the classical school critique of progressive vocationalism. The president of the local school superintendents organization complained about the torrent of facts to be learned and the time that doing so would take away from the crucial work of keeping students at grade level in reading and math.[9] As in 1994, an important and legitimate pedagogical dispute was washed away by a torrent of ideology.

There is a tide in the affairs of men, and Glenn Youngkin caught that tide in 2021. The former co-CEO of a private equity firm, Youngkin won the Republican nomination for governor that year and then ran for office less as the technocrat he appeared to be than as a deep-dyed conservative intent on transforming public culture. He rode the vogue hobbyhorse of "parental control." In a debate with his Democratic opponent, Terry McAuliffe, Youngkin said, "I believe parents should be in charge of their children's education." McAuliffe then delivered what he must have thought was a standard riposte: "I don't think parents should be telling schools what they should teach."[10] The pandemic had made that a disastrous misstep. At that moment, McAuliffe became a dead candidate walking.

Once he became governor, Youngkin benefited from a target-rich environment. In 2020 his Democratic predecessor, Ralph Northam, had impaneled the Virginia Commission on African American History Education in The Commonwealth. (The governor's critics observed that he issued the executive order only months after he was publicly shamed by a thirty-five-year-old photograph—whose authenticity he later contested—of himself in blackface.) In its final report, the commission recommended the kind of culturally responsive pedagogy that Illinois would adopt at about the same time as well as "culturally responsive leadership," which called on school leaders to "mitigate power imbalances based on race, culture, ethnicity and class" and to ensure "an anti-racist school culture and climate." The commission proposed its own revision of state standards, including what seemed like an extremely overdue correction of the claim that "Reconstruction policies were harsh and created problems in the South," but also insisting that first-graders learn "how the relationship between diseases and weapons of the English settlers impacted the Virginia Indians."[11]

Having replaced Northam's school superintendent with Jillian Balow, who had made a name for herself as Wyoming's superintendent of schools by rooting out any and all evidence of critical race theory in that extremely conservative state, Youngkin issued Executive Order One directing Balow to identify, and remove, "inherently divisive concepts" such as CRT within the Department of Education. Balow found quite a lot to identify and remove, including virtually any directive containing the word "equity," which many conservatives view as a progressive demand for equality of outcome rather than of opportunity. But she also found a department document that spelled out the basic tenets (misspelled as "tenants") of "anti-racist education," including "All members of society have been socialized to participate in racist systems" and "White people benefit from racism, regardless of intentions." Suggested resources included major texts on antiracism and critical race theory as well as a tract titled "No BS (Bad Stats): Black People Need People Who Believe in Black People Enough Not to Believe Every Bad Thing They Hear About Black People."[12] Balow promptly rescinded the offending programs, though the Democrat-controlled state senate rejected bills to ban the teaching of "inherently divisive concepts."

Neither Youngkin nor his superintendent could rescind the standards; that was the purview of the Board of Education. Virginia was hardly a problem state. The Fordham Institute, which had given Illinois an F for its history and civics standards, had awarded Virginia a B+ in both, suggesting modest improvements but calling the content in both subjects "impressive." Governor Northam had tasked the Department of Education with delivering new standards in 2022, little imagining that by that time he would give way to a conservative Republican.

After department officials finished presenting the new standards to the board in August 2022—and been duly praised for their work by Northam appointees—Balow, their boss, unexpectedly requested a delay. "I'm asking for one month to brief individual board members," she said. Balow emphasized that she was not interested in "digging into the content." It wasn't clear what she wanted. Now the board split along partisan lines. Bill Hansen, a former official in the U.S. Department of Education under George W. Bush, said that he had been getting "a lot of phone calls about the George Washington or James Madison issue." He didn't think it should be taken lightly. Andy Rotherham, an educational consultant who had previously served on the board under Virginia's Governor Mark Warner, a Democrat, added that while "the media will portray this as left-right," the real issue was whether they should endorse the "inquiry-based" approach within which the standards were framed. The first twenty-odd pages of the Virginia Department of Education's draft had been taken up with elaborate graphs and flow charts illustrating concepts such as "Learning content THROUGH developing social science skills." Years spent visiting classrooms had shown Rotherham that teachers who have learned precious little history in ed school are left adrift without strong moorings in historical fact. "That's why you get these classes where everyone's talking but no one's saying anything about content," as Rotherham later told me. Board president Dan Gecker, a lawyer and Northam appointee, told Balow that he would accept a delay so long as whatever revisions she had in mind would be finished in a month and would not entail "a wholesale rewrite of the standards." Balow did not demure, and the board voted for a one-month pause.

In mid-September, the Civics Alliance sent both the Virginia Board of Education and the state Department of Education an eight-page letter outlining its objections to the new standards. The letter combined self-evidently accurate observations, arguable claims, and ideological fixations. The authors observed that the draft had become confusing once officials decided to combine "standards of learning" with "curriculum frameworks." The document's goals, whatever they were, had been obscured by "vague, inflated prose." The standards also suffered from a "Misguided Skills Emphasis" and a "Misguided 'Inquiry' Emphasis"—the point that Andy Rotherham and others had made. The authors objected to the inclusion of exercises in action civics—and in social justice—such as the directive to students to "Identify an area of need in your community" and devise a plan to correct it. They similarly took umbrage at "material that supports radical ideology" and identity politics, including such progressive vocabulary as *"advocacy, engagement, a people with contemporary debate and possibilities."* They pointed to what they regarded as implicit endorsements of "DEI," which "forwards Critical Race Theory." The easiest way to fix the draft's myriad problems would be simply to adopt the "American Birthright" K–12 standards that the Civics Alliance itself had developed. They also proposed that Virginia appoint a new commission, as Governor Noem had done.

Like Noem, Glenn Youngkin and his education officials wanted to fight both the culture war and the pedagogy war, but given Virginia's very purple ideological complexion, they couldn't afford to be quite so candid about their goals. Jillian Balow had requested a brief delay for procedural reasons; in fact, she wanted a longer delay for substantive reasons. Even before the board meeting, in early August, Youngkin's secretary of education, Aimee Rogstad Guidera, had turned to an education consultant, Sheila Byrd Carmichael, known for working with classical schools. Guidera had also asked for a list of historians from the conservative Jack Miller Center. All of this had happened out of sight of the board. A school official told me that Balow complained that the same progressive historians had always advised on standards, and she wanted more balance. At the October board meeting where she was to present her modest edit of the existing standards, Balow instead explained that she would soon present a new draft that was not only "accessible, succinct and accurate" but also "neutral in content and approach," "balanced with content," and "inclusive of more voices." Balow may have enjoyed hijacking the progressive cant word "inclusive" to refer not to "marginalized" voices but to conservative ones.

On November 11, five days before the next board meeting, an entirely new set of standards landed in board members' email accounts with a mighty crash. While the prefatory material of the Northam standards had spoken of instilling in students "a thoughtful pride in the history of America" on the basis of the nation's continual effort to live up to its own professed values—the classical liberal formulation of patriotism—the new version celebrated "the world impact of America's quest for a 'more perfect union' and the optimism, ideals, and imagery captured by Ronald Reagan's 'shining city upon a hill' speech." Included in the "foundational principles" was the claim, apparently regarded as self-evident, that "Centralized government planning in the form of socialism or communist political systems is incompatible with democracy and individual freedoms." And lest teachers sought to smuggle in CRT, they were admonished to "engage students in age-appropriate ways that do not ascribe guilt to any population in the classroom."[13] First-graders were to learn civics by "singing patriotic songs like 'You're A Grand Old Flag.'"[14] It was as if the Youngkin administration wanted to pick a fight with the kind of people who could refer to George Washington without his mythic title.

No one was prepared to explain to me, either then or later, how or by whom this polemical document had been prepared. Balow, Carmichael, and Governor Youngkin declined to speak to me. Guidera was, however, made available. When I asked why the Youngkin administration had thrown down the gauntlet on history and civics, the first thing she mentioned was the allegedly nonchalant treatment of the Founders. "That," she said, "was just crazy." Such errors could, of course, have been easily fixed without the massive endeavor of redrafting, but Guidera said that she and others also found the document extremely confusing, for the reasons that the Civics Alliance had identified. What's more, Guidera added, in some cases the standards did not stipulate the grade in which they were to be taught. This still seemed to constitute a technicality. Guidera, generally considered an orthodox conservative rather than a dedicated culture warrior, did not address the Reagan-worshiping preface. The hill on which she preferred to stand was that of rigor. "Across the nation," she said to me, "there has been a lowering of expectations and a systematic decline of what we expect of our kids." She regarded the standards that the department had presented in August as part of the problem, not the solution.

In Virginia, as in South Dakota, political and cultural conservatives supplanted professional educators, whom they regarded as clandestine ideologues. The influence of the Civics Alliance was patent. The new document separated standards from curriculum frameworks, infused overt patriotism into elementary grades, and restored the centrality of white men to the Revolutionary cause—as the alliance letter had suggested. What's more, all references to participatory activities in civics had been dropped. Eighth-graders would now examine "how civic participation can address community needs and serve the public good"—but by reading about it rather than doing it. The head of the organization was later quoted as saying that virtually all of their suggestions had been adopted.[15]

The new draft was riddled with errors and absurdities, including describing antisemitism as one of the consequences of the Holocaust instead of the other way around, and listing the Treaty of Versailles under the section on World War II rather than World War I. Documents that came to light as a result of freedom of information requests by the press show that Youngkin's education officials had been thrown into a panic by the impossibly short period they had to rewrite the standards, itself a consequence of their unwillingness to admit just what they were doing. Though officials seem to have decided early on to produce an entirely new draft, Carmichael's contract, remarkably, was dated October 26, just two weeks before the new version would be presented. Education secretary Guidera had urgently requested names of conservative history professors the week before. But many of the figures Carmichael contacted, including highly regarded conservative historians, refused to review the standards in as little as forty-eight hours. Carmichael did receive feedback from Hillsdale College and almost certainly consulted Hillsdale's own K–12 curriculum.

Like George Allen before him, Youngkin provoked the culture war he appeared to be seeking. Indeed, history repeated itself with an almost wonderful fidelity. At a meeting called by the board, parents, students, and activists lined up to condemn the new standards, as they had three decades earlier. The critics fell into their stereotypical roles almost as faithfully as Youngkin had his own. The representative of an Asian group accused the authors of erasing from history people like her late Filipino grandfather. A representative of the Henrico County NAACP (an area adjacent to Richmond) said the document would legitimize white supremacy. Sikhs complained that they had been denied a place in Virginia's history. The head of the Jewish Community Federation of Richmond claimed that the draft would "undermine the teaching of the Holocaust." Still others assailed the absence of explicit skills instruction. A social studies teacher said that students can "find facts in five seconds on their cell phone." Why, she asked, were children being prepared "to be *Jeopardy* contestants"? Yet if the objections often felt like a parody of identity politics and progressive pedagogy, there was no mistaking the intensity of feeling. Though Youngkin had campaigned on returning control over the schools to parents, virtually every parent who spoke was infuriated by the new standard, just as parents had been in George Allen's day.

The Northam appointees to the board were no less outraged. Anne Holton, Virginia's former secretary of education, told Balow and Sheila Byrd Carmichael, whom Balow said was chiefly responsible for the document, that while she had defended the administration from charges of whitewashing, "I no longer have that confidence." Dan Gecker, a stickler for process, accused Balow of misleading the board and called the new standards "a breach of faith with the public." Even Andy Rotherham said that he was baffled to find that the draft did not describe slavery as the cause of the Civil War, though unlike Holton he attributed the failure to "sloppy drafting." Balow felt she had to apologize for a characterization of Native Americans as America's "first immigrants." The dam seems to have broken when Alan Siebert, a Youngkin appointee, finally said, "I can't do this." The board voted unanimously not to grant first review. Then things got even worse for Youngkin. Carmichael had grown so flustered under insistent questioning that she had listed Susan Wise Bauer, an educational consultant who had declined to respond to a request for help, as a source of the new document. Bauer subsequently demanded and received an apology, which she then posted on Twitter. Carmichael conceded that the standards were "deeply flawed" and said that she regretted "not pushing harder for more time and/or not removing myself from the process altogether."[16]

Youngkin's apparent bid to join Ron DeSantis and others in the red-state anti-woke pantheon failed not out of faintheartedness but apparent incompetence. Yet comparing the Youngkin to the Northam standards does not quite yield the neat culture-war dichotomy that the inflammatory preface seemed to promise. The new version drifted into overt polemic every time it got near free-market issues, including an implication that the New Deal had harmed as many Americans as it had helped. Little kids would have sung a great many patriotic songs. They would not have learned about Sikhs. But on the supreme issue of race, the Youngkin standards did not "whitewash" history, much less legitimize white supremacy. To take only a single example, students in sixth-grade American History would have had a slightly more detailed grounding in the Reconstruction era under the Youngkin than under the Northam standards. Study of the civil rights movement would include "Martin Luther King Jr, Rosa Parks, Malcolm X, Ruby Bridges, John Lewis, Medgar Evers, Ralph Abernathy, boycotts, Selma, Massive Resistance." (Rosa Parks was included twice, a typical drafting error.)

The greatest difference between the two documents was the pedagogical scaffolding. Sixth grade U.S. History begins with westward expansion. The November draft opened with a brief list of "essential sixth grade skills": "synthesize evidence from multiple informational sources," "determine cause and effect to analyze connections between the past and the present," and so forth. Teachers were then directed to ask students to apply those skills to analyze westward expansion by, for example, "detailing the events and developments associated with the Northwest Ordinances, Oregon Treaty, Pacific Railway Act, Gadsden Purchase, Pony Express, annexation of Texas, Treaty of Guadalupe Hidalgo, and the Homestead Act." Teachers were referred to the more elaborate curriculum frameworks for guidance on how best to teach those events.

The Northam standards featured a massive armature of skill acquisition. Sixth-graders were to acquire "workplace readiness skills of respect for diversity" and "teamwork," as well as "initiative" and "self-direction." They were to attain "understandings" about, for example, the difference between primary and secondary documents or about "contextualization"—twenty-nine understandings in all, plus fourteen sub-understandings. The study of westward expansion would be governed by an "overarching inquiry": "what are the benefits and challenges of movement?," which in turn would generate discussion of master themes, including the nature of freedom and of power and the influence of "people, places, and environments."[17] Among the list of understandings were several that must have elevated the blood pressure of Right-thinking patriots, including, "Westward expansion destroyed ways of life that Indigenous people had practiced for centuries and dispossessed them from their homelands." (The November draft asked students only to explain "the effect that westward expansion had on Indigenous Peoples.")

Yet Virginia's standards, unlike those of Illinois or a great many other states, were in fact highly detailed and did not treat content knowledge as a kind of inadvertent by-product of the acquisition of content-neutral skills. The truth was rather that the endless accumulation of skills mastery had almost wholly obscured the objects of learning. Youngkin's standards, on the other side, had pared much of that material away but not eliminated it altogether and had not actually bowdlerized the story of America despite the howls of outrage. The two drafts weren't quite as incompatible as they seemed. But the process of drawing up and presenting the standards had seemed so disingenuous that it wasn't at all clear that a reconciliation was possible. Youngkin had behaved as if Virginia were South Dakota, and he could impose his vision on hopelessly outnumbered progressives. But Virginia wasn't South Dakota.

The Virginia debate would have been much more interesting, and much more clarifying, if the November standards had not included all the nonsense about Ronald Reagan and all the fife-and-drum patriotism. There were figures in the middle, such as Andy Rotherham and perhaps even Sheila Byrd Carmichael, who wanted to have an argument over pedagogy rather than politics. In the ill-fated November meeting, Carmichael had said, "skills absent from content are leaving our children bereft of actual content knowledge." Young children, she added "love great stories." History, told chronologically, was not a bleak desert of enforced memorization but a great unfolding narrative. It's no coincidence that Carmichael is an instructional consultant to classical schools.

But it was precisely the content density of the new draft to which mainstream educators objected. State education groups complained that second-graders would be required to engage in "rote memorization" and to learn about the War of 1812 and "complex historical figures" such as Jonas Salk and Neil Armstrong, expectations that were "developmentally inappropriate."[18] Ed Ayres, an American historian who has long been a consultant to the Virginia Department of Education and testified eloquently on behalf of the Northam standards, which he helped formulate, told me flatly that programs such as E. D. Hirsch's Core Knowledge were "just a list of things you need to know." That, of course, is simply not so, though it reflects the almost a priori repudiation of content-rich curriculum in progressive circles. It is possible, but unlikely, that Ayres himself, who was born in 1942, gained his profound grasp of history thanks to a pedagogy that scanted factual knowledge.

In late 2022, Youngkin beat a retreat, as George Allen once had. Balow consulted with some of the organizations that had criticized the standards and brought school officials back into the drafting process. (Carmichael, who had been hired on a consultancy basis, was no longer involved.) At the same time, a consortium of state and national social studies groups worked furiously to revise the Northam draft by including some of the language from the Youngkin version along with some new suggestions.[19] The Youngkin administration did not acknowledge the so-called Collaborative Draft but appears to have incorporated some of its language. The new version, delivered in January, stated explicitly that slavery was the cause of the Civil War, as the November draft had not; included Juneteenth among holidays children were to study, and returned non-Western civilizations to the third-grade curriculum. It restored the sequence of subjects that Virginia's teachers were accustomed to teaching. Mistakes had been corrected. But the tendentious preface remained intact.[20] The Northam appointees still didn't like the draft; Anne Holton complained that the document was silent on the effects of "structural racism." She and others still preferred the Northam draft. But after six months of sometimes bitter dispute, the board was eager to lay the issue to rest and voted unanimously to grant first review.

In March 2023, the board held six public hearings around the state. Amber Northern, who evaluates state standards for the Fordham Institute, decided to attend the hearing in Charlottesville. She wanted to speak up on behalf of the new draft, which she felt had retained the strengths of the 2015 standards while making more explicit exactly what it was students needed to learn. Northern was amazed to find a line of would-be speakers stretching down the hallway of the Piedmont Community College. "It was refreshing," she told me later, "that people cared this much about such an arcane topic." That said, with the exception of herself and a solitary fan of Core Knowledge, every one of the fifty-plus speakers opposed the new draft. Given the stock talking points about racism and identity, Northern inferred that very few of them had actually read the document. Picketers outside claimed that "those in power" had eliminated the history of labor unions from the standards because "they're terrified of the power of working people."

Board members sat through all six sessions, absorbing the public wrath and taking copious notes. Dan Gecker had assigned two of his colleagues—both Youngkin appointees—to incorporate those comments into the January draft. Jillian Balow was now gone; after a series of missteps, including the November draft and meeting, she had stepped down in March. The board convened on April 18 and spent six hours going through the draft line by line. They added labor history and reduced some of the long lists of names. The preface still rankled. They softened, but did not eliminate, the anti-CRT message. The following day the board unanimously approved the new standards.[21] Gecker, a measured figure who had generally stifled his growing sense of pique at the high-handed behavior of the Youngkin administration, said, "There's no reason this had to be as controversial as it became."

But is that true? Until quite recently, the public paid little if any attention to state standards, and the work was left up to professional educators. That era is over. While it is culture warriors on the right who most object to the default progressivism of the educational establishment, the outpouring of identitarian protest in Virginia shows that many of our citizens now demand to see themselves—that is, their community—fully represented in American history and government. Standards in Physics—and even in literature—may still be decided quietly, but that will not be so when it comes to our civic identity. In South Dakota on the one hand, and Minnesota on the other, one side will typically carry the day. Purple states such as Virginia are probably condemned to civil strife for the foreseeable future.

The Virginia debate was an absolutely terrible experience for everyone involved, yet the standards the board finally approved achieved something almost miraculous: acceptance. The Civics Alliance announced that "Virginia finally has the social studies standards its students deserve."[22] On the other side, Chris Jones, executive director of the Virginia ASCD, a school advocacy organization that helped write the Collaborative Draft, told me, "I'm actually quite pleased with the final product" and congratulated the board for its almost heroic devotion to detail. And somewhere in the middle, Amber Northern of Fordham described the standards as "among the best in class." Apparently, it is still possible to reach compromise on the teaching of history and civics in today's America. But you have to wade through blood to get there.

7

You Realize That Everyone Has Reasons for What They Think

At 9:00 a.m. on December 5, 2023, the whole senior class at West Chicago High School assembled in the school's auditorium for the climactic session of the semester-long Legislative Simulation. The caucuses, assembled according to students' self-identification, were spread out across the room—Far Left to the far left, then Left Democratic, Liberals 1–4, Moderate Democratic, Centrist, Moderate Republican, and Conservative Republican. The speaker gaveled the meeting into order with a stern admonition—no cell phones, no personal attacks, no interruptions. She was, like all the senior officers for the legislative exercise, a member of the AP elite in West Chicago's highly stratified student body, but the rules dictated that everyone had to participate. The house began considering HB 5943, which would raise the federal minimum wage to $17 by 2027. The bill's sponsor talked about the rising costs of rent, mortgages, and car payments. I assumed the measure would pass overwhelmingly, but then the roof fell in. The Far Left opposed the bill because $17 was too low. The Lib Dems opposed the bill as inflationary, citing a study of the subject by the National Bureau of Economic Research.

A very striking thing happened as the debate moved from left to center: students whose parents ran small businesses, as so many of the immigrant parents did, began arguing—as free-market conservatives long have—that the bill would put those firms out of business. "My cousin just started an ice-cream stand," said one. "How is he going to stay in business if he has to pay $17 an hour?" (Leave aside the fact that a federal minimum wage would cover only federal employees.) Another young man said that he worked on his father's landscaping business. "We work in hot weather up to 100 degrees and cold weather down to 30 degrees. It requires a lot of physical stress. It doesn't seem fair for a highly skilled worker to be paid the same as an unskilled worker," which he felt would happen if a "McDonald's cashier" got $17 an hour. The minimum wage, for these students, was not just an interesting abstraction; it was their lives. The bill's sponsor all but conceded, and it went down to a handy defeat.

The Legislative Simulation has some important features in common with Gilder Lehrman's Hamilton Education Project. Both bring something remote much closer through acts of personal engagement: the Founding, in the case of Eduham; the operations of American government, in the case of the Legislative Simulation. Neither is a class, a lesson, a unit, a curriculum; both fuse knowledge and experience, though knowledge is more central to Eduham and experience to the simulation. Embedded in the legislative exercise, especially, is the premise, dear to many thinkers about civic education, that young people need to gain the "dispositions" that will be required of them as fully engaged democratic citizens. Yet neither exercise enlists students in progressive campaigns of social justice. Both thus expose the simple-mindedness of the right-wing onslaught on civics-outside-the-classroom. Abolishing such "experiential learning," as David Bobb of the conservative Bill of Rights Institute puts it, "would be like the Boy Scouts without the camping experience." To deliver high-quality civics instruction, Bobb now works closely with groups that the organized right anathematizes.

These exercises nevertheless raise questions about the role of school in shaping young lives that are different from those raised by a straightforward academic domain. The habits that civic education seeks to form and to reinforce are not merely cognitive ones; they have to do with the future behavior of students as citizens. Civics, done right, *changes* students. But is that, as Dr. Liu, the orchestra teacher at Metea Valley, asked me, the proper role of schools? In what way, and to what extent, do we wish schools to change students, beyond making them more knowledgeable? This is not at all an obvious question. What form of shaping is consistent with the liberal individualism that governs our public world? Dr. Liu answered his own question by addressing the orchestra as a "harmonious community," a model of collective behavior, if only the members would make it so. He had made his own little world inside the giant utilitarian machine of Metea Valley.

The cultural Right, of course, suffers few inhibitions over limiting the autonomy of students. One of the most influential conservative texts, *Battle for the American Mind* by Pete Hegseth, the former Fox News commentator who now serves as President Trump's defense secretary, and David Goodwin, a leading Christian educator, argues that public schools are already profoundly molding young people according to the dictates of an implicit "Cultural Marxist Paideia" that undermines traditional morality and authority and the United States itself. Hegseth and Goodwin would restore the "Western Christian Paideia" that they believe formed the world of public schooling until Dewey came along, though such is their extreme loathing of liberal secular culture that they deeply doubt that their project can be achieved absent a full-scale privatization and Christianization of the schools.[1] Even the folks at Hillsdale would counter that the public classical schools are well positioned to achieve that transformation of values. But it is a premise of cultural conservatism that the alleged liberal neutrality of the schools is a self-serving myth.

The Left, on the other hand, would abandon pretenses of neutrality for an overt commitment to building a more just society. Today's progressives, like those of the 1960s, believe that students already are radical critics of society and would have schools meet them on that terrain. Thus Meira Levinson, mentioned earlier, argues for a form of civic education that involves "teaching through and for group solidarity," allowing students to move fluidly back and forth between the ethnoracial identity that is native to them and the civic identity that school wishes to impart.[2] Others argue that any attempt to teach civic values such as honesty and responsibility to students who regard the system, including the schools, as deeply unjust will fail unless teachers directly confront that injustice.[3] This is the implicit, and sometimes explicit, view of polemical historians such as Howard Zinn. Schools, that is, should furnish students with a civic identity fitted around their tribal identity as members of marginalized groups or enlightened critics of the state.

For both the Left and the Right, civic education entails indoctrination, though of course with very different doctrines. Liberalism offers something different, but also thinner. Liberal thinkers tend to argue that the commitment to cultivating individual autonomy takes precedence over any attempt to inculcate "character," or love of country, or virtually any affirmative code of conduct or belief. The philosopher Judith Shklar has written that any attempt by the state to direct "character education" is incompatible with the tenets of liberal democracy. The British philosopher Harry Brighouse writes, "If the state helps form the political loyalties of future citizens by inculcating belief in its own legitimacy. . . it will be difficult to conclude that their consent is freely given, or would have been freely given." An overview of liberal thinking on the question finds a consensus only around the promotion of "critical thinking," that is, helping students learn to examine rival propositions. Anything more—including inculcating belief in the legitimacy of the state—would be coercive.[4]

Yet even many liberal thinkers who recoil at the language of virtue, or for that matter of patriotism, recognize value-neutrality and critical thinking as a flimsy foundation for citizenship. In her book *Democratic Education*, the philosopher Amy Gutmann described a "liberal moralism" that seeks to cultivate personal autonomy rather than respect for tradition—the core of conservative moralism, as Gutmann understood it. Schools can't directly teach moral autonomy, she acknowledged, yet they can teach the "cooperative virtues" upon which a democratic society of individuals must rest: "empathy, trust, fairness and benevolence."[5] Gutmann is only thinking of elementary schools. Thereafter, she says, schools should cultivate the capacities for democratic participation. As the child develops into a moral agent, civic education thus moves from the inculcation of virtues to the shaping of democratic dispositions.

This comes much closer to the actual practice of schools than does the single-minded protection of the autonomous, choosing self that other thinkers regard as the foundation of liberal schooling. Few elementary school teachers would call the explicit teaching of those cooperative virtues coercive. Many public schools are committed to programs of "restorative justice" that teach children how to behave nicely, how to acknowledge and apologize for harm caused. By the time of high school, however, that formal emphasis on character—on virtue—tends to be miniaturized into a slogan delivered over a PA system. Perhaps that was why Dr. Liu felt impelled to establish an ethos of his own for orchestra class. A school that polls students about their preferred electives, as Waubonsie Valley does, is offloading a portion of its own authority in the name of encouraging democratic participation.

Perhaps one way of describing the liberal approach to civic education is that while schools encourage certain virtues among small children, thereafter they show respect to the developing young person by inculcating "dispositions." One of the appeals of the vocabulary of dispositions is that it describes civic habits that can be instilled without violating the autonomy of the individual students. Or, to put it more exactly, liberal civic education means fostering the habits most likely to fully reconcile individual self-development with the forging of a good society. The thinker who has done the most to advance this vision is Danielle Allen, a professor of political science at Harvard, a celebrated Black intellectual, a classically trained philosopher, and a prominent activist and innovator in civic education. Aristotle is Allen's touchstone, though not quite in the same way as he is for Jason Caros and the classicists. In her very first book, *Talking to Strangers*, Allen wrote about Aristotle's idea of "civic friendship" as a model for the relation of citizens in a democracy, for democracy requires reciprocity, acknowledging the legitimate interests of others, tempering self-interest in the name of solidarity. "No consensually-based form of social organization," she writes, "can, over the long term, sustain relations of cooperation in the face of unrestrained self-interest." The ultimate goal of civic education is to develop the dispositions that make such a society possible.[6]

Yet while a conservative such as Jason Caros or Kevin Gillett would say that this conception of a good society that lies beyond self-interest requires an education in the self-denying virtues, Allen uses a political rather than a moral vocabulary. What, she asks, is the political world we seek? In a recent work, *Justice by Means of Democracy*, she writes that only "a fully inclusive, egalitarian, participatory constitutional democracy" will secure justice for all its citizens. That is her substantive vision of what she calls "democratic eudaemonia."[7] The world of classical republicanism was, of course, neither inclusive nor egalitarian; the freedom of citizens was made possible by the servitude of slaves. How are we to bring about a society in which none are marginalized and all may flourish? What does it mean to teach, and to practice, "civic friendship" where all are equal citizens? The "dispositions" that Allen wishes school, and indeed all of society, to impart are those that make it possible to realize an inclusive, egalitarian, participatory democracy.

Because no such society can be founded on an ethic of self-interest, Allen writes that we must learn to accept the full agency of others, to acknowledge the legitimacy of their interests, to seek ways to connect our purposes with those of others. We must learn the skills of deliberation, by which she means disagreeing in a way that converts rivalry into mutuality. She uses the expression "fair fighting" to describe a form of robust, truth-seeking advocacy. Elsewhere Allen extols what she calls "difference without domination." Civic education thus models the way citizens relate to one another in a well-functioning democracy. Participation is central to Allen's view of democratic life; she rejects the libertarian conception of liberty as the right to be left alone. In *Education and Equality*, Allen adopts an argument that she attributes to the philosopher Hannah Arendt: people have an intrinsic wish to participate in the world, to be agents of their own destiny. Democracy is the system that fulfills that need to the greatest imaginable degree. Citizenship is active, and people are free to choose among many roles—as advocate, as political professional, as engaged citizen. Allen recommends training in what she calls "participatory readiness"—the cognitive and psychological capacity to take on whatever roles the future citizen chooses.[8] As a practitioner of civic education, Allen believes strongly in activities that require students to act as engaged citizens.

Allen is far more explicit about the kind of skills or habits that students need to acquire than she is about the knowledge that will allow them to deploy those skills. She observes that democracy, unlike personal systems of rule such as monarchy or oligarchy, is a complex abstraction that places great cognitive demands on citizens, and thus requires the linguistic and conceptual skills needed to make nuanced judgments about collective goods. For that reason, she writes, the "verbal empowerment" imparted by a liberal arts education is "the foundation of civic competency."[9] But Allen does not say whether she believes schools now offer such an education or suggest what they would have to do to approximate that good.[10]

Danielle Allen had not written a word about civic education when West Chicago High School first developed the Legislative Simulation. But, perhaps because both arose from a liberal conception of civic education, the exercise almost perfectly embodies Allen's understanding of the schools' role in preparing students for democratic life.

After the delegates to the Legislative Simulation voted on the minimum-wage legislation they took up a proposed constitutional amendment to preserve affirmative action. This provoked a debate no less heated than the minimum-wage proposal had. The sponsor, a white girl, said, "We're fighting against white supremacy." Her partner pointed out that the great Ivy League colleges had been founded by slave-owners and so were "inherently racist." Yet none of the other speakers availed themselves of the vocabulary of doctrinal combat. Many of the students identified their own ethnicity, though for different reasons. A Hispanic student argued that affirmative action violated "the core American value of equality as contained in the 14th Amendment." A girl who described herself as Chinese American said that, while she was fortunate, many other Asians were not, and needed the boost provided by affirmative action. In this case, the Left voted Left, and the Right voted Right. The final tally was 161 to 51, with 28 abstaining, which left the measure just shy of the required two-thirds majority of all present.

During a break, I sat with one of the Liberal caucuses while they prepared for the remaining debates. A Hispanic girl sitting in the back raised her hand and asked the caucus leader, a South Asian boy, if he would read her speech, because she feared she had made mistakes. "It's your speech, Ma'am," he said gravely. I had never before heard one student address another as "Ma'am." I was struck not only by the boy's elaborate courtesy but by the evident fact that these two seniors had plainly never met before. The AP track had been brought into contact with the regular track.

The last two bills would have legalized abortion and prostitution. The sponsor on abortion responded pungently to the pro-life argument against mothers seeking to end an unwanted pregnancy: "He could grow up to cure cancer or he could grow up to be a mass murderer," she said. "But what's certain is that the mother will suffer." The students turned out to be overwhelmingly pro-choice but opposed to legalized prostitution, chiefly on the grounds that it would legitimize the exploitation of women. In the middle of the program they stopped to listen very attentively to speeches from representatives of their state senator and congresswoman, as well as from their state representative herself—a regular feature of the Legislative Simulation.

Afterward I talked to half a dozen of the seniors; I was allowed to use their first but not last names. Most of them said that they had had no idea how hard it was to make government work. Fernanda said, "I realized that government is less paper and more talking. You kind of have to do bargaining to get a law passed." Tyler said that he had felt "demoralized" when a bill that he had drafted with great care was not accepted by committee—for bad reasons, he thought. He realized, he said, that "you have to persuade people to get your bill passed." ("Democratic knowledge," Danielle Allen writes, includes understanding how to bridge differences in the name of a common good.) Trinity said that she had learned that you have to speak to people in a civil manner in order to get them to listen to you. "You can't make it personal," Scout added. (Aristotle's "civic friendship," Allen writes, is founded not on love or fraternity but on the imperative for citizens of a republic to enact law.)

The most intriguing conversation I had was with Dan, the leader of the Far Left caucus, a Punjabi boy who served as editor of the newspaper.

"You look at the Internet and everyone is down in the mud," he said. "But I felt like this humanized people. You realize that everyone has reasons for what they think." He had been forced to listen, and to reflect; he had changed his vote on legalizing prostitution after listening to the arguments against. But what had been most powerful for him was meeting students he had never exchanged a word with in the past. Dan was taking six AP classes; like the South Asian boy who addressed his fellow student as "Ma'am," he lived inside the world of the 250-odd AP kids. "There were people in my caucus group I had never met before in my life," he said. "I had no idea that they had a point of view on anything." (Allen: fully accepting the agency of others.) Dan and his friends were aristocrats who had been forced to mingle with the *hoi polloi*. Some of them, it turned out, were worthy of respect.

I made a point of asking the kids, as I generally did, where they got their news from. The answers were: TikTok, TikTok, parents, and Univision, the Spanish-language channel. Only one student appeared to read anything. These were among the most intellectually and civically engaged students at West Chicago High School. The war in Gaza had begun two months earlier, and Jocelyn told me that she had voted against the foreign aid bill because it would have provided assistance to Israel, and she had seen videos on Instagram of Palestinian civilian deaths. That was the first she had learned of a conflict that had been consuming the news. One of the precepts the students had learned in Government was that you cannot formulate a view of your own without hearing the arguments from the other side, so I asked Jocelyn if she had sought out the pro-Israeli argument. She hadn't; she and Fernanda agreed that the pictures were so powerful that there couldn't possibly be another side.

The Legislative Simulation prepared students for the Arendtian life of democratic action that Danielle Allen describes as the heart of civic education. The program showed them both the difficulty and the satisfaction of crafting rules for society in a way that no class on "how a bill becomes a law" could ever do. It furnished lessons in both aggressive advocacy and civil discourse. And it had the additional civic value of bridging the academic divide that otherwise separated West Chicago into two worlds, like a public agora in a deeply stratified society. As with Eduham, one would wish all high school students to have the same opportunity.

These students had learned things; some had even consulted an article published by the National Bureau of Economic Research. Yet West Chicago was also a school where all but the most gifted students knew little about American government and history. Even the most engaged kids made do with TikTok when it came to learning about current events. The same students who were gaining precious experience in democratic life were barely learning the rudiments of American history; West Chicago seemed much more effective in imparting dispositions than knowledge. You could argue that what Danielle Allen calls "democratic knowledge"—the knowledge, often tacit, of how citizens of a democracy act toward one another—equips students quite adequately for a future as citizens. But it's not a very persuasive claim. As Kelly Rose, the AP teacher at Waubonsie Valley, had said to me, citizens are called on to make choices that depend on knowledge, not only of this or that issue but of how our nation and other nations have succeeded or failed in the past. How do we resist the polemical claim that America has always been righteous or that it is irremediably racist if we know so little about the past? How can we apply the wisdom of our founding documents if we lack the vocabulary to make sense of them?

I had sat down with West Chicago's history teachers just before the simulation began. None of them was inclined to put a shiny gloss on the difficulty of teaching American History to the non-AP kids, many of them far behind in reading and analytical skills. "That's a conversation we have almost daily," said Joe Zeman. They used the case study method to focus on specific events that they thought might resonate with the kids. Jamie Garcia said he had spent a great deal of time on the Dred Scott case because it raised a question so pertinent to immigrant students: Who gets to be a citizen? They talked about Bacon's Rebellion and other uprisings. They lingered on Malcolm X, always a student favorite. They did not believe, as more doctrinaire educators such as Meira Levinson do, that teachers had to expose an unjust power structure in order to reach alienated students, but they recognized that the kids in front of them would not identify with George Washington or Abe Lincoln; they responded to the underdogs and the rebels.

But the teachers didn't think they were making much progress. Close to half of their students worked after school to support their families, some at almost full-time jobs. Few of their parents saw school as the route to a better life. "He's not a troublemaker," said Mr. Garcia, paraphrasing what he often heard. "He's not failing; so all's good." I had sat in on a class in which Mr. Garcia implored his students to take advantage of a policy that allowed them to retake a test in order to improve their grades. Only four of eighty to ninety kids ultimately took him up on the offer. By sophomore year, Nick Caltagirone said, most of the students had decided whether or not they were college material. If not, they drifted quietly through their last few years.

Mr. Caltagirone wondered if schools should offer some kind of associate's degree that would allow students to graduate at sixteen. But that was an admission of failure. How could they, instead, hold the kids to higher standards? "We'd have to fail them for a few years," Mr. Garcia conceded, to force elementary and middle schools to make more rigorous demands. Yet they all took deeply seriously the obligation to teach students what it meant to be an American and to help them become good citizens. "If we can't give these kids the ability to be an effective citizen by tenth grade, when we've had them for ten years," said Mr. Caltagirone, "that's probably on us."

8

The One True Curriculum—or, Failing That, a "Roadmap"

In the summer of 2019, just weeks before the *New York Times Magazine* would publish the "1619 Project," the National Endowment for the Humanities, in collaboration with the U.S. Department of Education, issued a request for proposals for a $650,000 grant to universities and nonprofits to "highlight innovative approaches, learning strategies, and professional development practices in K-12 civics education." Given the source, the proposal was hard to take at face value. Donald Trump had tried to eliminate the NEH, though Congress had blocked him as it had previous Republican efforts to zero out the agency. The Department of Education was headed by a hard-core ideologue, Betsy DeVos, who had devoted much of her time in office to defending the private profit-making higher education industry. But the proposal was real.

The idea was the brainchild of John Peede, a Mississippi folklorist and veteran arts administrator whom Trump had appointed as interim director of the NEH and then left in place when it survived. Peede was so worried that Trump would succeed in getting rid of the agency that he had turned to the Department of Education to fund the proposal. And he was so worried that serious scholars would laugh off the whole thing that he called James Grossman, head of the American Historical Association to say, "This is an absolutely open competition; please get the word out." Two years later, just such a bipartisan group would produce "The

Roadmap to Educating for American Democracy," which may be as close as the United States can get to a national curriculum of American history and government.

In much of the world the idea of a national history or civics curriculum would be unexceptionable; in some countries it is regarded as indispensable. In France, where the schools have long been regarded as the source of transmission of the nation's republican ideals, students all over the country read the same passages from Pascal or Voltaire. This has never been true in the United States, where the content of schooling is left up to states and localities. Yet because we, too, look to the schools to transmit our founding principles, educators have periodically sought either to disseminate a locally designed curriculum to schools across the country or to devise one at the national level and then persuade states and localities to adopt it. Those efforts have failed.

Perhaps the most ambitious private attempt to draft a national curriculum came in the aftermath of the National Educational Association's 1916 "Report of the Committee on Social Studies." The following year some of the nation's leading progressive school reformers, including Charles Eliot and Abraham Flexner of Harvard, helped establish the Lincoln School, a "laboratory school" at Teachers College of Columbia University modeled on the famous lab school at the University of Chicago that John Dewey had pioneered in 1894. The Rockefeller Foundation provided the bulk of the funding. In 1920, Harold Rugg, a leading educational scholar at Chicago, agreed to head the new effort. Rugg's goal from the outset was to design a model curriculum. He began with social studies. Rugg thought that the NEA report had offered a meaningless jumble with no regard for larger meaning. The goal of the social studies, he believed, was "to understand modern life and how it came to be."[1] The subject needed to be studied synthetically, not as separate domains. He would ultimately call his curriculum "Man and His Changing Society."

An engineer and statistician by background, Rugg mapped out his program systematically. First he and his colleagues determined the leading issues of modern life by canvassing the major social science journals, categorizing the books held in Columbia's research collections, and, most important, studying what Rugg called the "frontier thinkers" of the day, among them Thorstein Veblen, Bertrand Russell, George Bernard Shaw, and Charles Beard. They also made a systematic study of existing social studies curricula to understand what students were then learning. Ultimately they whittled down the issues, or "problems" as Rugg called them, from three thousand to three hundred: the pell-mell growth of industry, the rise of modern transportation and communication systems, threats to democracy, and the like. They gathered age-appropriate readings for each problem. Starting in 1922, the Rugg team began producing a series of pamphlets containing texts for a junior high school curriculum; they would later produce a series of elementary school pamphlets as well. Teachers at the lab school and at an ever-widening circle of progressively minded schools across the country began using "Man and His Changing Society."[2]

Between 1929 and 1932, Rugg's team combined the pamphlets into six "Reading Books" covering each of the six master themes: Economics, World Geography, American Civilization, American Government and Culture, Problems in American Culture, and America's March Towards Democracy. For each subject, they also produced a "Teacher's Guide" and a "Workbook for Directed Study" containing student exercises. Rugg had absorbed from Dewey the idea that learning required doing; the workbooks suggested field trips, debates, the preparation of "original briefs," map-reading exercises, and the like. He complained, like Dewey, that traditional schooling discarded meaning in favor of a mindless chronological march. Yet Rugg's sense of how children learned sounded very much like that of the 1892 and 1897 committees of scholars. History, he wrote, "must be treated as a pageant of living personalities, of stirring scenes of conquest, conflict or cooperation." He mocked the vogue proposition that "growth in generalizing ability comes from the learning of increasingly more difficult generalizations." In fact, he argued, students learned to think by acquiring information and learning how to choose among alternative explanations.[3]

Over the ensuing decade, schools (and some general readers) purchased four million copies of the reading books, teacher guides, and student workbooks. By 1941, it was estimated that five million students in five thousand junior high schools had used "Man and His Changing

Society."[4] It's easy to see why. At a time when most textbooks recycled patriotic clichés, the Rugg texts were vivid. The very first volume, *Our Country and Our People*, began with a cross-country trip in which the author speaks to ordinary Americans, who tell the story of their lives. At the end of each unit, students were asked to review information and to answer broad questions such as, "What do you think decides who is an American?" Or, at the end of a unit on race that includes readings from Booker T. Washington and W. E. B. Du Bois, "As a result of studying about the Negro, what important problems do you see that must be solved in the coming years?"[5]

The texts were exemplary. But there was a problem: Rugg was a New Deal social democrat who made no secret of his views. The chapter on work had real stories about real people, but many of them illustrated the sense of despair of the unemployed in the depths of the Depression. "While some have much more of this country's goods than they can use," the text lectures, "many live actually close to starvation." The answer to this market failure, the text concludes, as FDR had, was active and compassionate government. Elsewhere, Rugg asked whether America really was "a land of opportunity" and answered, "Only for some. The majority do not have any real security." In 1932, most Americans probably would have agreed, but as the Depression lifted, the nation's sentiments began to return to the pro-market status quo ante. "Man and His Changing Society" came increasingly under attack from conservatives. As one columnist cuttingly, if hyperbolically, asked, "If their parents believe in the capitalist way of life . . . should teachers indoctrinate them with Socialism and Communism?" By 1939, the American Legion and other right-wing groups had organized a mass campaign against the Rugg textbooks. Use of the social studies curriculum began to taper off in 1941; by 1944, in the heart of the patriotic effort to win World War II, the curriculum had virtually disappeared.

The crusade against "Man and His Changing Society" became a cause célèbre among civil libertarians. Rugg himself believed that he was a victim of a "manufactured conflict" promoted by a small group of zealots. Yet Jonathan Zimmerman, a leading historian of textbooks, concludes that the campaign took hold thanks to widespread support among parents; many critics, he notes, took up the cause after a child came home from school to ask why, for example, "World War I was fought for the bankers." American politics had shifted, and Rugg's texts came to be seen as an attempt by a liberal elite to impose its views on American parents.[6]

The Rugg texts came to grief even though they did not bear the imprimatur of the state, and adoption by individual schools was wholly voluntary. A true national curriculum, imposed or even suggested by the federal government, had always been treated as beyond the pale. Neither the 1892, nor the 1897, nor the 1916 reports had proposed one. Yet the panic over the dismal performance of American students exposed in the 1983 "A Nation at Risk" report and in early returns from the National Assessment of Educational Progress led to a clamor for national action. In 1988, the Bradley Commission on History in Schools, commissioned by a conservative foundation, called for a new curriculum that would introduce history in elementary school and require at least four years of history in middle and high school. The authors also specified that certification for middle and high school social studies teachers should include substantial training in history—one of the central recommendations of "A Nation at Risk."[7]

It appeared, at first, that critics, educators, and historians shared an understanding both of the need for a more rigorous history curriculum and just what such a curriculum would look like. In 1988, Lynne Cheney, the conservative head of the National Endowment for the Humanities under President Ronald Reagan, established a National Center for History in the Schools at UCLA; its codirector, liberal historian Gary Nash, had written a K–8 history textbook to be used in conjunction with stringent new state standards in California. The broader idea that schools needed to be guided by, and held accountable to, rigorous academic standards seemed to be an idea whose time had come. Soon after taking office in 1989, President George H. W. Bush convened an education summit at which Albert Shanker, the head of the American Federation of Teachers, called for national academic standards as well as national assessments. Bush himself vowed that America would adopt "world-class standards" in the major subjects.[8] The president had the public behind him: a Gallup poll found that 68 percent of Americans favored a national curriculum; 77 percent supported national tests.[9]

In 1991, Bush established the National Council of Education Standards to recommend action. Recognizing that whatever Americans might say to pollsters, the tradition of local control over schooling was deeply entrenched, the group proposed adopting national standards rather than a single curriculum and a national system of assessments rather than a single national test. The Department of Education established task forces to draw up those standards in the major academic fields. The history task force was cochaired by Cheney, now a private citizen, Gary Nash, and Lynn Crabtree, the codirector of the national center at UCLA. The whole standard-writing effort was overseen by Diane Ravitch, whom Bush had appointed assistant secretary of education. Four years earlier, she and Chester Finn had excoriated the state of history instruction in *What Do Our Seventeen-Year-Olds Know?* At this moment it appeared, incredibly, that a Republican president had authorized an unprecedented nationalization of education policy.

From the outset, according to a later account by Nash, Crabtree, and one other colleague, the effort was riven by the debates that beset the field in the 1990s. How "multicultural" should their version of American history be? They agreed that they would balance a full respect for diversity with an expression of shared civic values. Outside of American history and government, should they be devising a course of study in Western Civilization or World History? To what extent should that account reflect the American preoccupation with the progress of democracy? They were divided over pedagogy. They agreed on the need to encourage "historical thinking," but what exactly would that entail? All these thorny questions were resolved by the twenty-eight-member body over the course of two years. Finally, in May 1994, the group met to put the final touches to the National Standards for United States History. Amidst much celebration, Chester Finn, a traditionalist like Ravitch, warned that the document was way too "politically correct" for "the Wichita Rotary Club"—which would have made a fitting epitaph for "Man and His Changing Society."[10]

In fact, the standards took incoming fire long before they reached Wichita. Finn, Albert Shanker, and a number of more conservative historians publicly opposed the document. Lynne Cheney, once the patron of the whole effort, published a jeremiad titled "The End of History" two weeks before the standards were even unveiled. Cheney noted, variously, that none of the thirty-one stipulated standards mentioned the Constitution; that George Washington made only the briefest appearance while the Ku Klux Klan merited seventeen references and Joseph McCarthy and McCarthyism nineteen, and that "white males" including Thomas Edison and Albert Einstein were neglected while Harriet Tubman's name appeared six times. Cheney argued that Nash's own California text, *Lessons from History*, had offered a far more balanced version of history, fully acknowledging the nation's failures while nevertheless striking "a tone of affirmation." She urged that the standards be repudiated.[11]

The same waves that had overwhelmed Harold Rugg now threatened to submerge the national standards. The consensus of 1932 had dissolved by 1940; in this case, the apparent consensus had always been an illusion, enabled by the fact that all parties wanted to change the way history was taught and were eager to have the federal government sponsor such an effort. Cheney, Ravitch, Finn, Shanker, and others believed that students had failed to learn history because it hadn't been taught in a serious, coherent, and consecutive fashion. The historians and educators on the task force believed that students hadn't learned because history had been taught as mere facts disconnected from truths that mattered to them, and because a narrative of white men felt impossibly remote from an increasingly diverse student body. Nash was quoted as saying that their goal was "to bring about nothing short of a new American revolution in history education . . . we want to bury retro learning and the emphasis on dates, facts, places, events and one damn thing after another."[12]

Though by this time the Democrat Bill Clinton had become president, the cultural politics of the moment overwhelmingly favored the conservatives. In January 1995, the Senate voted 99 to 1 against the new standards. (The one holdout sought a yet harsher condemnation.) The vote did not, however, prevent states from adopting the proposed standards. After a body called the Council for Basic Education reviewed the standards and concluded that many of the teaching examples offered "a disproportionately pessimistic and misrepresentative picture of the American past," the authors produced a new version in April 1996.[13] The very first words of the new document were "The study of history . . . rests on knowledge of facts, dates, names, places, events and ideas." But, the authors went on to note, "true historical understanding requires students to engage in historical thinking," and they then explained precisely what that kind of thinking entailed.[14] The new standards won broad acceptance from scholars, but it was too late. States declined to adopt the standards, and no one would ever again make the mistake of trying to frame such a document.

Students of educational history could have predicted that Harold Rugg's debacle would await the history task force. Indeed, the effort now looks like one of those utopian projects of the immediate post–Cold War moment, like President Bush's "new world order." The Berlin Wall may have fallen, but the walls separating progressives from traditionalists and the history profession from parents and local school folk had not. Even in that era of relative comity, no consensus could be reached either on the American story or how to teach it. Whatever happened henceforth would be piecemeal and local, as education reform had always been in the past.

The collapse of history standards had not, of course, abated underlying fear over the disintegration of America's civic fabric. Foundations, think tanks, and universities sought to fill the void, proposing local and private initiatives in lieu of national leadership. The word "history" having become radioactive, almost all of the calls to action deployed the more anodyne word "civics." The 2003 Carnegie report, "The Civic Mission of Schools," mentioned earlier, had proposed action at all levels. The federal government, the authors argued, should increase funding to states for civic education; states should devise rigorous standards for civics; schools of education should offer courses in civics education; public schools should develop civics curricula.[15] In a 2011 follow-up report, "Guardian of Democracy," the authors repeated their "urgent call for action to restore the historic mission of our schools." None of these hopes bore fruit.

But in fact civic education had a strong advocate in an ideal position to make something happen: John Peede of the National Endowment for the Humanities. Peede was a professional arts administrator who had worked in the NEH as a political appointee under George W. Bush, and then as a civil servant under Barack Obama. Donald Trump's failure to eliminate the agency meant that Peede had a real job in an agency to which the White House was largely indifferent. He was far from a MAGA activist. Peede says of himself, "I have some conservative views and I have some straight-up views as a citizen that wants people to know about the country that I love." The Department of Education had asked him to oversee the release of the new and discouraging results of the NAEP civics test. He had, he thought, the power to do something to encourage what he calls "informed patriotism" as opposed to "blind nationalism." And because he was well regarded among the career officials in the Department of Education, he knew that he could both work with them and draw on their budget—whatever happened to the NEH—in order to award a grant to improve civics education. It was Peede's decision to issue the request for proposals, and to stipulate their bipartisan character, in July 2019.

One of the first scholars to seize the opportunity presented by Peede's request for proposals was Danielle Allen. Though herself a liberal who had briefly run for governor of Massachusetts as a Democrat, Allen had devoted her philosophical work to exploring the means by which democratic citizens could manage disagreement. She was convinced that no national effort could go anywhere unless it were bipartisan. The NEH proposal—if it could be trusted—was the vehicle she had been waiting for.

Louise Dubé, the head of iCivics, had also taken note of the NEH initiative. So, too, had Kei Kawashima-Ginsberg, head of the Center for Information and Research on Civic Learning and Engagement (CIRCLE) at Tufts University, which had coproduced Carnegie's "Civic Mission of Schools" report. Allen, Dubé, and Kawashima-Ginsberg had long worked together and agreed to join forces to draw up a proposal. Peter Levine, the founding head of CIRCLE and a scholar of civics education, agreed to join. Allen recruited Jane Kamensky, a prominent historian and her Harvard colleague, because Allen was determined that whatever they produced cover history as well as civics. All four were progressives, as was virtually everyone they worked with in the academic world. They made the crucial decision to reach out to Paul Carrese, a conservative political scientist, scholar of George Washington, and founding director of the School of Civic and Economic Thought and Leadership at Arizona State University. Carrese, in turn, brought in conservative colleagues at ASU as well as Allen Guelzo, an eminent Civil War historian—and conservative—at Princeton.

Kamensky says that she assumed at first that the proposal had been "cooked" in some way to ensure a right-wing winner. Nevertheless, she felt a professional obligation to try. Over the previous half-century, she believed, historians had paid far more attention to the splintering narratives of marginalized and discordant voices than to the binding national faith presupposed by civic education—a signal failure, she thought. Historians had a special civic obligation of their own to at least seek to supply a national narrative that Americans could broadly accept.

The group started with little beyond the conviction that their work had to not only appear but actually *be* bipartisan. As Kamensky put it, "You can't produce something that will pass muster with a broad ideological swath of the American public unless you are actually talking to a broad ideological swath of the American public." Whatever doubts they may have had about that proposition were laid to rest in real time, for the "1619 Project" appeared at almost the exact moment when they began working together on a proposal for the NEH. The members of the group had very different views among themselves about the merits of the 1619 argument, but they knew that it would repel many Americans. Beyond that, they understood, despite Kamensky's initial hopes, that no one narrative would "pass muster" with a deeply fragmented American people. Some, including Peter Levine, had been involved with the failed effort to create national standards; all regarded it as a painful object lesson. (The saga of Harold Rugg was less well known.) The group quickly settled on an approach that would promote "inquiry" rather than offer a single coherent story.

Some among them embraced an affirmative rather than merely prudential argument for a pluralistic and open-ended approach. "There isn't one American story," Louise Dubé says. "There are American stories."

For the past generation progressive scholars had been arguing that the old-fashioned single narrative had been devised to universalize the experience of the dominant group—white men—and minimize the role of others. Of course, conservatives had been loudly objecting to this displacement of great white men at least since Lynne Cheney had complained about too much Harriet Tubman and too little Thomas Edison. Yet this new endeavor depended on strategic compromise; the conservatives in the group had to accept the value-neutrality and pluralism of the inquiry approach. The obligation to compromise went both ways. Carrese had objected to the initial title of the proposal, "Educating for Democracy." "Where?," he asked. "On Mars?" Some of the progressives had responded that the United States had appropriated to itself a word that applied to all the countries of the Americas, but they stood down on that.

In November, the NEH announced that it had awarded the grant to iCivics, the lead institution, for a proposal entitled "Educating for American Democracy: A Roadmap for Excellence in History and Civics Education for All Learners." At that point, the initial small group expanded to include primary and secondary school educators, museum officials, civic organizations, and many more scholars, all organized into task forces on history, civics, pedagogy, and other subjects. These bodies, like the Rugg team a century before, commissioned "landscape surveys" of the major questions in their field. They convened monthly and issued reports to a steering committee, which in turn sent findings and new questions back to the subject-matter groups.

Again and again over the course of this period, progressives and conservatives found themselves bristling at language that the other side had taken for granted; each side had been accustomed to producing its own narrative free from the irritations of heterodoxy. Conservatives wanted to speak of America as a "republic," a system based on representation and consent, while liberals wanted "democracy," to denote a participatory system based on citizen engagement. They settled on "constitutional democracy." Conservatives wanted more focus on what binds the nation together while progressives wanted more diversity; they met in the middle. Identitarian leftists objected to the whole enterprise. Kei Kawashima-Ginsberg says that scholars on the left refused to join a working group on citizenship, because the very word "citizen" excluded illegal immigrants and asylum-seekers. Louise Dubé says that Nikole Hannah-Jones, the organizer and key author of the "1619 Project," "wouldn't even return our calls." (Hannah-Jones says that she does not recall any contact.)

Though the expanded group included more conservatives, they were vastly outnumbered by the liberals, mirroring the reality of the academy if not of the nation. The conservatives fought what they regarded as a rearguard battle on patriotism. "Should the questions be critical about America?," Paul Carrese asked. "How much should we feature marginalized points of view as against the core of *e pluribus unum*?" They won what they regarded as an important compromise: the final document would call for "reflective patriotism." Peter Levine, who objected from the left to what he regarded as an overemphasis on the nation-state rather than sources of civic vitality in localities and non-state bodies, says that while the deck was stacked in favor of people like himself, "the conservatives were always conservative, but the liberals were not always liberal" and were broadly open to being called out for their implicit bias. That was, no doubt, the liberal view.

Both sides understood that the way they had amicably settled their very real differences offered both a moral and a pedagogical lesson. They would "teach the disagreements." They decided, remarkably, to use an appendix of the final report to illustrate their own disputes and the means by which they had nevertheless reached agreement. Thus the report's authors detailed the complex meanings contained in the word "American" and explained that students should learn the sources of those different understandings; so, too, with "citizen," "democracy," and the tension between unity and diversity. "Civic education," they wrote, "is less about learning answers to a set of contested and contestable questions than about learning to disagree well with one's fellow citizens."

The framers of the EAD Roadmap thus struggled through both the ideological and the pedagogical questions that shape the debate over the teaching of history and civics. The earlier civics reports, including the 2013 C3 Framework that had proved so influential in Illinois and other progressive states, had borne the stamp of the social studies profession, scanting knowledge of history and government in favor of cultivating vaguely defined capacities of "thinking like a historian." The lead participants were as conscious of avoiding this pitfall as they were of the partisan one.

Allen, who chaired the executive committee, says that the group sought to "break down the binary" between disciplinary knowledge and the Deweyesque focus on learning by doing. The "guiding questions" that would shape the EAD Roadmap could not be answered without consulting primary texts, though the texts themselves would not be specified. In the name of pluralism, the EAD Roadmap would "leave entry points open," as Allen put it, so that, for example, in a lesson on the Bill of Rights, kids from the suburbs might choose to learn about freedom of speech while inner-city kids, all too familiar with police stops, could study the Fourth Amendment prohibition on unreasonable search and seizure.

The group convened on the campus of Louisiana State University in the spring of 2020. There, according to Kamensky, educators explained to academics what would and would not work in the classroom, while state officials cautioned them about what would not fly back home. Nobody wanted to get on the wrong side of the Wichita Rotary Club; changes were made. Later that year, a more finished draft was sent out to three hundred outsiders to get wider input. The final document was published in March 2021, two months after both the Capitol riot of January 6 and the release of Hillsdale's "1776 Report." Both events served as reminders of just how stiff a partisan gale the EAD project was sailing into.

The report that accompanied the EAD Roadmap began by invoking the indispensable role of civic education in a democracy and went on to lament that Americans had nevertheless allowed civics and history to fall into neglect. So much was conventional in all such documents. Tellingly, however, the authors asserted that one reason for the decline was "adults' damaging inability to disagree productively about the purposes and content of these disciplines." This was the stalemate that they had managed to break among themselves. They delivered a jab to the Left by noting that scholars' "laudable concern with the diversity of historical experiences" had led to "fragmentation" and the loss of "integrative frameworks for understanding the American past." Then they reminded conservatives that opportunities to learn civics and history had been distributed inequitably; a commitment to equity entailed not just a redistribution of funds but a realignment of narratives. George Washington "was a foundational leader but also enslaved people."[16] No mention was made of Paul Carrese's point that, uniquely among the Founders, Washington had freed all his slaves upon his death, wrecking his estate in order to serve his conscience.

The EAD Roadmap itself began with seven overarching themes incorporating both history and civics. "A New Government and Constitution" covered the nation's history in the founding era, as a course in American History would do, as well as "the theoretical underpinnings of our constitutional design," the heart of a traditional Civics or Government class. "Civic Participation," a very Danielle Allen theme, explored the history of the relationship between citizens and the state with the ultimate goal of encouraging civic participation by young people. "A People in the World" focused on America's global role. "A People with Contemporary Debates and Possibilities" furnished the historical background to contemporary issues. The whole structure very much resembled Harold Rugg's multidisciplinary "themes"—but without the specific content that would cohere into a distinctive point of view.

The themes did, it was true, include arguable assumptions, such as that encouraging civic participation was an intrinsic good, but they had been formulated to forestall partisan carping as far as possible. Spanning all of the themes, the report somewhat confusingly listed five "design challenges" for educators and administrators charged with turning the EAD Roadmap into curricula, standards, and tests. The underlying purpose seemed to be to treat inherent tensions as sources of productive inquiry rather than conflict. Thus under the design challenge, "America's Plural Yet Shared Story," teachers were to ask themselves, "How can this more plural and therefore more accurate story of our history and foundation also be a common story, the shared inheritance of all Americans?" How to balance the *pluribus* with the *unum*?

The EAD Roadmap contained the competencies to be mastered and the questions to be posed for each theme, organized by grade bands. Thus among six "key concepts" for "A New Government and Constitution," students in grades 6 to 12 were expected to "explore the relationships between equality, equity, justice, freedom, and order in American constitutional democracy" and to "analyze the role of groups without formal decision-making power in influencing change in the U.S. government." This last assignment in effect treated the master theme of Howard Zinn's *People's History* as a question to be posed rather than an assertion to be accepted.

Teachers would structure lessons under these themes through "driving questions" and more specific "guiding questions" for both history and civics. Thus among the history "driving questions" for students in grades 6 to 8 were, "What was the nature of the U.S. government when it was new? What were its central ideas? What were its shortcomings?" Driving questions in civics included, "What is power? How is power reflected in your lived experiences?" Guiding questions were more numerous because they were intended to lead to more particularized understanding. Those listed were only "suggested." Among the questions for history was, "What historical precedents (classical, British, Native, and other) shaped the founding documents of the United States?" The civics question included, "Why is majority rule an important principle? Why are mechanisms to protect minorities (whether racial, sexual, religious, ideological, or cultural) also important?"[17] The inquiry model felt at times like an incredibly cumbersome means of avoiding the problem of assigning actual content, but the authors believed that the high degree of specificity of the questions would compel the acquisition of content knowledge.

The report confronted the complex relationship between inquiry and content knowledge in a list of "Six Core Pedagogical Principles," which were discussed at greater length in an accompanying document called "The EAD Pedagogy Companion."[18] Teachers were to "appreciate student diversity and assume all students' capacity for learning complex and rigorous content"; "engage in continuous self-reflection and cultivate self-knowledge"; "cultivate students' capacity to develop their own deep and critical inquiries about American history and civic life"; and model civic virtues "through democratic practices and promoting civic responsibilities, civil rights and civic friendship in their classrooms." Civic friendship—that was a little hat tip to Aristotle and to a more classical conception of civic education.

One obvious impediment received only glancing attention: the document's far-reaching pedagogical expectations presupposed an exalted level of professionalism and preparation among ordinary teachers. The report's recommendation of "continuous strengthening of the teacher corps for history and civic education" sounded like the kind of pious wish so often expressed in blueprints for school reform.

The EAD team then began the work of implementation. Task forces began to research the classroom practices that would advance EAD goals, to work with museums and other cultural institutions to align their educational programs with EAD, and to promote professional development. Many of the nation's leading civics instructional providers joined the effort in order to provide material that teachers could draw on for lessons. A number of organizations, including iCivics, began to write curricula based on the EAD Roadmap. One of them, strikingly, was Core Knowledge. John Ballen, the executive director of the national organization, said that he regarded the EAD Roadmap as fully compatible with Core Knowledge's belief in a content-rich curriculum. His instructional experts set to work on a K–8 curriculum for school systems in Louisiana.

The EAD team had, they thought, assembled four-fifths or so of the spectrum of opinion on American history and government. Of course, it's the other fifth that has churned up the waves. The Left, for reasons unclear to the authors themselves, paid no attention to the EAD Roadmap. Not so the Right, for the participation of well-regarded conservatives in a consensus document threatened to blur the battle lines of the culture war. The first blast appeared in the conservative publication *City Journal* two months after the EAD report was published. Sounding very much like Lynne Cheney responding to the initial draft of proposed national standards, Mark Bauerlein, an emeritus professor at Emory University, wrote that the EAD Roadmap included only twelve references to the nation's founding—and eight of them "cast doubt on its merits." Bauerlein noted that students were asked to link the founding to "U.S. national self-interest and power," thus casting suspicion on America's origins. He also observed a preoccupation with "victim groups" and an implicit faith in the efficacy of protest politics.[19] These fleeting references probably did furnish evidence of an implicit view of the American story, though, as with the faith in civic participation, it was one widely shared among the four-fifths. If an AP History text could have somehow been reconstituted as a series of questions, it might have closely resembled the EAD Roadmap.

A more direct and personal attack came two years later when John Fonte, a doughty culture warrior who had served under Lynne Cheney in Reagan's NEH and was thus a veteran of the earlier skirmish over history standards, accused the EAD's conservative participants of lending their name and credibility to a project that was, in fact, "decidedly Left." Fonte's diatribe, "No to Conservative Accommodationism," demonstrated the obsession with the politics of word choice that marks polemicists of both Left and Right. To label George Washington an "enslaver," he wrote, was to acquiesce in the specious claim that the Founders had reduced people to slavery rather than merely owned them. To speak of "civic participants" was to place citizens and noncitizens on an equal footing. The EAD Roadmap asked students to speculate about the role "mass incarceration" had played in American life and to consider the benefits of "diversity"—code words for the woke Left. It had endorsed "action civics," that bogeyman of the Right. Yet, Fonte went on incredulously, Carrese, James Stoner, and the other conservatives claimed that they had been able to make common cause with the progressives: "This assumes, naively, that progressive educators are operating in good faith, motivated more by principles than power." Fonte concluded by declaring, "We are in the middle of a thoroughgoing cultural and political revolution. Education is a major front, in many ways *the* major front in this conflict."[20]

The attack was clarifying. The difference between figures such as Bauerlein and Fonte, on the one hand, and on the other Carrese and Stoner or David Bobb of the Bill of Rights Institute, who had agreed to head one of the EAD implementation task forces, was not that the former were more conservative than the latter, though they may have been. Rather, the participants in the EAD project had accepted the good will of those on the other side, while the critics did not. Carrese did not need to be convinced of Allen's doctrine of "political friendship"; that language came naturally to him. Like Jane Kamensky, he was dispositionally attracted to the question of what unites us and morally and politically committed to seeking common ground. The whole idea of a "culture war," by contrast, required acts of sharp clarification about sources of division. Fonte would have had the conservatives leave the panel and recommend instead the nationwide adoption of the Hillsdale curriculum.

Carrese and Stoner responded precisely to this point with a blog post of their own titled, "What's Un-American About Accommodationism?" They offered a long list of passages from the EAD Roadmap that endorsed patriotism, discussed the Christian faith of the Founders, and encouraged students to adopt such values as civic duty, courage, justice, and volunteerism. But the heart of their response to Fonte was that the Constitution had established institutions that allowed difference to flourish within an ordered system. If civics education was "nothing but partisan indoctrination," they wrote, how could that framework endure? They themselves, they went on, shared many of the views expressed in the Hillsdale curriculum, but noted that demanding its nationwide adoption "is unlikely to pull anything like a plurality let alone a majority of K-12 districts and schools across America out of the defensive crouch that avoids any improvements to civics education for fear of getting caught in the crossfire of precisely the kind Fonte delivers."[21]

The liberals watched the assault with real alarm. "If you could peel off Carrese and Stoner," Jane Kamensky thought, "and get them to say, 'You know, they made us say this and we don't really believe it,'" the project could be stripped of its bipartisan support. "The fact that it didn't work," she said, "is a testimony to their courage." Carrese found the whole thing dismaying but also faintly ridiculous. "Do they know what a Pyrrhic victory is?," he asked. For the right-wing warriors, of course, shattering bipartisan consensus would have amounted not to a Pyrrhic victory but a glorious triumph in the cultural and political counterrevolution.

The EAD Roadmap, unlike the National Standards for United States

History, did not have to be adopted by states or voted up or down by the Senate. Though commissioned by the federal government, it was, like the Rugg curriculum, a private effort that would succeed through propagation at the school level. Scarcely anyone outside the ranks of the culture warriors even noticed when the report was published. The very fact of its publication was a success, or at least a proof of concept, because it demonstrated that public-spirited scholars and educators could reach agreement on a framework for history and civics instruction that could be used throughout the country. It was mind-boggling to consider that the administration of Donald Trump had given birth to such a triumph of civic solidarity. The question henceforward would be whether the EAD Roadmap would be widely adopted in what was once again Donald Trump's America—and, no less important, whether it could survive contact with the reality of the schools.

9

The New Vision Struggles to Be Born

Peter Brown, the social studies curriculum coordinator of the Oklahoma City Public Schools, was born to serve. His father was a minister who left Oklahoma City to become a missionary in rural Thailand. His brother is a minister. He met his wife in church in the very poor neighborhood where they both grew up. He fell in love with history as a boy and decided that he would grow up to be a history teacher and a football coach. The coaching fell by the wayside, but in 2006, Brown, who at forty-four has a thick brown beard, a smooth skull, and a burger-and-fries paunch, began teaching social studies at a high school in Texas.

Moving back home, Brown joined the Oklahoma City Public Schools curriculum department and then became the one-man social studies department. "We're kind of a stepchild," he told me when I first visited the city in early October. "We lose out because of the singular focus on reading and math." Brown would tell school principals that social studies instruction had been shown to improve reading scores, but they dismissed that as special pleading. "They think if it isn't labeled reading, you're not teaching anything." Brown saw that what little social studies existed was taught in a rote manner. "It was either, 'Here's a worksheet,' or the teacher lectured for an hour." One principal confessed to him, "We don't have standards for social studies; we just make them up."

Brown tried to bring in whatever outside help he could find. He worked with Generation Civics to bring project-based, participatory civics to the schools—to give the kids something fun and possibly inspiring to do. He got a grant from the Hewlett Foundation to promote civics education throughout the schools. That brought him in contact with the folks at CIRCLE, the civic education group at Tufts. They, in turn, mentioned Brown to iCivics, which had developed an eighth-grade curriculum based on the Educating for American Democracy Roadmap and was looking for a school district to pilot the program. And that is how, in the 2022–23 school year, Oklahoma City became the first school district in the nation to implement the EAD Roadmap.

No one could claim that the district had been chosen for demographic or academic propitiousness. Oklahoma ranks second-to-last in the country in average SAT scores. Among the nation's fifty largest metro school districts, Oklahoma City stands thirty-ninth in academic achievement in third through eighth grade; the ranking improves only to thirty-fourth once the scores are weighted for socioeconomic status. In part because so many middle-class students have left for private schools or for charters, which form a separate district, the city's schools serve a highly impoverished population; in 2020–21, 91 percent of students were classed as economically disadvantaged; a little over a third were English-language learners. The school population is 57.6 percent Hispanic, 19.7 percent Black, and 11.7 percent white. Given the overwhelming correlation between poverty and academic performance, it's hardly a surprise that average scores on state reading and math tests are abysmal and only two-thirds of students graduate from high school, far below the national average.[1]

Teachers in Oklahoma City are poorly paid; some are still working toward their college degrees. Peter Brown had to find his candidates for the new program among the middle school teaching cohort he actually had. He sounded out the ones he thought would be most amenable, and then began to train them on the mechanics of an inquiry-based curriculum. He paid the teachers to write their own "driving" and "supporting" questions. iCivics later brought in trainers to demonstrate how to use, and to pace, the highly detailed lesson plans. Brown began the year with three teachers. One proved to be so inept that on a visit, Brown found kids wandering around the room, paying no attention to the teacher, in the name of some alleged inquiry-based exercise. Brown is an extremely mild-mannered person, but this was beyond the pale; he took over the class himself. The man was fired later that year. Another teacher, an old friend of Brown's, told him at the end of the year that the kids just couldn't do the work; he was going back to the old curriculum. That, Brown said, "broke my heart."

By the time I came along, in year two, Brown had two newbies and one returning veteran. Whether out of calculation or accident of schedule, he brought me first to Belle Isle Middle School, where his veteran, Nancy Brewer, taught. Brewer was an atypical teacher in an atypical school. Belle Isle is one of the system's "application schools," which accept students with better academic records, a device many districts use to keep middle-class children in the public schools. (Of course this has the effect of increasing the concentration of disadvantaged kids in the regular schools.) Belle Isle is 40.6 percent white, 27.5 percent Hispanic, and 16.7 percent Black; 55.8 percent are disadvantaged. Belle Isle looks a lot like America but not so much like Oklahoma City.

Belle Isle also seems to have an unusual esprit de corps. Every morning before class begins, all students, teachers, and administrators gather in the school gym. The morning I was there, the principal, Lynne Zahn, stood in front flanked by students. She reminded them of a few rules—no hats indoors, no roaming the hallways at lunch. Then she turned it over to the kids. One student led them in the Pledge of Allegiance, another in a moment of silent prayer; a third read a quote on honesty. Every week had a theme. This was Honesty week; next week would be Patriotism. Then all students recited the Belle Isle motto: "We love one another and ourselves. . . . What we do today will determine who we are tomorrow." I was reminded of the Founders Classical School, though in a lower key; here was the kind of unself-conscious promotion of virtuous behavior that might have been taken for granted in 1960 but now had been largely reduced to slogans.

Nancy Brewer turned out to be a very small woman with silver hair, square glasses, black-and-white checked Vans sneakers, an Oklahoma drawl, and, at age sixty-seven, a very active motor. I first saw her outside class reaching up to hug a Black kid about a foot taller than her. She later told me that he had been acting out at home and in school; she had, she said, reminded him that his choices ultimately were his own responsibility. That felt consistent with the Belle Isle motto—loving one another and oneself. In the classroom, nineteen kids—a small class—were ranged around six rectangular tables. On a board in the back of the class, Brewer had written the driving question for the unit, "What do *you* expect from *your* government?," as well as today's supporting question, "What does it mean to be a Framer?"

This was a new approach for Miss Brewer. While the kids worked on an opening assignment, she said to me, "For twenty-two years I did lecture; I used the usual material. The fact that I've had a paradigm shift is crazy because I'm old school." She had been won over by the well-designed projects that would take the place of tests and by the student-centered focus. "I want independent thinkers that can back up their opinion with facts," she said. "That's what we teach." By this time, Brewer was carrying on a simultaneous conversation with the students, who were talking about the famous Trumbull painting of George Washington standing among the delegates to the Constitutional Convention. "Why were there no women among the delegates?," Brewer asked. "You guys afraid of women? Wait 'til we get to Sojourner Truth."

Belle Isle budgets a double period for some of its classes, including American History. This gave Miss Brewer the luxury of allowing conversation to flow and even to digress into what might turn out to be fruitful areas. The focus of today's class, which was stipulated in Brewer's iCivics lesson plan, was to pick a person you know of who had the attributes of a Framer. The delegates to the Constitutional Convention, Brewer said—though all men—had been bold figures prepared to chart a new path for the nation. Who was like that? One little knucklehead cracked, "Hitler." Brewer, who knew better than to take the bait, said, "American." I walked around and talked to the kids. One boy, a flutist, hesitated between his musical idols, James Galway and Jethro Tull. Another chose Lil Nas X, a gay rapper who had not only come out but given important support to LGBTQ causes. Others chose Martin Luther King, Jr., Kobe Bryant, Barack Obama, Rosa Parks, and the Black cosmetics magnate Madam C. J. Walker. If it were up to the kids in Miss Brewer's class, strikingly, the Constitutional Convention would have been virtually all Black; perhaps John Fonte would have taken that as a sign of woke indoctrination. The students read what they had written—except for the boy who had chosen Lil Nas, perhaps not so bold as his hero—and talked about what it meant to be a Framer.

At the end of class, Miss Brewer assigned an "exit ticket," a mini-essay included in each lesson plan. "What does it mean to be a Founder and a Framer?" The kids wrote a few lines, and then left. In many ways, the lesson illustrated just what I didn't like about progressive pedagogy. The students had been asked to abstract and apply to themselves a concept—"Framer"—that had a very particular meaning at a very particular moment. Miss Brewer had talked to them briefly about the actual convention, but the real subject of the class was now, not then, and you, not them. That was the inevitable consequence of the decision by the EAD team to pose questions rather than to specify content. That said, the class had been lively and energetic, and the students had been deeply engaged throughout. And perhaps they had brought a very remote idea closer to themselves.

Brown and I spent most of our time visiting social studies classes in middle and high schools. The tough graders at the Fordham Institute had awarded Oklahoma's history and civics standards a B+, among the highest grades in the country. Yet the actual experience of the schools showed how merely notional such standards can be. At a ninth-grade class in Oklahoma history at U.S. Grant High School, whose population is overwhelmingly Hispanic and impoverished, the teacher, Beatrice Mitchell, had written on the board the ambitious objectives for the day's lesson: "compare different perspectives on land ownership, the structure of self-government, religion and trading practices." The class was absolutely, utterly mute. It was painful for everyone—Miss Mitchell, Peter Brown, me, and possibly the kids. Miss Mitchell wound up instructing them on the most elementary issues: "You have to capitalize proper names, like the United States." At a tenth-grade World History class on the Enlightenment, I walked around and asked the kids whether they knew what the word meant. Some of them were too shy to answer, as clearly had been true in Miss Mitchell's class as well. But no one could explain the term, and no one could tell me anything about Locke, Adam Smith, or Voltaire, whom they had learned about the week before and were to discuss today.

When I sat down with Grant's history staff, I had a discussion very much like the one I would later have in Illinois. "We need to bring it down to a sixth- or seventh-grade level," said Michael Stephens, a veteran teacher. They used a software program that allowed them to adjust the language of primary documents to the kids' own level. Brian Gorny, Brown's friend who had dropped out of the EAD curriculum the year before, would later tell me that he felt he had spent all of his time doing "modifications" so that the kids could make sense of the assigned readings. I asked the Grant teachers whether they felt they were helping to "Americanize" their students (though many were second- or third-generation Americans). Like the teachers at West Chicago, they worried that they were not getting through: "the kids don't see themselves in U.S. history." Mr. Stephens said bleakly, "I don't think the kids care about World History. They don't love history. They don't love school."

One of the reasons for situating the iCivics curriculum at eighth grade was that the students were old enough, in theory, to grapple with difficult concepts but young enough to still be reachable by school. Maybe a rich exposure to serious questions could alter their trajectory in high school. Brown worried more about the teachers than he did about the kids. He and I met one afternoon with Sarah DeWitt, EAD's national director of implementation. They both talked about how hard it had been to persuade veteran teachers to adopt an inquiry mindset. Many of them, said DeWitt, resisted going deeply into a given subject because they just didn't have the historical knowledge. The teachers would need, they knew, intensive ongoing professional development. Brown and DeWitt were constantly revising the curriculum in light of experience, but they wouldn't dumb it down. "We scaffold the primary documents with headnotes and a glossary of unfamiliar words," DeWitt explained.

"Sometimes we'll just assign a portion of a primary document, but they read the real words, not a summary."

Brown also worried about his district and his state. Oklahoma's elected school superintendent, a religious conservative named Ryan Walters, had complained at a school board meeting that "the current national left-wing indoctrination is attempting to destroy religion as a way to destroy our country." Walters had proposed as a bulwark of faith a new requirement that the Ten Commandments be posted in every classroom. He had also notoriously insisted that teachers should not characterize the 1921 Tulsa Massacre, the most deadly racial pogrom in the nation's history, as a racial incident. That, he said, would constitute "critical race theory."[2] A more immediate threat to the history teachers I met was Walters's suggestion that the state endorse an instructional provider called PragerU, which is not a university at all but a company founded by a right-wing talk radio figure who, along with confederates, compiled an extremely one-sided array of short videos on American history. "If they ever tell us we have to use PragerU, I'm quitting," said Katie Rogers, an eighth-grade teacher at Southeast Middle School.

However things played out, Oklahoma City Public Schools would remain a kind of neglected stepchild. The district's better students were leaving for the "application schools" and the charter schools, which were also permitted to exercise selective admissions, something prohibited in much of the country. Worse still, in 2023 the state had passed the Oklahoma Parental Choice Tax Credit Act, which offered tax credits of up to $7,500 for private or home schooling. This would accelerate the departure of middle-class parents, but the poor could not afford the additional sum that private schools would charge. The loss of revenue and of talent would deepen the crisis of the schools, thus vindicating the conservative critique of public institutions. Perhaps that was the idea. Brown had come to see the state government as the enemy of the public schools. But Oklahoma was far from alone. As of this writing, ten other states—all in red America—had passed such "universal voucher" laws.[3]

I returned to Oklahoma City in February. The students in Miss Brewer's class were finishing up a unit on judicial review. They had studied *Marbury v. Madison*. Then each of them had chosen a historic case to study—*Brown v. Board of Education, Dred Scott v. Sandford, Miranda v. Arizona, Gideon v. Wainwright, Roe v. Wade.* A number of the kids had researched a search-and-seizure case involving drugs found in a girl's backpack at school. They had used Oyez, a website that offers very useful summaries of major cases. The unit set chronology aside in order to help students understand the meaning of judicial review in their own world—another example of trying to bring a remote concept home to students.

The students turned to a new unit on the nineteenth-century treaties the United States signed with Indian tribes. Miss Brewer had created a class of her own in order to introduce students to the whole idea of binding obligations. "What are laws?," she asked. The kids tried out some intuitive theories. "Rules set by a higher authority," said one.

Who gets to make a law?
The government. Otherwise it's just a rule.
Are rules good?
Yes!
What rules do we have at Belle Isle?
No cheating. Be respectful. No violence. No cell phone in class.

If any of the kids felt remotely ironical about these strictures, I didn't hear it. They really were pro-rule.

"What are promises?" That was harder.
Something you assure to someone?
Can you sign a promise?
No.

And finally to treaties, promises made between two sovereign entities that had the force of law—at least until willfully broken by the more powerful party. Miss Brewer had used half of her double-period block to bring students to this point, but perhaps it would leave them with a deeper understanding of the broken promise of the Indian treaties. At this stage, perhaps because the lesson had run its course, things got a little blurry as Miss Brewer talked about the importance of student government and the danger of civic apathy. As with the lesson on the Framers, Miss Brewer had helped the students feel the reality of an unfamiliar concept, though she hadn't shed any light on actual treaties or American history. That would be coming later in the week.

Miss Brewer had three different sections, and each one had a slightly different collective personality. Her next class was poorly behaved and had a perverse talent for forcing her away from her intended point until she had lost the thread entirely. Soon she was illustrating the importance of rules in the school cafeteria by talking about how her grandson could die if someone nearby ate a cashew, and then everyone was talking about nut allergies and one perilous thing or another. Once unmoored from content, a class could easily drift into the shoals of chitchat. The lesson plan, with its rigid ten-minute mini-units, was meant to keep the ship heading steadily downstream, but Miss Brewer had cut loose those stays.

The following day, I sat in on Miss Brewer's third eighth-grade class. Not only were the students more attentive, but the class felt more tightly structured, perhaps because Miss Brewer followed the iCivics lesson plan. She showed the kids a video that explained the concept of tribal sovereignty in a very clear and straightforward manner. She handed out a passage from the immensely long Iroquois Constitution. I was wondering whether the kids would hear the echoes of the American Constitution. So was Miss Brewer. "Have you guys heard this before?," she asked. One student immediately piped up, "It's *our* Constitution." The students talked about what it meant to be a "civilized" rather than "barbarian" tribe. The civilized tribes, it was agreed, had taken inspiration from the United States, but they had not thereby been granted the status of equals.

Oklahoma City Public Schools, Brown had told me, had recruited Generation Civics to work in the district's high schools. The organization was notorious among the right-wing critics of "action civics"; the founder, Scott Warren, had handed them ammunition. In his manifesto, *Generation Citizen: The Power of Youth in Our Politics*, Warren had called on young people to mobilize for social change through movement politics. He took an extremely dim view not only of representative democracy but of the traditional civics education that promoted its virtues. Warren believed that civic education should serve instead as a preparation for civic action, "a citizen-centered politics in which citizens work together to solve problems."[4]

Peter Brown's own politics were hardly progressive: he had regarded himself as a conservative until Donald Trump had become the face of the Republican Party. He had turned to Generation Civics because he felt that the organization had evolved into a more traditional support organization for civic engagement. The MAGA folk did not agree. In 2019, an organization called the Oklahoma Council of Public Affairs published an attack claiming that "Generation Civics is a social justice organization using civics education as a Trojan Horse to take over Oklahoma's K-12 school system." The author insisted that the organization "can, should, and must be banished from Oklahoma's schools—and so should all 'civic engagement,' 'experiential learning,' and 'social justice education.' "[5] Warren and Amy Curran, the head of the organization in Oklahoma, fired back that Generation Civics had "worked together with a politically diverse range of state education agencies and lawmakers" to establish a more "integrative" civics education and, rather than telling students what to think, to "acknowledge and affirm their hope for a more just society."[6]

Generation Civics believed that it was following, rather than dictating, the students' politics. Peter Brown didn't think it should be doing either. In 2022 he attended a Generation Civics panel in Oklahoma City and was shocked to see that all of the panelists, including a transgender activist, were well to the left of the local norm. This could have led to disaster had the local press paid any attention, which, fortunately, it had not. Brown had seen a few cases where he thought "teachers were pushing their views on the students." He bluntly informed Generation Civics' leaders that they had to state explicitly that students would study all sides of whatever issue they chose to examine. Apparently the message had gotten through: at the ensuing panel, held in fall 2023, the conversation had focused on working with people with whom you don't agree; the panel had been evenly divided between Republican and Democratic officials.

Brown brought me to see Ann Kennedy, a twelfth-grade Government teacher at Southeast High who had been working with the organization. Kennedy had long felt that the very disadvantaged population she served desperately needed the experience of civic engagement in order to make the idea of citizenship real. She had developed a project in which students prepared a policy notebook as if they were an advisor to the president of the United States. Once they had chosen a subject, they would do research, interview at least one local figure in government or politics, conduct a poll among friends or strangers, and reach out to no less than six interest groups—three on each side of the issue. Sometimes she would bring in experts to talk to the class. The policy notebook would include a one-page recommendation for the president, a background discussion, and a bibliography.

Now Miss Kennedy was doing pretty much the same thing with the help of Generation Civics. The whole class would choose a subject and then divide into groups variously devoted to writing legislation, talking to community members, and so on. In recent years, they had studied the local grocery tax, sex education, gun control, and investment in their impoverished South Oklahoma City neighborhood. The past fall, they had worked on drug prevention. Concluding that one of the root causes was idleness, they had recommended increased after-school programs—a very Bill Clinton–era solution. As before, they had to do equal research on both sides. One year they had focused on school lunch programs. A Republican state legislator had explained why federal funding mechanisms would frustrate their effort to increase local spending. Miss Kennedy proudly recalled that this local politician had spoken so plainly and sincerely—unlike some of the progressives—the kids concluded that Republicans might be okay. If this was an example of the "service learning" and "action civics" that the Oklahoma Council of Public Affairs and the Civics Alliance so deeply deplored, it was hard to see how it would "obliterate from our children's memory the America worth loving and defending."

The other eighth-grade classes that used the iCivics curriculum were located in a school named after Mary Golda Ross, the first female Native

American engineer. The school had long been known as Stonewall Jackson Middle School until the city agreed that a school serving an overwhelmingly Hispanic immigrant population should not be named after a Confederate general. It was in this very poor neighborhood adjacent to the old cattle yards that Peter Brown had grown up; his father had ministered to a nearby church. Brown had managed to recruit two new teachers at Mary Golda Ross to the inquiry-based approach.

In the first class to which Brown brought me, the desks had been organized into two vertical columns hugging either wall; the column near the hallway was almost all-girl, while the one near the windows was for the boys. For much of the class, one girl played with another's hair; one boy drummed almost continually on his desk. The teacher, Robert Matthewson, let it slide. The subject of the day was westward expansion; the compelling question was, "What caused the borders of the United States to change?" The lesson plan indicated that the students were to write a poem on the subject. This seemed like a very tough ask of the kids, but that's what the plan said. Mr. Matthewson asked whether anyone knew what a poem was. He was met with silence. He gave them a nudge: poems used phrases rather than complete sentences. What was a phrase? Silence.

Mr. Matthewson asked what they remembered about the Mexican War and the Republic of Texas, which they had just read about. Nothing, apparently. The silence in the face of this inquiry-based curriculum was in no way distinguishable from the silence of Miss Mitchell's orthodox ninth-grade Oklahoma history class, but perhaps because these students were a year younger, the behavior was worse. Halfway through class, a girl drew up two chairs, put her pocketbook down on one as a pillow, and stretched out at full length—a brazen act of defiance that would have been inconceivable among Miss Brewer's rule-obeying kids. Mr. Matthewson chose not to notice, perhaps because he had tired of trying to enforce schoolish comportment.

Mr. Matthewson had been told to expect a fire drill, but for some reason it hadn't sounded. He told his students, with what felt like increasing desperation, that the drill was coming. Finally it did, and we all trooped outside, milled around, and came back twenty or so minutes later. Mr. Matthewson asked the kids to start brainstorming about a subject for their poem. I walked around and asked the kids whether they had learned anything that seemed worth writing about. Shrugs. "So, guys!," Matthewson cried. "Let's wrap this up. So what are we writing the poem about?" No one threw him a lifeline—until the buzzer sounded to bring the period to a merciful conclusion.

Things got only a little better in the next class. Perhaps because he was also of Hispanic background, Mario Campos had an easy, ribbing relationship with his kids. He spent fifteen minutes of the fifty-minute period showing a video of the California gold rush in which cartoon figures alternated with archival footage. The kids watched raptly. This video would have been more gratifying to the anti-woke Right, because it concluded with a cascade of grim consequences of the gold rush—mercury poisoning, violent crime, drinking and gambling, oppression of Chinese immigrants, the death or dispossession of Native populations. Mr. Campos asked whether the gold rush had been good or bad on balance, which led to a meandering discussion about good things and bad things. Remember, he concluded cheerily, "it's up to you guys to form your own opinion on that."

Peter Brown had sat with me in Mr. Matthewson's class, though not Mr. Campos's. It had been a painful experience for him. He had been thinking about what he would have said if he had been in front of the class. ("Do you guys know any *songs*? Poems are like songs, but without music.") But he had to work with what he had, just as the teachers had to work with the students they had. So much of what was worthwhile about the EAD Roadmap leaked away in the reality of the classroom. Miss Brewer was an excellent teacher in a good school with cooperative and generally high-achieving kids; even she had gone astray when she had wandered from the lesson plan. Mary Golda Ross was a much tougher row to hoe. What's more, the inquiry-based approach asked more of teachers than did one more firmly rooted in chronological narrative. Brown knew that he had a lot of work to do on professional development, as did the leadership at iCivics. But all the professional development in the world might not be enough for midcareer teachers with modest credentials.

What the students at Mary Golda Ross or U.S. Grant lacked were the linguistic skills—in reading, writing, and self-expression—that students need if they are to play any of the democratic roles that Danielle Allen lists. If the kids at Belle Isle had more of that verbal facility, that may have had less to do with anything the school did than with the students who came there—middle-class kids who received a broad exposure to language and to books at home and in their own world. The kids at the high-poverty schools did not. This was a problem that the EAD Roadmap could not solve. Only a very different form of schooling in the lower grades could make up for what the students weren't getting at home. And those students, especially, would need teachers with a deeper knowledge of their subject once they reached the later grades.

Oklahoma's history and civics standards were coming up for renewal in 2025. Brown was hoping that the state would agree to make the iCivics curriculum standard in eighth grade. That kind of success would colossally increase the burden on the system and on him personally. Brown was as dedicated to his mission as was his father to living on peanut-butter sandwiches in his Thai village. But in some ways, the younger Brown faced a more hostile environment. Oklahoma was a relative latecomer to the culture wars over the schools, and the governor and school superintendent hadn't yet gotten around to rewriting the standards to make the state safe for patriotism. Brown feared that Superintendent Walters would stack the committee charged with rewriting social studies standards with right-wing ideologues who would share John Fonte's view of the EAD Roadmap.

In the summer of 2024, Brown's fears appeared to be realized. In late June, Walters announced that all public schools in Oklahoma would henceforth be compelled to teach the Bible, including the Ten Commandments. (One week earlier, Louisiana became the first state to require that the Ten Commandments be posted in all classrooms.) The state had already decided to allow parents to use the state voucher system to send their children to religious schools, though that had proved too much even for the state supreme court. (The Supreme Court declined to overturn the lower court decision.[8]) Then things got worse. Although a group of educators—including Brown—had been hard at work on revised social studies standards, in early July Walters announced a "complete overhaul" of the standards to ensure that they were "chronologically sound" and to inspire "love of country," incorporate the Bible, and "eliminate DEI, indoctrination, and return teaching back to the basics in Oklahoma." Leaving nothing to chance, Walters himself appointed a new "executive review committee" whose members included Dennis Prager, Mark Bauerlein (the avowed foe of the EAD Roadmap), and Kevin Roberts, president of the hard-right Heritage Foundation and publisher of the 2025 Project.

On September 10, when Brown's team of standards writers convened to engage in final review, the Oklahoma State Department of Education instead presented an entirely new set of standards devised by the executive committee. I got an anguished text from Brown: "It is all so bad. I can't even articulate accurately how bad it is." The new standards were, he wrote, "word for word Birthright"—that is, the Civics Alliance's American Birthright standards. I tried to cheer Brown up by sending him an article from the *New York Times* that quoted superintendents from highly conservative and religious districts in Oklahoma observing that no one had asked for Bible instruction in schools, and many teachers and even parents believed that scriptural lessons belonged in the home and the church, not the classroom.[9] He wrote back, "the Bible mandate pales in comparison to the standards issue." Brown said that he was trying to decide whether he should "go scorched earth." That sounded like a suicide mission.

Brown ultimately decided against strapping on the dynamite; he would hold off pending an outcome. Miraculously, in early November the chief advocate of the American Birthright standards stepped down, complaining that the State Department of Education had clung to the old curriculum. And the board directed all Oklahoma middle schools to begin using the iCivics curriculum that fall. The Lord, as Ryan Walters might have put it, worked in mysterious ways.

10

In Florida, American History Is What the Governor Says It Is

In Orlando in mid-October 2023, I attended the 66th Annual Conference of the Florida Council for the Social Studies (FCSS). Under Governor Ron DeSantis, who was then planning to challenge Donald Trump for the Republican nomination for president, Florida had become the tip of the spear of the right-wing culture war. DeSantis had pushed through the GOP-dominated legislature a law against teaching young children about gender issues; a ban on the teaching of divisive concepts, above all critical race theory; and a "Parents Bill of Rights" requiring schools to post all information about curriculum and extracurricular activities and to establish procedures for parents to lodge objections. He had overseen changes to the civics curriculum designed to make it more explicitly patriotic and had set aside days and even entire weeks in which teachers would be required to tell students about the virtues of the American system and the evils of rival doctrines. I wanted to understand what it was like to teach in such an environment, and I wasn't at all sure that I would be allowed to do so by sitting in on class.

Confabs such as the FCSS are sponsored by instructional providers and other vendors to the schools: officials man booths furnished with literature and penny candies while teachers mill around and exchange gossip. iCivics had a booth, as did the Bill of Rights Institute and the National Constitution Center and Sphere, the educational wing of the libertarian Cato Institute. In one such booth I fell into conversation with Josh Roberson, a veteran history teacher at Seminole High School in Pinellas County (of which St. Petersburg is the capital). Roberson was good enough at what he did that he had been named Florida History Day Teacher of the Year in 2022 (though he was too modest to tell me so himself). That summer, he said, he had taken a professional development course from one of the nonprofit providers, the Jack Miller Center, and had also been certified by Florida's Civic Seal of Excellence, a course created by DeSantis's education commissioner, Manny Diaz.

"The Jack Miller program really was in my mind the best of what these educational summer sessions are about," Roberson said to me. I knew of the Miller Center as the outfit to which Virginia officials had turned to recruit conservative historians to counter the progressive tilt of the state standards. I asked Roberson whether he had detected any ideological preachments. Not at all, he said. Like the Bill of Rights Institute, apparently, the Miller Center had a point of view but nevertheless played it down the middle when it came to professional development. "The lectures were very rigorous and serious," Roberson said, "and they invited conversation from the teachers." That suited him fine. "My feeling," he said, "is that the way to teach history or civics is to present the alternative and let every kid make their own choice."

It was precisely that prior experience with an allegedly conservative training program that had made Roberson so dismayed by Florida's fifty-five-hour course. "It was all, 'Clarence Thomas is the best thing that's ever happened to the Supreme Court,'" Roberson recalled. At that point, a history teacher named Kimberly who had also taken the class joined us, and Roberson asked her what her impressions had been. "A lot of it was good stuff," she said, "but there were . . . moments. At one point we were talking about the First Amendment, Ben Franklin and such, and one of them brought up Hunter Biden's laptop"—an obsession, at the time, of the right-wing conspiracy mill. That had seemed positively weird. Like any teacher in Florida, both Josh and Kimberly had grown weary of listening to right-wing critics explain to the world that the schools had become hotbeds of socialism and wokeness. Both, in fact, regarded viewpoint-neutrality as almost a sacred classroom obligation, and both felt that it was their state that was practicing indoctrination in the guise of professional development. "It's exactly what they accuse teachers of doing," Roberson pointed out.

That was Florida, where a teacher never knew how he or she could get in trouble. I heard quite a few examples. One high school teacher from Brevard County, on the Atlantic coast, immediately to the east of Orlando, told me that in 2020, when schools were meeting in hybrid session owing to the pandemic, he had received a call from his principal saying, "Jeff, I know this doesn't sound like you, but a parent says that she heard you say that you saw Donald Trump throwing puppies off the Causeway Bridge." The parent was calling for Jeff's head. Once he gathered his wits, Jeff had told his principal that in order to explain libel law, he had said that Joe Biden would not be allowed to assert that he had seen Donald Trump throwing puppies off the Causeway Bridge. It was a ridiculous story but not an altogether funny one.

Governor DeSantis was the trailblazer of the "war on woke": He had begun targeting what he regarded as a left-wing school establishment soon after he had been elected in 2018. The following year he proposed, and the legislature passed, a law ordering the Florida Department of Education to rewrite civics standards. The new standards were approved in June 2021 and had gone into effect at the beginning of the 2023–24 school year. I heard about that too when I first arrived at the FCSS meeting. The new standards, I was told, had eliminated all references to experiential learning contained in the old ones. And, like the Civics Alliance's American Birthright standards, they were overtly patriotic to the point of jingoism. Nicola Gerges, a veteran history and civics teacher at Kennedy Middle School in Brevard, said that the new standards boiled down to "America is best."

That turned out to be absolutely true, though also slightly incomplete. With a Republican-controlled State Board of Education, DeSantis had had the kind of free hand to rewrite state standards that Kristi Noem had in South Dakota but Glenn Youngkin had not in Virginia. Seventh-grade civics students would no longer be expected, as they had been under the standards adopted in 2010 under the moderate Republican governor, Charlie Crist, to "experience the responsibilities of citizens at the local, state and federal level," "conduct a mock election," "simulate the trial process," or "conduct a service project to further the public good." And while under the old standards students were to "compare different forms of government," under the new they would "analyze the advantages of the United States' constitutional republic over other forms of government in safeguarding liberty, freedom and a representative government." So, too, with "the advantages of a federal system" and "the advantages of capitalism and the free market." The civics standards had been subjected to so thoroughgoing an ideological makeover that the vogue right-wing term "constitutional republic" had even supplanted "democracy."[1]

Yet in Florida as elsewhere, the new conservatism had a pedagogical as well as an ideological dimension. The old version, like the original draft of the Virginia standards, had begun with a list of major skills to be mastered: "the student will use new vocabulary," "the student will use context clues," "the student will determine the main idea or essential message." All that was gone, replaced by factual learning rooted in a high regard for first principles. While the old standards had begun with the Magna Carta, the new ones asked students to explain the influence of ancient Greece and Rome, as well as "Judeo-Christian ethical ideas," on America's "constitutional republic." Students studying the Declaration of Independence would be expected to "explain the concept of natural rights"—the Hillsdale hobbyhorse—and to "analyze the relationship between natural rights and the role of government" in the language of the Declaration. Sixth-graders in Florida would be able, or so the standards now stipulated, to explain the influence of "Cicero, Marcus Aurelius, Pericles, Solon, Cleisthenes"—even Cleisthenes!—"on civic participation and governance in the ancient world."

Florida had been one of the first states to take civics education seriously, both by adopting rigorous standards and by requiring classes in middle school and high school. DeSantis had thus set out to fix what was not obviously broken. He had, in effect, ordered an immersion in conservative thinking as a corrective to a progressive bias that, at least on the evidence of the former standards and of the teachers' professed aversion to indoctrination, was very difficult to detect. That said, sixth-graders who could discourse fluently on Cleisthenes might be permitted an excessive deference to natural-law theory.

The Florida Department of Education developed the Civic Seal of Excellence course to prepare teachers for the new curriculum. Though the training was voluntary, teachers would receive a $3,000 stipend for completing it—a meaningful sum for someone earning $60,000 or so a year. In one of the first panel sessions I attended at the FCSS conference, John Duebel, the state education department's head of social studies and the arts, explained that not only had 20,000 teachers already taken the course, but many other states were now clamoring to imitate Florida's example. "In spite of what you may have seen in the media," he said primly, "the teachers were very happy." In fact, the teachers I discussed it with hadn't been happy at all. Local newspapers had had little trouble finding bewildered or just plain vexed graduates of the program. The *Tampa Bay Times* quoted Tatiana Ahlbum, a local twelfth-grade teacher, as saying that instead of helping teachers present their subject, as every training she had taken in the past had done, the Florida program "presented the history as if none of us had learned it before." That was hardly an accident: the presenters believed that they needed to shatter a consensual left-wing worldview. Ahlbum told the paper that a state education department facilitator had explained to a group of teachers that they would need to clearly explain the evils of socialism because students "think it's the best thing ever."[2]

The Florida Department of Education boasted of the "53 expert scholars and practitioners" who had agreed to present material for the course. Yet while even conservative-leaning instructional providers such as the Bill of Rights Institute typically seek to recruit a balanced slate of scholars, the Civics Seal of Excellence featured only one side. Of the ten speakers for Module One, "Ideas and Events That Led to America's Independence," five came from Hillsdale College; two from the Claremont Institute, another key node in the right-wing intellectual network, and one each from the conservative First Liberty Institute, the Christian Ave Maria University, and the free-market-oriented American Institute for Economic Research.[3]

While the lectures are not available to outsiders, the Florida

Department of Education had furnished the accompanying slides to the *Tampa Bay Times*. One of the slides on slavery in the first module noted that only 4 percent of the slaves sent to the Western Hemisphere ended in the colonies (far more went to Brazil), while another claimed—without attribution—that both George Washington and Thomas Jefferson wanted to pass legislation to abolish slavery, without noting that both were slave-owners, much less that neither made any serious effort to act on their abolitionist convictions. Another slide described the view that the Founders believed in a strict separation of church and state as a "misconception." Florida's new civics standards and its training course represent the Hillsdalification of the state's educational program.

I attended another panel at which the presenter, a teacher from Orange County, kicked off by asking how many "mandates" the audience could name in thirty seconds. The voices rang out: "Victims of Communism Day!" "Constitution Day." "Portraits of Patriotism." In educational terms, a mandate is a state law that bypasses or supplements the board of education; Illinois, for example, uses mandates to fill in some of the gaps left by the state's uniquely vague standards. What distinguishes Florida is both the sheer number and the polemical character of the mandates imposed under DeSantis. On "Victims of Communism Day," for example, all social studies teachers in the state devote the day's lesson to the superiority of American democracy.

Steve Masyada, director of the Lou Frey Institute at the University of Central Florida, which offers curriculum support and professional development (and played a minor role in the Civic Seal of Excellence course), said to me, "We tried to create a lesson plan for Victims of Communism Day, but it turned out to be very hard. We know what they want the kids to think, but is social democracy the same as socialism? Is socialism the same as Communism? We focused on the easy ones—North Korea and Venezuela. But what were we supposed to say about China?" Teachers have found "Portraits of Patriotism" easier to teach, because the Florida Department of Education has helpfully provided video portraits of immigrants from Cuba and Venezuela, who explain why they fled their home country and embraced their adopted one.

Florida has specialized in passing what are blandly known as "transparency" laws, which require schools to post all lesson plans and assigned materials on a searchable database and to establish procedures that allow parents to lodge objections to those materials. The latter provision is central to Florida's Parents Bill of Rights Act, which passed in January 2021, the very first of the pandemic-era restrictions imposed on schools in the state as well as the nation's first such law. In a report on what it called "Educational Intimidation" laws, the writers organization PEN found that from the time of the Florida law until the end of 2023, 392 such bills had been introduced, and 39 had passed, all in red states. PEN wrote that while the bills "do not constitute direct forms of censorship," they "facilitate the conditions for a chilled climate in public education" and were "part of a broader, ongoing 'Ed Scare'" whose purpose was to limit opportunities to read or discuss controversial ideas, chiefly about race and sex.[4]

At the heart of that broader campaign are laws explicitly prohibiting the discussion of particular ideas or subjects. In April 2022, Florida passed HB 7, the "Stop Woke Act," which—in language apparently drawn from Stanley Kurtz's Partisanship Out of Civics Act—prohibits schools from teaching that "members of one race, color, national origin or sex are morally superior to members of another race, color, national origin or sex" or that "a person, by virtue of their race, color, national origin or sex should be discriminated against or receive adverse treatment to achieve diversity, equity or inclusion." The law *required* teachers to express certain views, including that "meritocracy" and "a hard work ethic" are not racist "but fundamental to the right to pursue happiness and be rewarded for industry." Teachers could be punished either for what they said or for what they failed to say.

I did encounter trace elements of critical race theory at the conference. At a session titled, "'Whiteness as the Default: Reflections on Navigating Social Studies Education from the Perspective of Black Females," Clarence V. Walker, a professor of social science education at the University of South Florida, argued that critical race theory offered a framework for understanding the systematic disadvantage of Black students and "the micro-aggressions, micro-insults, micro-invalidations" that they endured at the hands of white teachers. Walker suggested that these students look for guidance to Black teachers at predominantly Black schools, who cared about and identified with their students as white teachers, he said, did not. He even approvingly cited Kimberlé Crenshaw, the scholar most closely associated with critical race theory.

That said, Walker was an academic, not a teacher. I never heard a teacher talk about micro-invalidations. The actual effect of the don't-say-this-or-that laws, from what I could judge at the FCSS, was to make everyone look over their shoulders when they said anything that might even be deemed controversial. "What I see is really great teachers who are terrified that they'll say the wrong thing," Josh Roberson said to me. Actually, veteran teachers such as Roberson worried less about themselves than about more vulnerable and less confident novices. Dr. Lindsay Brinkmann, a history teacher in Volusia County and the 2021 Gilder Lehrman Florida History Teacher of the Year, ridiculed the obsession with critical race theory. "If you teach civil rights as this group is bad and that group is good," she said to me, "you're not teaching it right." But the law, she said, had scared the bejeezus out of young teachers. She feared that the "anti-teacher" climate would make it that much harder to recruit talented young people into the profession.

I heard less about fear at the conference than I did about frustration and surrender. Jennifer Jolley, the head of high school social studies in Brevard, explained to me that a teacher who wanted to assign any resource not already in the posted curriculum had to receive special permission either from the school principal, the librarian, or the district office. Nicola Gerges, the Brevard middle school teacher, said that she typically won approval for new material—but only after a month or so, when it was too late to be useful. "Education should be fluid," she said. "You need to be able to act in the moment. You don't know when the moment is going to happen when a kid's going to get it. And when it does, you'll want to go off on a tangent." But she had to stick to her knitting. Gerges used the example of the Columbian Exchange, the transfer of goods, products, and people between the Old World and New World. "There's very little on that in the texts," she said, "so you have to find websites on your own. But you can't do that. So I have to say to the kids, 'You have to find it on your own.' They say, 'Why?' And what I say to them is, 'Those are the people your parents voted for. Don't yell at me; yell at your parents.'"

The twin zones of peril, in Florida and elsewhere, are of course race and sex. The most notorious of Governor DeSantis's many interventions in the schools is the so-called Don't Say Gay law, which passed in 2022. The law prohibited any classroom instruction on gender and sexual identity in grades K–3 and permitted such instruction in later grades only as developmentally appropriate. For all the furor over the bill, there is a perfectly valid argument that sex education of any kind need not begin so early—indeed, that sex education is one of those subjects, valuable and even necessary on its own, that takes up too much time in the school calendar. But yet another law passed the following year explicitly stated that "a person's sex is an immutable biological trait and that it is false to ascribe to a person a pronoun that does not correspond to such person's sex." The law prohibited school personnel from referring to students by "their preferred personal title or pronouns" if they did not correspond to their biological sex.

The law, mocked as "Don't Say They," had tied the schools in comical knots. One morning, as a group of teachers were regaling me with outrages, one of them said, "Does he know about the nicknames?" When I said that I didn't, she explained that she was not allowed to refer to Robert, if that was the name on the attendance roll, as Bobby, even if that's what he called himself, without sending a note home and receiving parental permission. Rather than singling out only the Evan-turned-Erin, the state had, in a gesture of even-handedness, subjected each and every nickname to the new test of "transparency." Parents had to know and approve. The sheer cumbersomeness of the process, the inane waste of time, seemed almost worse than the prospect of getting hauled on the carpet for nomenclatural transgression.

Practically everything in Florida had become a minefield. Not surprisingly, several of the panels were devoted to tactics designed to keep teachers out of trouble. A panel on "Hard Histories" suggested that teachers distinguish between "settled issues," such as the Holocaust or climate change, and "open issues," such as politics and policy. (Of course, many Florida parents might not regard climate change as "settled.") At the closing brunch, a representative from one of the curriculum providers demonstrated "some of the ways that we can tweak our lessons to protect ourselves." You can, she suggested, "insulate yourself from parents" by showing them a lesson plan in advance so they can see how carefully balanced it was. You could; yet this defensive, almost preemptive, approach to teaching seemed to mock the "fluid," spontaneous pedagogy that Nicola Gerges had rhapsodized about. Why would a great teacher want to teach in Florida?

The combination of the generalized atmosphere of fear and the intense politicization of race and sex had led to some bizarre outcomes. In early 2024, a parent at an elementary school in Miami—a liberal bastion, or so one might have thought—posted a permission slip he had received for a library event that his daughter's first-grade class would be attending. His daughter would need explicit permission in order to "participate & listen to a book written by an African-American." There was no suggestion that six-year-olds were to be indoctrinated with CRT; rather, the school couldn't take the risk of exposing them to a Black speaker without parental approval. The chairman of the State Board of Education blamed the local school for "grossly misinterpreting" the intent of the Parental Bill of Rights. Yet the week before, parents at *another* Miami school had received a permission form for "class and schoolwide presentations showcasing the achievements and recognizing the rich and diverse traditions, histories and innumerable contributions of the Black communities."[5] Better safe than sorry, apparently.

Like Glenn Youngkin—like all his conservative brethren—DeSantis regularly insisted that his goal was to clear away the fog of woke thinking in order to restore the rigorous learning that parents demanded and students needed. Yet teachers who could not assign interesting readings without running a bureaucratic gauntlet and who had to worry that any stray remark could land them in the stocks were in no position to provide rigorous instruction. The conservative self-contradiction went deeper still. In 2023, Florida became the first state to authorize teachers to use the free videos provided by PragerU—the provider that teachers in Oklahoma City told me they dreaded—for students in grades K through 6. This did not arise from a judgment about academic quality. Dennis Prager, the right-wing radio host who formed the company, explained that the material was designed to counter the "woke agenda infiltrating classrooms."[6] One video showed Frederick Douglass warning cartoon children of the dangers of radical abolitionists such as William Lloyd Garrison. (Douglass worked closely with Garrison but then broke with him.) Another showed a Dutch farm boy complaining that climate regulations would put an end to his way of life. As elsewhere, Florida's blessing emboldened other states to do likewise; PragerU soon gained approval in Missouri, New Hampshire, and, of course, Oklahoma.[7]

Teachers at the conference also told me about Dave Ramsey, an evangelical radio host whose "textbook" on personal finance had been approved for use in Florida's financial literacy curriculum. Ramsey's view of finance is biblical; he describes credit cards as "snakes," and he routinely cites scripture to justify economic claims. In the summer of 2023, after a new law making personal finance a mandatory subject took effect, one of the Ramsey Group's texts, *Foundations in Personal Finance*, was mysteriously removed from the state's "Not Recommended" list and was approved for use in Pasco County, north of Tampa. Though state officials claimed that the text had been revised to reflect new standards, an official from Florida Freedom to Read, a free-speech organization, told a TV reporter that she could find no meaningful difference between the old version and the new.[8]

No one could claim with a straight face that Florida had endorsed Dennis Prager or Dave Ramsey—or mandated Victims of Communism Day and Portraits in Patriotism—in the service of academic rigor. Under DeSantis, Florida was plainly prepared to sacrifice rigor to a greater good—the war for America's soul against the grandees who allegedly control the commanding heights of the culture. As DeSantis put it when he announced his presidential campaign in mid-2023, "These elites are not enacting an agenda to represent us. They're imposing *their* agenda on us, via the federal government, via corporate America and via our own educational system."[9] If schools have long since been politicized by the Left, then the Right is *depoliticizing* school by going to war against the system. That's why Stanley Kurtz could title his model law the

Partisanship Out of Civics Act. That objective supersedes the professed goal of intellectual rigor.

It's true, as we'll see in the next chapter, that in some left-leaning states, history and civics standards, curricular material, official pronouncements from school leaders, and indeed the entire atmosphere surrounding the schools is shaped by progressive views so pervasive as barely even to be recognized as views. *Some* programs of action civics—though certainly less than conservatives imagine—do feel like an extension of movement politics. Yet in Florida and other red states, the intense mobilization of right-wing forces operates not as a corrective to liberal bias but as a full-throttle attack on the very idea of a neutral middle—of teachers such as Josh Roberson inviting students to think for themselves. It is designed not to open up discussion and debate but to foreclose it.

Several of the Brevard County teachers I met suggested that I talk to Jennifer Jenkins, the one liberal on the district school board. Jenkins was a speech pathologist in the district; her husband taught eighth-grade history. In the summer of 2020, she ran for a seat on the board. It was the depth of the pandemic, and DeSantis, after initially complying with public health recommendations, had begun to gain a national reputation by defying recommendations for indoor masking. Jenkins ran against Tina Descovich, the conservative incumbent, on an agenda of mask compliance as well as increased teacher pay. She won an upset victory in a Trump-leaning area. Later that year, Descovich, along with another former school board member from outside Brevard, established a group called Moms for Liberty. In February 2021, the organization announced that it had become a national body. "The balance of power in education has dramatically shifted away from parents and communities to unions and bureaucrats," said Descovich. Moms for Liberty would right that balance, just as Glenn Youngkin was promising to do in Virginia.[10]

Descovich used the word "parents" the way DeSantis used the word "us," to mean "not them"—not, that is "the elite." In fact, of course, she had just been dislodged from office by parents who disagreed with her. Whether or not the schools should be ruled by plebiscite, the democratic will in this case was scarcely obvious. But populists cannot imagine that most people, including well-intentioned people, think differently from themselves. Moms for Liberty now adopted the kind of "movement" politics that conservatives in the pre-Trump era professed to abhor. After a district-level document explaining to administrators how to deal with LGBTQ issues became public, right-wing activists in Brevard, mistaking it for an ideological manifesto, organized a demonstration for the next board meeting. Both a small group of students and a small group of parents gathered outside the meeting. But while the students stood silently, the parents had a bullhorn. Some thundered about "ungodliness" and "uncleanness." One of the more unhinged participants can be heard yelling, "Faggots!" Members of the new organization, in their blue T-shirts, jammed the board meeting in order to speak out against this and similar violations of parental will. From this time forward, board meetings became wildly contentious; protestors began turning up in front of Jenkins's home and issuing dire threats. Jenkins says that she had to be escorted by security to and from board meetings, where protestors gathered in order to call her a Nazi or a witch or whatever other imprecation came to mind.[11]

Anger at pandemic restrictions helped fuel the growth of Moms for Liberty (and elect Glenn Youngkin). By the time of its first national conclave, in June 2022, organizers claimed to have ninety-five thousand members in thirty-eight states, though as only five hundred people attended the event in Tampa, those numbers may have been notional. Nevertheless, to Governor DeSantis the rapid spread of this homegrown body offered proof that ordinary Americans shared his outrage at the woke mandarinate. He delivered the keynote address for the convention, urging delegates to organize for upcoming school board elections in order to "solidify the state of Florida as this country's citadel of freedom."[12]

School board elections in Florida had been, and remained, legally nonpartisan, yet the crusade DeSantis inaugurated effectively put an end to the old idea that schools, and thus school boards, need to be shielded from partisan politics. Just as in recent years the courts, another historically nonpartisan institution, had been yanked off their pedestal and flung into the world of politics and dogma, so, too, would school boards. The neutral institution was anathema to the populist imagination. DeSantis endorsed thirty school board candidates for upcoming elections; most, with support from Moms for Liberty and other groups, won their seats. The new board members then began firing superintendents seen as indifferent or hostile to their agenda. The Brevard superintendent, Mark Mullins, resigned before he could be ousted, declaring, in a tribute to a now forlorn ideal, "This mission is bigger than any of us individually, including me."[13]

In early 2023, DeSantis published a list of fourteen liberal board members, Jennifer Jenkins among them, who would need to be challenged in 2024.[14] Jenkins, the combative daughter of a New York City corrections officer, said that while she had committed to serving only one term, now she was thinking of running again just to show her daughter how to stand up to bullies. In the end, however, common sense prevailed, and Jenkins decided to spare herself and her family any further abuse.

By mid-2022, school closures and mask mandates had waned and thus lost their political salience. Though Moms for Liberty had encoded the idea of freedom of choice in its name, the issue that really galvanized members was not liberty but anger over issues of sexuality and, to a lesser extent, race. During the pandemic, "book banning" had become an issue in Florida and across the nation. PEN found 1,586 instances of books being removed from school libraries or classrooms between July 2021 and March 2022. At that time, almost all bans had been initiated by school boards or administrators.[15] By the following year, the numbers had risen higher still, and far more of the books had been challenged by parent-led groups such as Moms for Liberty. Florida had risen from a distant third place, behind Texas and Pennsylvania, to a very close second, thanks in part to the mechanisms established by HB 1467, passed in March 2022, which obliged schools to create new procedures to respond to book challenges.

By the second half of 2023, the total number of banned books had shot up to more than forty-three hundred, with Florida easily overtaking Texas thanks to Escambia County, in the Panhandle, where sixteen hundred books had been temporarily removed from library shelves pending investigation.[16] Those volumes included dictionaries, encyclopedias,

Ripley's Believe It or Not, and biographies of Oprah Winfrey and Thurgood Marshall.[17] Here, too, the principle that you never know what you can get in trouble for had led to a ludicrous overreaction.

Teachers from both Brevard and Martin Counties, in southern Florida, told me that about one hundred books in their district had been banned. In Brevard, members of Moms for Liberty began showing up at board meetings in order to read the most sexually explicit passages from books they wanted to see removed. The board chairman, herself a conservative, frequently ordered them to stop. That was, in fact, the whole point, for Florida law stipulated that if a school board cut off discussion of a book deemed "pornographic," the school district had to at least temporarily "discontinue the use of the material."

Because "book banning" conjures up "book burning," and thus the Nazis and *Fahrenheit 451* and other dystopias, it is difficult to imagine that anything can be said in its behalf. Certainly you can search through all the reports on the subject published by PEN or the American Library Association without finding any extenuation of the campaign. Yet there are extenuations. First, books are deemed "banned" when they have been removed from libraries; in most cases, however, they are returned to the shelves after investigation. One study, by the conservative Heritage Foundation, found that three-quarters of the books listed by PEN as "banned" were in fact available in district library catalogs. Though activists have called for the removal of many classic works of literature—the Brevard branch of Moms for Liberty challenged Kurt Vonnegut's *Slaughterhouse Five* and Khaled Hosseini's *The Kite Runner*, among others—Heritage researchers found that no such works were unavailable in any district. All of the top ten actually banned books were young adult works that contained graphic sexual language or images.[18]

The book most frequently removed from library shelves, *Gender Queer*, a graphic novel by Maia Kobabe, is, to my mind at least, a moving story of a girl who finds herself unable to occupy any available gender identity and spends long and painful years trying to understand where she fits. It's quite funny about her absurdly progressive Waldorf school. But it does contain plenty of explicit pictures of masturbation and oral sex. Another top-finisher, *Milk and Honey*, a best-selling work of poetry by Rupi Kaur, is so completely preoccupied with sex, abusive and not, that the few explicit line drawings seem superfluous.[19] You would not have to be one of those Moms hurling invective at Jennifer Jenkins to feel that books such as these should not be available to kids below a certain age. Booklooks.org, a website established in Brevard, which claims, somewhat dubiously, to have no connection to Moms for Liberty, offers summaries of hundreds of books that have fallen under suspicion and gives each a rating from "For Everyone" to "Aberrant Content"—meaning, in effect, for no one. Both *Gender Queer* and *Milk and Honey* receive a "No Minors" rating, meaning that they should not appear in school libraries at all.[20]

What is the right framework within which to think about this vexed question? As a matter of constitutional rights, the U.S. Supreme Court seems to have settled the matter when it declared in the 1982 *Board of Education v. Pico* decision that school libraries have "special characteristics" that make them "especially appropriate for the recognition of the First Amendment rights of students"—to which the Court had already shown deference in the 1969 *Tinker v. Des Moines School District* decision. As a matter of democracy, PEN argues that surveys show more than 80 percent of Americans "oppose book bans"—though the poll in question asked only about banning works on American history and race. And as a matter of justice, the prohibitions weigh most heavily on marginalized groups. As the American Library Association notes, "titles representing the voices and lived experiences of LGBTQIA+ and BIPOC individuals made up 47% of those targeted in censorship attempts. Each attempt to ban a book represents a direct attack on every person's constitutionally protected right to freely choose what books to read and what ideas to explore."[21]

Perhaps these considerations should decide the question. Yet a school library is not a public library, much less a bookstore. In a school, questions of "the right to read" need to be balanced against prudential judgments. Is there really no book so vulgar, so reprehensible, so stupid that a librarian ought not purchase it or that the school administration ought not remove it once stocked? Does the fact that a book includes the voices of marginalized groups immunize it from such judgments? Is it wrong to make judgments of quality at all? If the framework that matters most is not the First Amendment but education for democratic citizenship, then we should be concerned not only about the opportunity to read young-adult novels or memoirs about someone just like yourself but also its opposite—the opportunity to discover in books a world utterly unlike your own.

As with sex education, a reasonable solution to an apparently intractable conflict was within reach; but that was never the goal in Florida. Like many districts, Brevard already had a system for adjudicating requests for the removal of books. A book review committee consisting chiefly of teachers and librarians examined each such request and voted on an outcome. But Jennifer Jenkins points out that after the district school board tilted more heavily to the right in the 2022 election, the school-based members were replaced by community members, including an activist for Moms for Liberty. The decisions were now taken by the board itself.

The group also gained control over the process at the state level. In order, he said, to enforce the provisions of HB 1467, Governor DeSantis created a committee to establish statewide guidelines for the restriction of books and for the training of librarians, who are now known as "media specialists," because most of them preside over so few actual books. The committee consisted of eight state education officials and media specialists—and then two others added by Commissioner Diaz, both members of Moms for Liberty. One of them, Michelle Beavers, was the head of the Brevard branch of the group. In their second meeting, in late 2022, Beavers sought to expand the committee's remit to eliminating books that advocated critical race theory, though the law applied only to sexual material. The other appointee, Jennifer Pippin, head of Moms for Liberty in Indian River County, proposed avoiding all books that conferred "glorification" on violence, suicide, cannibalism, and the consumption of drugs, tobacco, and alcohol, which would have eliminated a large fraction of adult literature.[22]

Cathy Boehme of the Florida Education Association, who followed the process with mounting dread, says that the training manual produced by the committee in December 2022 was professional and straightforward. But when the final version appeared after Christmas, it was plain that the text had been tilted toward the Moms and away from the professionals.

The manual defined pornography as "the depiction of erotic behavior (as in pictures or writing) intended to cause sexual excitement," which would eliminate whatever literature remained after the "glorification" standard had been applied. In selecting materials, the manual admonishes media specialists to avoid "unsolicited theories that may lead to student indoctrination."

HB 1467 had not dealt with "theories" of any kind, but of course earlier Florida laws had outlawed supposed theories of Black superiority. The manual went on to remind media specialists of the prohibitions on the teaching of CRT and the questioning of meritocracy and the like incorporated in the "Stop Woke" law. Moving from the forbidden to the required, media specialists were to purchase, "whenever appropriate," works that portray the harmful effects of tobacco, alcohol, and drugs, as well as those lauding the virtues of thrift.[23] The combination of prohibitions, exhortations, and the obligations of transparency virtually ensured that schools would purchase no material that would not pass muster with local conservatives. The manual reminded readers that violations of the law would be punished as a felony in the third degree.

Governor DeSantis had created the ideal condition for reducing Florida's schools to a republic of fear. Teachers had to worry about being betrayed, even inadvertently, by students. School and district administrators had to worry about local boards dominated by ideologues. Librarians had to worry about parents hunting for evidence of pornography and critical race theory. The safest course was to stock only the most vapid books and to teach only the most inoffensive material. One Brevard County history teacher said to me, "I'm very careful not to appear to be politically biased in a way that is opposite to the way they want you to teach."

This is what it was like to teach, if not in an authoritarian society, then in a deeply illiberal one. Florida offers a glimpse of the America that Donald Trump and the culture warriors with whom he has surrounded himself envision. Much of the language of the president's executive order on education, above all the definition of "discriminatory equity ideology," seems to be adopted from Florida laws. The order also draws on "transparency" laws like Florida's to threaten withholding federal funds from schools that "interfere" with parents' "statutory rights to information regarding school curricula, records, or physical examinations." The use of federal power to enforce these principles means that the kind of indoctrination that Florida has mandated could spread to blue states as well as red. Teachers everywhere will be "very careful not to appear to be politically biased"—in the wrong direction.

Or do I exaggerate? After all, by then I knew that behind the closed classroom door many teachers blithely ignored the admonitions of state standards and regulations. I wanted to see for myself; but, as I feared, I was not allowed to. After submitting an application to the Brevard Office of Accountability, Testing and Program Evaluation, I received a letter stating that my proposal would not "significantly improve conditions for Brevard County," would impose an undue burden on teachers and administrators, and lacked "problem clarity." I was also rejected by Volusia County farther south on the Atlantic coast. Several teachers I wrote to hoping for an invitation didn't respond. I imagine they were afraid. I can hardly blame them.

11

In Minneapolis, There Is Only Racism and Antiracism

Unlike most school leaders, Emily Palmer, the principal of Washburn High School in Minneapolis, welcomed me to visit her school and see whatever I cared to see. Palmer shared my view about the centrality of the schools' civic role. When we met in her office in early March 2024, she said, "As far as I'm concerned, the first reason why you have public schools in this country is so that kids can be educated to be citizens of a democracy. The second is so they can find out who they are. The third is being prepared for work." Civic education, for Palmer, was deeply bound up with questions of race and social justice. She had written her doctoral dissertation in educational administration on Minneapolis's failed experiment with desegregation. Her thesis was that teachers in white-majority suburban areas, to which non-white children from Minneapolis had been sent, were unprepared to teach these new students and refused to change their methods in order to do so. This view had shaped her own career. At a middle school where she had previously served as principal, Palmer had made Ojibwe mandatory in sixth grade so that Native children felt that others were studying their culture and not simply the other way around.

George Floyd had been killed in a neighborhood from which Washburn drew. The girl who had taken the video of his slow asphyxiation had been Palmer's middle school student; she felt proud that the girl had had the courage to disobey orders that she stop from abusive policemen. What made the tragedy all the worse for Washburn was that the killing had taken place during the pandemic, which prevented Palmer and her teachers from being able to guide and comfort their students, many of whom were out in the streets during the months of protest. It was a period of fury and anguish. Like all Minneapolis high schools, Washburn had been offering an Ethnic Studies elective since 2015; the class became mandatory after the George Floyd incident. Palmer said that the school spent so much time on the issue of racial justice that the kids had complained that they were feeling exhausted by the subject. But she felt impelled to do more, to place race and justice at the heart of Washburn's culture.

Palmer drew up two documents and distributed them to her faculty: "Washburn HS Practices for Racial Equity" and "Anti-Racist Understandings at Washburn HS." The first admonished teachers to ensure that "perspectives of color are present in the curriculum" in "all disciplines"; to assign seating so that each classroom was integrated; to give extra attention to students with the lowest grades; to "prioritize people over curriculum," taking time out from class work to build a foundation of trust with students; and to eliminate "racial discrepancies" by assigning the same fraction of letter grades to each racial group. Palmer established an "Equity Team" to work toward these goals. The premise of "equity" understood this way is that unequal treatment—rather than the cumulative effect of historical disadvantage—is responsible for differences in outcome. Those gaps can be closed by addressing that unfairness. But it wasn't at all clear, at least to many faculty members, what unjust practices needed to be rectified.

The second document was drawn directly from Ibram X. Kendi's work. Palmer cited Kendi's central claim that "there is only racism and anti-racism." Students who might wish to regard themselves as "non-racist" needed to recognize that "neutral sides with the oppressor." One proposed "action": "If you are not ready to be 'anti-racist,' look hard at why. What are the influences in your life that make this difficult?" This being Minneapolis, the teachers and students at whom the warning was directed were among the most racially enlightened, or at least sensitized, people in America. Palmer made a point of noting, as Kendi does, that "institutional racism does not require intention or malice. . . . We can and do desire great outcomes for students of color & still participate in the racism of the institution." The way forward was "to talk about race & experience discomfort in order to learn and grow," though not at the expense of "BIPOC colleagues or students" who may not want to spend their lives as racial therapists for guilty white people. Also, because "language evolves," white people need to "pay attention" to the latest usages in order to avoid inadvertent harm.

These two documents seemed to place a ring of fire around some of the most painful issues in our society; white students who recoiled at Kendi's formula would hesitate to say so lest they be accused of racism. And they sent a message to non-white students that society wanted them to fail—and that whatever failures they experienced were not of their own doing. I told Palmer that I had spent time at schools that consciously set identity aside and seek to treat each student the same. That struck her as naive. Years of studying and teaching racial equity had convinced Palmer that race and racism had to be confronted head-on. "None of us is colorblind," she said to me. "We have to process our lived experience in order to move towards color-blindness. That's why there's so little bullying in our school around identity. The kids know that they can dress how they want, they can identify in whatever way they want." They could learn the centrality of identity in order to move beyond it. "Once they're past that," Palmer said, "we're all Millers"—the name of the school's teams.

That was, in miniature, the progressive view of civic identity, which is to say precisely the set of ideas that Donald Trump would vow to suppress soon after coming to office. Palmer used equity in the group-conscious and compensatory way that Trump's executive order would describe as "discriminatory." And it was Kendi's view of "institutional racism" that Trump's order would target when singling out the view that an individual can be "inherently racist . . . whether consciously or unconsciously." Washburn High School, and perhaps much of the Minneapolis public school system, might prove to be a target-rich environment for the shock troops of the Department of Education.

Liberals regard "the culture wars" as a one-sided assault by conservatives on settled practices in curriculum and pedagogy and on mainstream views of race, gender, and identity. Conservatives, for their part, believe that progressives have hijacked the traditionalist consensus of an earlier age in order to dominate culture, above all in the schools. "The most extreme forms of leftist politicization are no longer confined to anecdotes," the ubiquitous conservative pundit Stanley Kurtz asserted in a 2023 article titled "The Blue-State Education Nightmare." "Entire states are now imposing CRT, ethnic studies, DEI—the whole panoply of left-wing indoctrination strategies—on every classroom. . . . Secrecy and subterfuge are the order of the day—unless you fight back." The big education story, Kurtz wrote, was not Florida's anti-woke crusader Ron DeSantis but the woke forces against which DeSantis was pushing back.[1]

I had seen how unchallenged assumptions about pedagogy had shaped both teaching and the development of state standards. But the conservative claim was much more sweeping. Was there, in fact, such a thing as a "Blue-State Education Nightmare"—Floridas of the Left? I hadn't seen much evidence. Though Illinois mandated "culturally relevant teaching" and Black, Asian, and Native American History, identitarian thinking seemed like much less of a problem than the state's vague and vapid standards. Similarly, the real defect of the Virginia standards had been pedagogical rather than ideological—unless, of course, you regarded the failure to call James Madison "the father of the Constitution" as an act of lèse-majesté. The big issue, it seemed to me, was ignorance, not CRT.

But was I being too blithe about the educational politics of the Left? In early 2023, Rhode Island passed new social studies standards that seemed to so completely take for granted a progressive worldview that you had to wonder whether the authors were even aware that they *had* a view. In a microscopic analysis of the new standards, David Randall, an academic affiliated with the National Association of Scholars, pointed out that the state's "anchor standards," which were meant to infuse the entire curriculum, simply assumed the primacy of marginalized identities and of the tension between those groups and the majority. Thus, in the Civics section, students were to learn "how power can be distributed and used to create a more equitable society for communities and individuals based on their intersectional identity and lived experience." Students in history classes would analyze events "through the lenses of identity, power and resistance." Randall also noted that the authors had incorporated the United States into a Genocide Education curriculum meant to teach the atrocities of the Nazis and the Khmer Rouge. Questions students were to ask about the United States included, "How did settler colonialism contribute to Indigenous genocide?" An issue very much worthy of debate was reduced to a flat assertion.[2]

It was Minnesota, however, that took the palm in the blue-state sweepstakes. In 2021, the state adopted new social studies standards that were even more resistant, though slightly less intersectional, than Rhode Island's. In the immediate aftermath of George Floyd, the state had decided to adopt Minneapolis's Ethnic Studies program as a requirement and to afford it equal standing with the major subjects of the field—History, Geography, Citizenship and Government. A local conservative group, the Center of the American Experiment, asked Wilfred McClay, the conservative historian affiliated with Hillsdale College, to review the new standards. In his report, McClay noted that he had been among the authors of *Education for Democracy*, a 2003 document produced by the American Federation of Teachers and which, McClay said, had served as the basis for Minnesota's previous set of standards. McClay described those standards, accepted in 2004 and updated in 2011, as a balanced account of the American story, "giving attention to the role of minorities, women and non-Western people as much as the role of men and people of European ancestry."[3] (The researchers at the Fordham Institute, less impressed, had awarded Minnesota a B– for both history and civics standards.[4])

McClay compared the "moral atmosphere" of the new standards with that of the "1619 Project," in which American history was understood as "an ugly and soulless competition between the narratives of the dominant classes and the stories of the marginalized and oppressed and forgotten." McClay went to town on the Ethnic Studies standards, citing one of the standards for kindergarten: "Resistance: Describe how individuals and communities have fought for freedom and liberation against systemic and coordinated exercises of power locally and globally." Ninth-graders were to "develop an analysis of racial capitalism, political economy, anti-Blackness, indigenous sovereignty, illegality and indigeneity." One almost wonders how the neutral expression "political economy" found its way into that witches' brew of radical polemic. McClay also noted that the standards paid "almost no attention to the foundational facts of American and European history."

McClay's account sounded like a caricature. It was, but not by much. In the lower grades, only Ethnic Studies overtly waved the freak flag. Even there, the standards, intended for teachers, sounded slightly less tendentious than the "benchmarks," which proposed specific tasks. Thus the benchmark for the "resistance" standard was "Retell a story about an unfair experience that conveys a power imbalance." By high school, the story of American—and world—history is, as McClay dryly notes, "oppression narratives as far as the eye can see." The age of exploration, which Miss Rose had so dazzlingly summarized in her AP class at Waubonsie, does not qualify for inclusion in World History 1400–1800; rather, students are to "analyze how caste systems based upon race, social class, and religion have been used to justify imperialism, colonization, warfare and chattel slavery." Neither the standards nor the benchmarks make any mention of individuals; students are to understand history as the play of blind "forces."[5]

The Center of the American Experiment, the outfit that assigned McClay to eviscerate the standards, also got hold of the reports submitted by the expert reviewers hired by the Minnesota Department of Education. One wrote that both he and teachers he showed the standards to found them hopelessly vague. He added that, while he was "one who favors most of the ideas of the political left," he had done a "careful semantic analysis" that confirmed the standards "have a decidedly leftward slant" and "marginalized valid moral concerns of the political right." He found the Ethnic Studies standards both "age-inappropriate" and "bizarrely unbalanced." Other reviewers found the new standards so vague as to be almost useless. Minnesota seemed to be stipulating a point of view but not the actual knowledge that a student would need to sustain that point of view.[6]

I had long since learned that state standards have only the most tenuous relationship to the reality of the classroom, even as they establish a kind of ideological weather pattern for the schools. Conservative critics read one another's reports of abuse and convince themselves that the diktats contained in standards and official statements and speeches by teachers' organizations are transmitted directly to the classroom. That's why "action civics" has become such a cockpit even though most things done in the name of this doctrine seem quite tame. Stanley Kurtz had suggested that teachers had hidden the truth when I had visited. He could far more easily imagine left-wing propagandists fearful of exposure than teachers who as a matter of principle left their own politics at the classroom door. One could say the same of progressive critics who insist, on the basis of carefully selected public statements, that classical schools are engaged in a covert program of Christian nationalism.

The entire history of school reform stretching back to the Committee of Ten is of theses boldly nailed to the wall and then actual priests and congregants going about their business according to their own needs. So it was with "child-centered pedagogy" and "life adjustment" and, no doubt, today's "culturally relevant teaching." But we mistake the manifestos for reality, first, because we seize on any evidence of doctrinal clarity as a weapon to be wielded in our ideological debates, and, second, because it's far too time-consuming and troublesome to actually spend time in classrooms. I needed to go to Minneapolis in order to see the reality for myself.

My initial approach to Minnesota almost seemed to vindicate Kurtz's view of a mass cover-up. I contacted first one, then another, highly regarded high school teacher recommended to me by my friends at the Gilder Lehrman Institute. Neither responded to multiple emails and phone calls. I don't really think either had anything to hide; by now I was so accustomed to school paranoia that the silence seemed almost normal. Finally Adrienne Diercks, who runs Project Success, an admirable after-school program in Minneapolis, connected me to Emily Palmer and to Vernon Rowe, principal of Northeast Middle School, who was equally excited to welcome me for a visit.

Washburn is, as Emily Palmer puts it, a "bi-modal" school. The school's immediate neighborhood is largely well-to-do and overwhelmingly white. These parents used to send their children elsewhere; owing in part to Palmer's leadership but also very much to Washburn's adoption in 2012 of the International Baccalaureate diploma, a kind of global Advanced Placement program, local parents now send their children to the school. The student body is 60 percent white; 19 percent Black, many of them Somali or Ethiopian; and 14 percent Hispanic, of whom a significant part are very recent immigrants come from Ecuador and elsewhere. The school's Black graduation rate of 76 percent, and its Latino rate of 64 percent, are far above the Minneapolis average, though also far below the white rate of 93 percent. Palmer and the faculty worried very much about the implicit caste boundaries between the 20 percent of the kids who graduate with an IB diploma, almost all of them white, and everyone else, and have sought to narrow the gap by encouraging as many kids as possible to take IB as well as AP classes. Even so, those classes look starkly different from the regular ones. This is the hard core of the problem of equity; holding uncomfortable conversations about race with one's BIPOC colleagues seemed very unlikely to make a difference.

Soon after meeting with Dr. Palmer, I sat in on Eduardo Romo's twelfth-grade History of the Americas class, part of the global orientation of the IB program. Students were expected to trace the political and economic development of Latin America through historical texts—including, as Romo proudly pointed out to me, the works of Bartolomé de Las Casas, the sixteenth-century Dominican friar and historian who argued for the civil and political rights of subject peoples, a counterintuitive figure for students primed to see neocolonialism everywhere. This morning the kids were preparing for a debate that Mr. Romo had puckishly titled, "Che Guevara: Revolutionary Hero or Pedantic Thug?" The students seemed to fall pretty strongly on one side: after reading a short profile, a number of them had chosen Che in an exercise on "political heroes." Others had listed Fidel Castro, Bernie Sanders, and Alexandra

Ocasio-Cortez. Nevertheless, other students had chosen Barack or Michelle Obama, Machiavelli, and Arnold Schwarzenegger (possibly a jokester there). One of Mr. Romo's students said that Che's critique of American capitalism and imperialism was plainly right. A girl sitting next to me agreed. "Capitalism really hasn't worked."

"Really?" Mr. Romo rejoined. "What about your families?" Romo knew perfectly well that most of his kids came from prosperous families. "It's worked for the top one percent," my neighbor responded, "but not for the bottom 50 percent." The conversation turned to "structural racism." Here, too, the students, at least the ones who spoke, seemed to be of one mind. "Minneapolis was a Jim Crow city until the 1960s," one boy said. "It's still totally segregated. I don't see how you could argue otherwise."

Mr. Romo arched an amused brow. "Would anyone," he asked, "like to try?" There were no takers. "The U.S. is always claiming to do the right thing," another student said, "but it acts for selfish reasons." Another said that she hadn't given much thought to police brutality because it had never affected her; and then George Floyd happened. "I don't think you can reform the system," she said. "It's built on systematic racism." Most students favored defunding the police, though one had the temerity to say that you'd need to have them around to respond to violent crime.

Mr. Romo didn't think it was his job to foist his own more moderate convictions on his highly progressive students. "I consider Donald Trump a danger to the nation," he told me while the kids were writing, "but I've voted Republican before and I'll vote Republican again after Trump is gone." (This was, of course, before Trump was reelected.) He did, however, have a cautionary motive for the Che debate. "These kids are going to go off to college and they're going to see posters of Che all over the dorms," he said. "They need to learn about the horrible things he did. He killed people for having a different viewpoint; he killed someone for snoring too loud." In Mr. Romo's carefully guarded inner recesses, he may well have considered Che a pedantic thug. Afterward he told me that the debate had tilted heavily toward "hero" until the "thug" side pushed back, leaving many of the kids in "a muddled mess"—a modest victory for complexity.

In other classes I sat in, I got the impression that the students were a good deal more politicized than the teachers or the material. Matthew Pronley assigned a down-the-middle textbook called *The American Promise* for his U.S. History class, though he said he used primary documents whenever possible. But classroom discussion had a slightly more politicized cast than I was used to. Students in Mr. Pronley's class looked down at their hands when he asked them to explain the connection between the Great Migration of Blacks from the South and the so-called Red Summer of racial violence in 1919, about which they had just watched a video. But when he asked about the intrinsic tension between "collective security" and "personal freedom," the air was suddenly filled with talk about the Patriot Act, surveillance, and restrictive measures imposed during the pandemic.

These students seemed more alive to current events than those I had seen elsewhere, but they were every bit as much at sea when it came to history. The eleventh-graders in AP U.S. History took a "gallery walk" among posters taped up around the room and into the hallway with excerpts from FDR's "Arsenal of Democracy" speech. They wrote their thoughts on each poster. Most thought the United States shouldn't tell other countries what to do, though some conceded that that general principle might not apply to the Nazis. The kids I talked to had a very hazy idea of who the Nazis were. In "Rights and Protest," another IB course, students made an art project to illustrate the concepts of liberalism, socialism, fascism, and the like. (IB offers history teachers different thematic strands; at Washburn, most elect "Rights and Protest.")

After school, I spoke with several teachers. Melissa Beukema told me that she urged students in her Government classes to get involved in nonpartisan activities; some had worked as election judges. When it came time to learn about voting behavior, she had the kids write to politicians about a local issue. Current events played an important role at Washburn; Miss Beukema says that she sometimes had her students watch clips from CNN, Fox, and MSNBC so that they could see how very different the same issue looked on different news networks. Jason Morzenti said that he assigned students the introduction to Howard Zinn's *People's History* and a comparable passage from Larry Schweikart's conservative

Patriot's History of the United States—"which," he said, "they don't like." Both taught Ethnic Studies. Unfortunately, all of the Ethnic Studies classes were offered in the fall rather than the spring. I would return then to get the full picture.

Vernon Rowe, the principal of Northeast Middle School, is too busy putting out fires and keeping kids' heads screwed on tight to formulate doctrines on institutional racism; he would, however, say that Northeast is a victim of it. The school is located in a historically Polish neighborhood now rapidly filling up with immigrants, many of them Somali. Northeast is 41 percent Black, 32 percent white, 23 percent Latino. Rowe spends a lot of his time in community meetings pleading with white parents to send their kids to Northeast rather than shipping them out to wealthier suburban schools or to local charters. He pitches Northeast as "a bridge" among communities, a school dedicated to bringing diverse groups together. He tries to dispel rumors of violence and chaos. That's not always easy: The morning I visited, two sixth-grade girls had brought a beef that began on Snapchat into school and begun fighting in the cafeteria. Rowe had to call in the moms. But one mother had already called the police, and Rowe had to explain to the officers that it was just one of those things. They took notes and left. Everyone, apparently, knew the drill. Another fight flared up at the end of the day, when an eighth-grade boy called a girl a lesbian.

Like Washburn, Northeast began teaching Ethnic Studies well before it was mandatory. Mr. Rowe's reasoning, however, was wholly pragmatic. Even before George Floyd, police killings had triggered local demonstrations. "The wrong element got involved," Rowe recalled, by which he meant alcohol and drugs. "Our kids got involved and I was worried they were in over their heads. We needed to start teaching them about social responsibility." The school worked with the University of Minnesota to devise a curriculum appropriate to sixth-graders who needed to learn about respect for difference. Rowe added a class called Youth Participation Evaluation, which gave seventh- and eighth-grade students the opportunity "to use their voice."

Mr. Rowe is the kind of principal you see on television more than in real life. He is a Black man who spent many years in sales and marketing at Monsanto, and then left to teach high school economics before coming to Northeast. He still dresses corporate—gray flannels and crisply pressed shirt—but his manner is Big Brother. Mr. Rowe strides through Northeast's halls in a torrent of fist bumps and hugs and shouted greetings—"Whassup, dude?" He tells a boy that he has to improve his dribble with his off hand. He shouts to a girl at the water fountain, "Your grades lookin' better!" She looked up, amazed. "My grades are good?" "I didn't say 'good,'" Mr. Rowe ripostes. "I said 'better.'" I took another tour with him toward the end of the day. Shy immigrants came up for a hug. More fist bumps, a hug, another, and then, suddenly, "STOP!" A boy seemed to freeze in midair as Mr. Rowe fixed him with a glare. He was about to jump another boy. "Weren't they playing?," I asked Mr. Rowe. "That's how it starts," he said. "It goes from pretend to real."

At Northeast, in short, Ethnic Studies is less an ideological commitment than a bridge-building program. Melissa McCann, who teaches Ethnic Studies as well as a World Studies class for second-language students, had posted a series of questions on one wall of her classroom: "Can struggle bring us together? At what point does identifying with our ethnic group become dangerous? How can someone with few roots gain some roots?" This last question seemed especially piercing for the World Studies class, where four Afghan girls in headscarves sat at one table, a brother and sister from the Democratic Republic of Congo at another, Ecuadorian kids at yet another. Mx. McCann (who identifies as nonbinary) placed the kids strategically so that the ones who understood some English could help the ones who understood almost none. She had taught them to use the Translate function in Google Docs so that they could look up assignments in their own language. And she used a voice translation system that allowed her to speak in English and create a simultaneous Spanish version on her smartboard. The work of translation was so laborious that little time and energy was left over for the actual course material. The more pressing goal was to teach the students to read in English. That was no easy task; many of them came from countries with extremely weak educational systems and thus had poor reading skills in their native language.

The Ethnic Studies class that I attended focused on the Harlem Renaissance. After briefly airing a CNN news clip on humanitarian aid in the Gaza war, Mx. McCann showed a video on the rather abstruse question of whether works of art reflect the artist's intention. She asked the students about their opinion; some thought they did, others not. It was not a question to which these twelve-year-olds had given much prior thought. She then distributed cutouts of works of art from the Harlem Renaissance. The students were to answer some questions: "What kind of feelings did you see in the artworks? Do you think every work of art we looked at came from a person of color? Why or why not?" The images were so tiny that I wouldn't have known how to answer myself. The students spent the rest of class gluing sections of the artworks together. It was the kind of class that might have upset E. D. Hirsch more than Wilfred McClay or Stanley Kurtz.

At Northeast, as at Washburn, current events kindled a spark. Rick Davis's sixth-grade Minnesota History began with a news clip on "shrinkflation," leading to a lively conversation about whether it was better to pay more for your cookie or less for a smaller cookie. But when Mr. Davis asked them to turn to the chapter in their text about the Civil War and define the words "abolitionist," "secede," and "Confederate," the kids were stumped. The Somali girls I sat with had, not surprisingly, no idea what the Civil War was, though it seemed that many of the kids who grew up here didn't either. Mr. Davis, perhaps a bit embarrassed, pointed to a group of girls sitting on the floor and said to me, "You should ask them; they'll have a good answer." They were the white girls; and they did, in fact, know all the words, though none had a clear idea who Abraham Lincoln was. Elsewhere, a Chinese boy laboriously copied out all the definitions though he hadn't been able to read the text, while hilarious noises burst from a group of disruptive kids in the back. I was reminded of Oklahoma City.

Mr. Rowe brought me to meet Jennifer Huster, an eighth-grade science teacher who was one of Northeast's stars. She turned out to be a sort of poster girl for action civics, right down to the Gay Pride banner and Black Lives Matter poster fixed on upper walls of her classroom. She had assigned her kids a project on urban heat islands. After proving that you could take steps to mitigate heat islands in high-poverty neighborhoods such as their own, 161 of her students had written to the city's progressive young mayor, Jacob Frey, asking about the city's plans for northeast Minneapolis. The mayor had responded, pointing out that he had, in fact, agreed to plant fifteen thousand trees in the area, which would reduce temperatures. Far from being mollified, the kids wrote back to ask where, exactly, the trees were to go. They strongly implied that the mayor was lying. Rowe said that a furious Mayor Frey now demanded that the school board fire the science teacher who had provoked the kids. The board's HR department had conveyed the demand to Mr. Rowe. Now he laughed as he recalled his response: "That's not the teacher, it's the students who wrote the letters. You're not going after the teacher." Miss Huster thanked him for sticking his neck out. "Good trouble, man," said Mr. Rowe. "That's what we teach our kids."

Much though it was the motto of John Lewis, the saintly civil rights leader and congressman, "good trouble" is exactly what conservatives think progressive educators are infusing into innocent children. Black Lives Matter and Gay Pride flags are far from the principled neutrality that many teachers, including very progressive ones, make a point of cultivating. And schools really shouldn't encourage students to accuse their mayor of lying. But I couldn't find it in my heart to condemn either Mr. Rowe or Miss Huster. There was something wonderful about newcomers to America, many from places where citizens get thrown in jail or killed for criticizing the regime, discovering that they, a bunch of fourteen-year-old kids, could get a rise out of the mayor of Minneapolis, a figure as remote to them as the Wizard of Oz. And it turned out that even Mayor Frey couldn't punish them for their impertinence. Isn't that a lesson about democracy that we should be proud to teach?

Northeast Middle School didn't strike me as a place in thrall to a woke ideology—or to any ideology, for that matter. Ethnic Studies as it was practiced there seemed less a matter of resistance and intersectionality than of what used to be called "life adjustment"—getting along with one another. Miss Huster, it was true, had taught the kids to fight the power, but at least in doing so she had also imparted the central lesson of Youth Participation Evaluation: their voice could make a difference. What was really troubling about Northeast was how much energy and effort had to go into keeping the place from flying apart, how passive most classrooms felt compared with the electric hormonal energy pulsing through the halls. Here, as elsewhere, the limits of civic education were set not by political commitments, and not by relative class time, but rather by what felt like the intrinsic problems of the classroom.

I returned to Washburn High School in November 2024. Ethnic Studies was now in full swing, and I began the day at a class called Race and Identity Studies. On my earlier visit, several teachers in the program had explained to me that the class began with a discussion of "identity" itself—something each of us had rather than a walled-off zone of privilege and disadvantage. Washburn had originally offered the class in ninth grade, so that, as Dr. Palmer had said, the issue of identity could be demystified and students could then see one another as fellow Millers. But the district had decreed that students would take U.S. History in ninth grade and Ethnic Studies as juniors. This morning, Jason Jirsa was talking with his students about the Harlem Renaissance. The class very much resembled the others I had seen on the topic, including at Northeast Middle School. First, the students watched a very good video on the subject featuring Henry Louis Gates, Isabel Wilkerson, and other leading figures. Then they made "Harlem Renaissance trading cards," choosing a figure and learning enough about that individual to put on the back of a card. The material seemed pretty elementary for eleventh-graders.

I happened to pick up the class text—*Stamped: Race, Antiracism, and You,* a "remix" of the Ibram X. Kendi original for younger students. Leafing through it, I was struck by a passage on W. E. B. Du Bois, which mocked the pathbreaking scholar as "the Black king of assimilation," desperately seeking white approval and denigrating the capacities of ordinary Black people. Du Bois, students would learn, had blamed Black people "for being lynched" and "for wanting to live" before becoming more enlightened later in his career. Even Frederick Douglass had shared the elitist view that "Black men were bad." Further on, I found a passage on Stokely Carmichael, the civil rights militant who had coined the expression Black Power, and on the Black Panthers, that glowingly compared their brave race-consciousness with the "assimilationist vomit" spewed by elites such as Roy Wilkins, head of the NAACP.[7]

Mr. Jirsa explained to me that he had not chosen the book; it was the only one provided for the class by the district. It was, he conceded, "pretty strong." When I suggested that students might need to look at a text with a different view, he conceded that that might be a good idea. Later I asked Emily Palmer about the book. She told me that she objected to its juvenile language; the youth edition of *Stamped* is recommended for students in elementary school and is written at that level. Palmer didn't really understand my substantive concerns. "Isn't it obvious," she asked me, "that Black people in America have suffered from systematic racism?" Of course it is, I said; but do we really want to tell students that the neutral position between racism and antiracism is a fraud? Is it ever a good idea to discredit the idea of a principled neutral position? Dr. Palmer patiently heard me out, but she plainly found it hard to believe that one could disagree with Kendi in good faith.

I stayed in Mr. Jirsa's class for World History, the IB class that I had attended earlier with Mr. Romo. I was back in a different world. Students had begun researching their mandatory 2,200-word paper, a more ambitious exercise than any of them had undertaken before. They were free to choose any historical subject. That weekend they had convened at the Hennepin County library to find books—actual books!—to consult. A Hmong student who planned on writing a paper about the Vietnam-era secret war on the Hmong had found two books on the subject; she also planned to interview family members who had lived through the terrible slaughter. A Somali girl was looking for articles on the 2018 terrorist attack by Al Shabab on the Westgate Mall in Nairobi; she, too, would interview relatives. One boy was researching the underlying causes of the Salem witch trials. He recalled studying it in elementary school, but he had never understood what it was all about. A girl working on the assassination of Gandhi had found the memoir of his Hindu nationalist killer, Nathuram Godse. The students had to hand in an annotated bibliography with ten sources. There would be a lesson on note-taking; Mr. Jirsa suggested they learn the archaic art of the index card. Students in the IB program were learning to value scholarship, but only the school's elite breathed that atmosphere on a regular basis.

From IB I moved on to more Ethnic Studies—the impeccably titled Chicanx/Latinx Studies class. The teacher, Kevin Zonnefeld, explained to me that when he had first started teaching the class in 2016, he had been told, "You don't have to do what the white people in the district tell you you have to do." So, he said, he typically asked the kids what they wanted to study. They had been talking about the presidential election the week earlier, and several of the kids had asked about Project 2025. Mr. Zonnefeld had found a short introduction to this massive document, and they had spent the past few days discussing it. The students had raised some questions. Mo, who had been raised in Kurdistan, wanted to know what life had been like in the first Trump term. "Pretty much like normal," one student answered, "and then Trump would say some crazy thing." (Mo welcomed the return of Trump, who had, he said, chased ISIS out of Kurdistan.) Another student said he didn't see any difference between the parties: "Democrats and Republicans just lie, and then they get into office and don't do anything they promised." Matteo, a year-abroad student from Spain, rejoined, "You don't lie, you don't achieve the goal you're proposing." This hard-headed pragmatism was far from the class consensus. Mr. Zonnefeld was content to let the students guide the conversation, though he did point out that fears that Trump would deport legal immigrants were hardly groundless, because American citizens of Mexican background had been summarily flung out of the country during the Depression. It was, however, the only article of Chicanx/Latinx history they had learned in the course of class.

Teachers at Washburn took to heart Dr. Palmer's admonition to include "perspectives of color" across disciplines. In a tenth-grade IB class called Language and Literature, which all Washburn students took, teachers had chosen *Citizen*, a collection of prose poetry by the Black poet Claudia Rankine, to illustrate a unit on citizenship. Each of the two teachers of this double class, Andrew Groettum and Mary Manor, supplied a cautionary introduction about the book. "It might be a little close to home," said Mr. Groettum. "In your groups you can discuss this in a safe space." Miss Manor issued an outright warning: "If you're a white person, never say the 'N' word," though Rankine herself used it. "If you're a person of color, I won't police your language." I had never before heard a teacher address a class this way, but Miss Manor was only following Dr. Palmer's admonition to white students, in "Antiracist Understandings," to accept discomfort but not at the expense of BIPOC neighbors. What was most bizarre about Miss Manor's proviso was that most of the students "of color" in the class were recent Latino immigrants who might not even have known what the "N" word was. Washburn divided the world between "white" and "BIPOC" even if the students themselves didn't.

The subject of *Citizen* is the systematic, if endlessly subtle and fully deniable, ways in which, Rankine believes, white people deny Blacks their full citizenship. It is, as Wilfred McClay put it, a 1619 version of American citizenship. The teachers had pasted on large cardboard squares passages from the book in which, for example, a white colleague had nattered thoughtlessly about affirmative action in ways that could hardly fail to wound the Black narrator. In another, the narrator sat in her car in the garage letting the day's racial struggle wash over her, thinking about how Black people "achieve themselves to death trying to dodge the pain of erasure." The students I sat with were more puzzled than discomfited; many did not understand that the subject was race. "It's about being stressed," said one girl. "I don't understand what she means by 'erasure,'" said another. I wasn't sure that the arrow of justice had hit the target.[8]

Language and Literature was not wholly devoted to antiracism. In the previous unit, "Media and Communications," students had learned how the language of marketing and persuasion works; they had each selected a dystopian novel from a list compiled by the IB authorities. The next unit, however, would be Prison and Abolition. The claims of literature seemed almost quaint in the face of this relentless attention to injustice. The teachers themselves were very much committed to their mission. The next day I saw Mr. Groettum sitting by himself in the library. "I'm thinking about something very difficult," he said. When I asked what that was, he said, "This whole question of whiteness." He would be talking about that in class, and he knew how tricky it was. "There's this idea that if you say 'race,' you're only talking about people of color. Being white means you're exempt from race; you don't have to think about your own privileged situation." Like Dr. Palmer, Mr. Groettum insisted on interrogating his own privileged standing. But did anyone at Washburn question the endless questioning of privilege?

After school, I sat with Dr. Palmer and her Instructional Leadership Team. At first, while department heads talked about grading rubrics, Dr. Palmer sat quietly, methodically cutting up student lists. Then she stood up and distributed a cut-up list to each teacher. The lists showed the grades that each had given to students of color in their class. Dr. Palmer put up on a screen the language from her "equity plan for grading." Teachers were to "monitor for racial discrepancies to address. The percent of each letter grade earned by any racial group should match their representation in the class." Dr. Palmer is a clear-spoken, fast-talking, tough-minded leader. She has given a good deal of thought to her convictions about equity, and she wanted to make sure that her team was fully aboard. She asked everyone to look at the A's and F's they had handed out and then consider the discrepancy between white students and those of color. She had also included attendance data, because students who didn't show up in class could hardly be expected to receive the same grade as those who did. She did not include students' reading level or any other academic factor that typically shapes outcomes. "We want to make sure," Dr. Palmer said, "that our structures are not part of the grade outcomes."

Each of the teachers silently scrutinized their list. "Isn't she white?," a teacher near me whispered to a colleague. Identity wasn't always self-evident. The first to speak up was Christian Hoogheem, a science teacher and Dr. Palmer's designated devil's advocate. He did not disappoint. "I like the first statement," he said. "I very much disagree with the second. Are you saying that we have to have the same proportion of A's for students of color that we have for white students?" The Black kids in his IB Chemistry class did much less well than the white kids. Dr. Palmer was not backing down.

> Yes, Christian, I'm saying that is the goal. What does it look like to create opportunity for students of color?
>
> "Creating opportunity" does not translate into grades.

You don't think that's a good goal?

Yes, it's a good goal. I would like everyone to get an A. It's not a good statement of reality.

The devil's advocate was hardly alone. Mr. Romo said that he agreed. Another teacher said, "I have a problem with 'should.' Everyone *should* be housed tonight. But 'should' is not a goal." Yet another asked why they didn't focus on gender disparities as well as ethnic ones, because girls did so much better than boys. If anyone agreed with Dr. Palmer's understanding of equity, they kept it to themselves. Dr. Palmer did not back down. Trump's victory had, if anything, increased the intensity of her convictions. She was very upset that 14 percent of the kids in the school's mock election had voted for him. She was outraged to hear that someone had written "MAGA" on a blackboard when the teacher wasn't looking. "I'd have them sit down and write down who was the perpetrator," she said grimly. "And I wouldn't let them leave until they did." That sounded pretty old school. The next day, on reflection, Dr. Palmer sent around a memo specifying that teachers should reflect on the low number of A's and high numbers of F's among students of color, without comparing those figures with those of white students. That might produce more equitable outcomes without making a mockery of grades, as her teachers apparently thought she was doing.

Washburn's faculty was divided over equity and antiracism. When I met with a group of ninth-grade social studies teachers, I asked about *Stamped*. Mr. Jirsa didn't see a problem, but Lindsay Sykes said, "That's a very hard message for ninth-graders. Many parents have a hard time with that too; most of society has a hard time with it." She wondered whether that kind of accusatory language had helped Trump win. On the grading question, Jason Morzenti said, "I'm a radical. I would just get rid of F's. You already have so much pressure from the denigrating information about your culture." Ms. Sykes asked, "What if you don't show up?" Mr. Morzenti said that he would give such a student "no credit," which was less stigmatizing than an F. Cayla Baumann, head of Dare to Be Real, which she described as "an antiracism leadership club," talked about an unexpected benefit of Ethnic Studies: "The Black kids know about this material and the white kids don't. It's good for our white kids to have that reality check."

I was very happy to learn that Mr. Romo was prepared to speak with me during his prep period. His class, the previous spring, had been my favorite at Washburn. I already knew that he was not a fan of Dr. Palmer's grading dictum. He pointed out that the teachers who had spoken up the day before were "two social scientists and a chemist"—all of them accustomed to carefully measuring and assessing reality. Washburn's reality, Mr. Romo said, was that well-to-do Black parents typically moved to the suburbs, while parents deeply engaged with their children's education often sent them to charter schools. That was why the school was so "bi-modal." The Black kids at Washburn on average had reading levels far below those of the white kids; you couldn't equalize their grades without making academic performance meaningless.

Mr. Romo had had it with BIPOC. Che, he said, "was an upper-middle-class white guy." What did it mean to identify him as "Latino," much less "of color?" Mr. Romo considered himself a "white Latino." Why, he asked, did so many Latinos vote for Donald Trump? Maybe they bridled at being reduced to an ethnic category. "We lose sight of the individual kid," he said. That was the most important thing—connecting with each student. Mr. Romo did, in fact, have an answer to Dr. Palmer's question about what the school could actually do to make a difference. We should, he said, assign every student at risk of falling through the cracks to one teacher or administrator, who would take responsibility for that young person. That might not produce equity, but it could make a difference in the lives of these students.

We may come to look on the killing of George Floyd as one of the great polarizing events of our radically polarized era. Along with the publication of the 1619 Project and Kendi's *Antiracism*—all occurring within the space of a single year—the explosion of anger and pain provoked by Floyd's death led to new ways of understanding what America's white majority owed to its Black minority and also to a very powerful backlash against that sudden shift in values. Washburn High School exemplified the post–George Floyd view of "equity" and of "structural racism." The new emphasis on the salience of group identity, and of collective guilt, constituted a very sharp departure from the American tradition of individualism. Perhaps this view, for all the moral force behind it, was unsustainable. Yet the backlash, at least in the form commandeered by Donald Trump, with its evident wish to erase the reality of race and of systemic injustice, posed a deep threat to the schools and to America's civic culture. Were schools like Washburn now to fall under the lash for insisting on their view of race? Were leaders like Emily Palmer to be forced to curb their views on pain of defunding? The new "patriotic" dispensation seemed likely not only to falsify American history but to lock the vise grip of orthodoxy on classroom debate. Students should be able to decide for themselves whether Che was a revolutionary hero or a pedantic thug.

12

Great Books Can Set You Free

Every spring the Great Hearts Institute, which oversees a network of classical schools based in Phoenix, hosts a "National Symposium for Classical Education." Classical schools have become a world unto themselves, with dedicated programs of professional development, learned journals, and, of course, national symposia. Here, in one place, I could see the larger culture from which Lewisville Founders had sprung. I already had a sense of how such confabs reflected other school cultures. Much of the Florida social studies conference I had attended had been devoted to helping teachers stay out of trouble with parents, administrators, and political leaders. I had also gone to Civics for All!, the annual convening of Illinois's Democracy Network. One of the breakout sessions there offered advice on compliance with the Teach Equitable Asian American History Act (yes, Pacific Islanders are included); another explained how schools could create a safe space for students of color through building "Equity Action Teams" and a "District Equity Leadership Team." Just from looking over the schedule of events, I could see that the classical symposium reflected a very different milieu. The opening keynote address was titled "Fairy Tales as the Music of the Spheres." Breakout session subjects included "What Makes a Great Book?" and "The Jewish World of Alexander Hamilton." Classical people apparently shared the archaic view that education revolved around books.

In fact, the symposium bore a superficial resemblance to the other convenings I'd attended. Instructional providers lined a sort of midway in the Phoenix Convention Center, though in place of iCivics and the National Constitution Center were Christian colleges and the Heritage Foundation. The book booth offered the complete works of C. S. Lewis, J. R. R. Tolkien, and G. K. Chesterton—the literary deities of the classical world—as well as the *Patristics* of St. Athanasius and *Sayings of the Early Christian Monks*. The whole collection would have made for a very pious, not to mention ponderous, reading list.

In his keynote address, Jonathan Pageau, who has written a series of "symbolic retellings" of classic fairy tales such as "Snow White," cautioned his listeners against reducing fairy tales to allegories. These works matter, he explained, because they have endured; and they have endured because they offer joy. Pageau apparently knew his audience: several of the teachers who came to the microphone to ask questions groped for the moral ground he had just cut out from under them. "For those of us tasked with cultivating virtue in children," one asked, "what is the importance of teaching fairy tales?" Or another: "How can we learn to read scripture like a fairy tale?" They seemed to want to convert these magical tales back into allegory. That said, they all seemed to be serious readers; every question included a reference to a text, or to several.

I spent much of my time circulating around the crowd. I met three women who taught at a classical school in Arlington, Texas, whose population was heavily Middle Eastern and Central Asian. When I asked why these immigrant parents had chosen to send their kids there, one said, "What they love about us is the lack of technology." The school had no TVs, no computers, no smartphones; just blackboards and books. That sounded very much like Lewisville. The following morning I sat down next to Robert, an eighth-grade Earth Sciences teacher at the Great Hearts school in Prairie View, north of Fort Worth. Robert reminded me a little bit of Dr. Tutuska at Lewisville—heavy beard, thick specs, whirling hands. In fact, he had planned to get a PhD in Philosophy, but the pandemic had gotten in the way. Now, he said, he talked to his middle school kids about "natural philosophy"—the ancient grounding of science in philosophical precepts. He brought science back to first principles; and, he reassured me, he found a receptive audience among both students and his colleagues.

Returning to first principles was the implicit subject of many of the talks at the conference. A speaker in a panel titled "What Are Great Books?" said, very much in the spirit of Jonathan Pageau, "Great literature is not summarizable. It is the experience of it, not the knowledge of what it says." In her talk on "Virtue and Liberal Learning," Dr. Jennifer Frey asserted, as Aristotle did, that "there is no human freedom without virtue." That being so, only a liberal education grounded in moral as well as intellectual virtues offers a path to individual liberation (surely a confounding thought for progressives). This brought Frey, too, to the subject of great books, whose truth transcends their own time or any time. Several days of virtue talk had made me wonder how classical schools could deal with an audacious novel such as Gustave Flaubert's *Madame Bovary*, a work from which God is conspicuously absent even at the climactic moment of Emma's death. And then Dr. Frey led off her list of great nineteenth-century novels with—*Madame Bovary*. The moral checklist was less restrictive than I thought.

I sat at lunch one day with Constance Ford, who in 2011 had founded the Parnassus Prep School in the inhospitably progressive setting of Minneapolis. Ford told me something that I heard from many other of the educators there: she had found her way to classical education after first discovering Core Knowledge. "My daughter's school was movies galore," she said sardonically; "*so* progressive. The only question was how fast she could graduate so she could go to college." Ford had learned about classical education at a Core Knowledge conference. Three-quarters of the students at Parnassus Prep were non-white; half received free or reduced lunch; many were English-language learners. Though her board chair was the nephew of Foster Friess, the billionaire donor to right-wing causes, Ford bristled at the conservative label typically applied to classical schools. "I want poor children to get the same education that rich kids get," Ford said to me. The disadvantaged kids started off way behind the others, but at least they narrowed the gap over time. She wouldn't, under any circumstances, dilute the curriculum to ease their path. Ford ended our conversation in the way that almost everyone I talked to did. Please come to my school, she said. I was in a land of true believers. The contrast with Florida could scarcely have been more drastic.

The keynote speaker of the first full day of the symposium was Roosevelt Montás, a peculiar kind of classical school celebrity. In 2021, Montás had written a memoir, *Rescuing Socrates: How the Great Books Changed My Life and Why They Matter for a New Generation*. The story he tells is as inspiring as it is remarkable: arriving in New York City at age twelve from a mountain village in the Dominican Republic, often living hand to mouth, Montás had fished out of the garbage a copy of Socrates's last dialogues as recorded by Plato. Socrates's search for truth, his rationality, his stoic calm in facing death, had spoken to this sixteen-year-old immigrant across the immense gap of time and culture.

Montás had gained admission to Columbia and fallen under the spell of the classics in its famous Core program. He had gone on to get his PhD in literature at Columbia, remained as a professor, and became chief administrator of the Core from 2008 to 2018. In *Rescuing Socrates*, Montás championed liberal education as a transformative force for the disadvantaged and marginalized. He writes that he often tells parents "there is a long tradition of steering working-class children towards an education in servitude, an education in obedience and docility. . . . The idea that liberal education is only for the already privileged, for the pampered elite, is a way of carrying on this odious tradition."[1] Like Constance Ford, Montás wanted poor kids to have access to what rich kids take for granted. As a former poor kid, a Hispanic immigrant, an Ivy League scholar, and a New York liberal, Montás offers living proof that classical education is not a conservative plot to subvert public education.

Montás's talk that morning was clarifying in many directions. He used the word "liberal" rather than "classical" education in order to emphasize Aristotle's idea of education as the instrument of liberation for free citizens rather than as an explicit commitment to antiquity. Montás noted, in fact, that classical democracies had been slave societies; only with the Emancipation Proclamation had America attempted to forge a democracy in which all were citizens. All Americans now needed to benefit from an education once reserved for the few. Montás jokingly suggested that he should call his talk the "1863 Project"—a gibe, presumably, both at 1619 and 1776.

A central theme of Montás's talk was that any effort to subordinate a liberal education to a political program was destined to fail, for it was precisely the open-endedness of such an education that made it so powerful for children of all backgrounds. The ultimate goal was not the mastery of a body of knowledge but the mastery of self—that is, true self-knowledge. Montás cited the example of Michel de Montaigne's *Essays*, which circle around truths without ever arriving at an end point. Liberal education, he said, "is an education in the contestability and incompleteness of any account of the human good." Montás had, in effect, taken the subtext of Lewisville Founders Classical Academy—that we cannot ultimately know what is beautiful, true, and good—and raised it to an organizing principle. The great books permit us to pose ever deeper questions. Few in the audience would have missed the allusion to Hillsdale and other right-wing champions of classical schooling. Montás said that he had long felt compelled to defend liberal education from progressives who regard the "canon" as an instrument of white supremacy. Lately, though, he had been more concerned about "the embrace of liberal education on the right."

This was a pervasive worry at the symposium. Helen Baxendale, chief of staff at Great Hearts, told me that she worried Hillsdale's ubiquity cast a shadow over classical education. "We're trying," she said, "to thread the needle and democratize this form of education." Yet despite figures such as Montás—an outsider, after all—the culture of classical education remains largely conservative and white. There were few Black or even Latino or Asian faces in the crowd. Quite a few of the panels had a plainly conservative valence. In "Navigating Difficult Conversations," the Black principal of Vertex Prep in the Bronx spoke of how he had brought his students to hear Justice Clarence Thomas talk about the dangers of affirmative action. Two of the three members of the panel on book banning regarded the issue as a left-wing obsession. In the final keynote speech, Tony Abbott, the conservative former prime minister of Australia, slammed then President Joe Biden on both domestic and foreign policy, lamenting the declining hold of Christianity on Western publics and furnishing a long list of personal heroes, including Winston Churchill and John Wayne. "Those were the days when Hollywood was a moral teacher," Abbott fairly snarled. This was precisely the kind of advocacy Montás had in mind when he talked about the dangerous embrace of the Right.

The mansion of classical education has many rooms. In the leftmost sit Constance Ford of Parnassus Prep and Rakeem Person, a Black spoken-word poet who teaches English and creative writing at Piedmont Classical High School in Greensboro, North Carolina, where, he told me, most of the staff and student body is Black. There, too, sits Roosevelt Montás, who does not dream of returning America to an imagined golden age of moral and civic solidarity and thinks of liberal education as a lever of social justice. In the middle, one finds the Founders schools and those in the Great Hearts network, which began as a Christian academy and has begun to open up new religious schools now that Arizona's voucher law has created a market for them. (Jay Heiler, Great Hearts' CEO, told me that "we made a big mistake when we took religion out of the schools"—at which point a mildly panicked Helen Baxendale clarified that Jay meant that "we should study the Bible as a key text," not as scripture.)

Further to the right lies Hillsdale, whose Barney Initiative charter schools use Hillsdale's distinctly right-wing curriculum and presumably reflect Hillsdale's explicitly conservative orientation. And to the right of those, if that metaphor still applies, lies the whole world of private Christian classical schools. I did not seek to visit any private schools, but I did read *Battle for the American Mind*. In the "Western Christian Paideia," Hegseth and Goodwin write, "there is a divine order, revealed in Christ." In the "American Progressive Paideia" that now holds sway, "There is humanist anarchy." Christian classicism does not, like the secular version, regard supreme goods as intrinsically unknowable. "Beauty is not in the eye of the beholder," Hegseth writes. The child is to learn "God's absolute standards of Truth, Beauty and Goodness." Hegseth looks forward to a day when America, and its schools, will be fully Christianized and God's kingdom will stand supreme.[2]

Classical schooling is all those things. But insofar as it is understood as the educational wing of the culture war—the Hillsdale view—its spread beyond the conservative world will be limited. Only if it advances under the banner of beautiful content, and the dedicated pursuit of ultimately unknowable goods, will it make major inroads among the infidels.

While I was in Phoenix, Jake Tawney, Great Hearts' chief academic officer, had invited me to spend a day at Veritas Prep, Great Hearts' flagship school, and at its affiliated elementary school, Archway Veritas. Great Hearts now enrolls twenty-eight thousand students in forty-six schools in three states; the majority of students are non-white. Veritas, by contrast, draws on middle-class and well-to-do neighborhoods near Scottsdale. Almost all of the little kids I saw were blond; the little girls all seemed to have their hair in neat ponytails. The elementary school students enter and exit the class in single file, as they do at Lewisville. Even the middle school kids are courteous; you don't see much whooping and jostling in the hallways. Jake himself is a well-scrubbed, rigorously upright, bow-tie-wearing, deeply pious. He is also, like Jason Caros, an educator with a sense of calling in which the intellectual and spiritual are fully blended.

The Veritas hallways are lined with artwork by students. All of them, strikingly, are copies of classic paintings. Here's a fifth-grade copy of a still life from Paul Cézanne; there's a giant reproduction of a work by John Singleton Copley overlaid with a grid whose squares were filled in by high school students. When I asked Tawney why the kids didn't paint anything of their own, he said, "True creativity comes first from imitation; then you can depart on your own." The same, he said, was true with great books: first you read for understanding, then you can begin to interpret those works on your own. Veritas seemed actively scornful of the cultivation of the subjective self that lies at the heart of progressive schooling. Even the language of personal virtue was less obtrusive than at Lewisville. "Our character education," Tawney said to me at one point, "is our reading list." Children are exposed early to the good, the beautiful, and the true. The elementary school poem, which fourth- and fifth-graders were expected to memorize, was Gerard Manley Hopkins's acoustically magical, and obliquely Christian, "The Windhover." It, too, was posted on the wall. Tawney had worked as a social studies teacher, not an English teacher, but he loved Hopkins and knew his work well. As we walked away he began to recite: "I caught this morning morning's minion, king / dom of daylight's dauphin. . . ."

Archway Veritas is a Core Knowledge school with a sort of booster shot of classicism. Students take a class called Phonics in every grade, though as they grow older, the emphasis shifts from decoding to spelling, reading, and, of course, cursive handwriting. All children take Latin in elementary school, starting in kindergarten. Tawney brought me across the campus to the middle school, where we sat in on seventh-grade Medieval History. Many of the students had something to say about sumptuary laws. When the subject turned to Scholasticism, quite a few were able to distinguish between the thought of St. Anselm, Abelard, and Aquinas. The teacher asked them, not which one they liked best, but which one they thought would have been most popular at the time. One girl said that it must have been Anselm, who believed that faith preceded reason, because most people were very religious at the time. After we left the class, I told Tawney that I had been struck by the question. This gave him a chance to reinforce his earlier lesson: "We discuss the text, not what we personally think about the text. Your first responsibility as a reader is humility before the text." I'm fairly certain that I never heard a teacher in a conventional school utter those words. Or recite Hopkins.

The Great Hearts curriculum is narrow but deep. All schools must assign the same core texts; each school—not each teacher—can add 20 percent of its own material. All students take fine arts every year, and music—which at Veritas means chorus and music appreciation—from kindergarten through tenth grade. There are no electives until senior year. All high school students take a two-hour class called Humane Letters, a combination of literature and history something like what I had seen in Illinois save on a vastly more elevated plane. When I mentioned to Tawney my complaint about the lack of chronology in the "Society" classes in DuPage County, he contradicted me, though for a striking reason. "We don't want to historicize the novel," Tawney said. "For example, we shouldn't read *A Tale of Two Cities* right after we study the French Revolution. A great work should stand on its own."

We ended the day at two Humane Letters classes. In the first, juniors were talking about Aristotle's *Nicomachean Ethics*. Their desks were arranged in a square; the teacher sat at one corner. At one point, the teacher had to leave class for ten or fifteen minutes. No one seemed to notice; the conversation flowed on without him. More remarkable still was the senior class on Dante—not the *Inferno* but the *Paradiso*, a work that until then I had regarded as an obscure and unread sequel, like Milton's *Paradise Regained*. (The students had already read *Inferno* and *Purgatorio*.) The teacher seemed rather ineffectual, so the students did all the talking, sometimes tumbling over one another to get in a word edgewise. Their subject was, What failings consign us to Hell? "We choose pleasure so many times in life," one student pointed out. "What happens if we die at that moment—like we're at McDonalds?"

"It's not just pleasure that makes you go to the Inferno," another rejoined. "It's *misdirected* pleasure. If you went to McDonald's and you were totally gluttonous and had five Big Macs, that would be a sin."

I never attended a New England prep school, but the class reminded me of what I imagined a seminar at Exeter or Andover looked like. Though I had been faintly appalled at Veritas's almost eighteenth-century preference for imitation over originality, copying Cézanne—and memorizing Hopkins—did not seem to have crippled the students' critical faculties; as Jake Tawney had suggested, they appeared to have emerged into the mature world of interpretation. I was, however, surprised at the square configuration of desks, and asked Tawney whether teachers were free to design their own seating format. Not at all, he said. "In elementary schools, the kids face forward. The teacher is the shepherd of their soul." Tawney, a conservative Catholic and father of eight, quickly corrected himself. "In the Aristotelian sense, of course, not the religious sense." In upper-grade Humane Letters, however, "the authority in the room is no longer the teacher, it's the text. You're going to have a civil discussion; of course you're going to face each other."

"That sounds pretty progressive," I said.

"One thing the progressive and the classical approaches have in common," Tawney replied, "is that we're both student-centered. But we mean something different by that term. We believe in the unique desire of every child to learn." So do progressives, of course. But Tawney would have been right if he had said that classical schools believe in the child's desire to learn about the world *beyond herself.* Kelly Rose of Waubonsie Valley, who had jokingly asked me how she could apply to a classical school, would have felt very much at home.

13

The War Over African American Studies

TWO IRRECONCILABLE NARRATIVES

In 2018, the College Board, which in addition to administering the SAT test publishes Advanced Placement courses, began to work on a new course in African American Studies. The rising national consciousness about race provoked by the Black Lives Matter movement, and then the rage and the soul-searching in the aftermath of the death of George Floyd, imparted a sense of urgency to the deliberations. How could there be AP classes in U.S., European, and World History, Microeconomics and Macroeconomics, but not in a subject so constitutive of American life as Black history and culture? It felt like a grave oversight. In 2020, the organization convened a symposium for scholars in the field in order to lay the groundwork for the new course. Administrators understood that they were embarking on a contentious subject, but they had successfully negotiated just such a minefield a few years earlier and thus felt that they had learned the necessary survival skills.

That earlier crisis had occurred in 2014, when the College Board published an updated version of its AP U.S. History course. The draft framework appeared to incorporate a point of view about history in a way that previous versions had not. And that view was left of center. Students, for example, were to "analyze ways that philosophical, moral and scientific ideas were used to defend and challenge the dominant economic and social order in the 19th and 20th centuries." The unit on "European

Settlement" asserted that "Many Europeans developed a belief in white superiority to justify their subjugation of Africans and American Indians, using several different rationales." A passage on Ronald Reagan asserted that the president "initially rejected détente with increased defense spending, military action and bellicose rhetoric" before joining with Mikhail Gorbachev to reach arms agreements.[1]

These were assertions that most mainstream historians would regard as unexceptional. But they were assertions, and conservative groups, including the Republican National Committee, were outraged by them. Some conservatives mused that the time had come to produce a rival version of the course. At the very least, the College Board feared that some states might reject the new course. The organization "listened and learned," as one figure close to the process recalls. "There may have been some political bias in that document." And so the College Board asked the scholars who had produced the new course to make revisions. A less delicate way of putting it is that the organization beat a strategic retreat. A new version issued the following year took the edge off sharp questions, removed the implied criticism of President Reagan, deleted the words "racist" and "xenophobia," and substituted for the straightforward assertion about "white superiority" the bland assertion that settlers disagreed among themselves "about how non-Europeans should be treated."[2]

And it worked. Although Stanley Kurtz and John Fonte pronounced themselves unmollified, more moderate conservatives Frederick Hess and Max Eden of the American Enterprise Institute described the revised version as "a sea change," adding, "It's not just better—it's flat-out good."[3] The moral was clear: you could find a middle ground with reasonable critics if you listened to them. "We took a lot of lessons from that process," said my informant.

In February 2022, the scholars and educators who served as consultants for the African American Studies course produced a preliminary document called a "Course Framework and Exam Overview." The framework document offered the mix of primary and secondary texts, the exploration of culture and daily life as well as high politics, the balance of theory and narrative content, and the encouragement of thoughtful debate that has made the AP the gold standard of high school history. The framework felt more polemical than did a typical AP course in the social studies; but only in the final units, which covered recent and contemporary history, did the authors' bias, or shared presuppositions, become manifest. The proposed subjects were not only clotted with contemporary academic jargon—"womanism," "metalanguage," "racecraft"—but also notably radical, at least by the standards of the world beyond the academy. "Black Studies" itself would be a subject of this Black studies class—twice—as would "Black Queer Studies" and "Afrocentrism."[4]

A fair argument could be made that even the most apparently outré of these topics belonged in an advanced African American Studies course, but unlike in other such curricula, highly tendentious material was to be taught as unrebutted or mainstream doctrine. Students would read an excerpt from *The Afrocentric Idea* by Molefi Kete Asante, an immensely erudite but also radical (and ponderous) scholar who argued that Africa was the true source of "Western culture" and that the Black American heritage was thus free of the taint of "Euro-linear" culture.[5] This is a premise that would have shocked a great Black thinker like W. E. B. Du Bois or a great novelist like James Baldwin, both of whom insisted on the profound American-ness of Black culture. For a class on "Black Liberation Theology," students would read James Cone, a leading Black theologian of the 1960s and 1970s who justified violence as the proper Christian response to white oppression. "The Black experience," Cone wrote, "is the feeling one has when throwing a Molotov cocktail into a white-owned building and watching it go up in flames."[6] The curriculum included no Black conservatives, or for that matter non-Black conservatives, who would present a different view of the place of Black people in America.[7]

This early draft became a cause célèbre thanks to the indefatigable Stanley Kurtz. In an article in *National Review* in September, Kurtz announced that he had procured a copy of the draft, which the College Board had treated as a working draft rather than an early version of the final course, and thus refused to release to the public. The curriculum, he wrote, "clearly proselytizes for a socialist transformation of the United

States, although its socialism is heavily inflected by attention to race and ethnicity." The proposed curriculum was "positively filled with CRT," including assignments from several of the doctrine's founding figures, including Derrick Bell and Kimberlé Crenshaw. Kurtz observed that the very title of one of the weekly topics, "'Postracial' Racism and Colorblindness," which "labels attempts to treat individuals without regard to race as racist," directly violated state laws prohibiting the teaching of colorblindness as a form of racism.

Florida had, of course, passed just such a law five months earlier. Governor Ron DeSantis had become the national standard-bearer of the "war on woke." The politics of culture had become vastly more toxic since the College Board had learned its lessons in 2014. Now states were prepared to try to force change by threatening to reject a proposed course. Over the summer, the Florida Department of Education had told the College Board that the proposed course would violate the Stop Woke Act. (Kurtz may have gotten his leaked copy of the early draft from contacts in the department.) On September 23—eleven days after Kurtz's article appeared—the department notified the College Board that it would not accept the curriculum without revisions. After further discussions with the College Board, Florida education commissioner Manny Diaz announced that the state had rejected the new program, though as yet it existed only in pilot form. The proposed course, Diaz stated, violated Florida law, which it almost certainly did, and "lacked significant educational value," which it plainly did not.

The announcement unleashed a torrent of outrage. More than eight hundred African American studies scholars, administrators, and "allies in higher education" released an open letter describing Diaz's assertion as "a proposition supported by white supremacist ideology, because it fundamentally demeans the history, culture, and contributions of Black people."[8] (Diaz had not, of course, claimed that students should not learn African American history.) On February 1, 2023, the College Board, putting to use the lessons learned from 2014, released a "revised framework" that eliminated or soft-pedaled many of the most controversial topics. Florida education officials promptly took credit for forcing the College Board to back down, gleefully itemizing nineteen banished subjects, including "Anticolonialism," "the Nation of Islam," "Intersectionality," "Afrocentricity," and "Reparations."[9]

But the playbook no longer worked. The appearance of throwing Black scholars overboard to appease Ron DeSantis constituted a reputational catastrophe for the College Board, which felt called upon to rebut Florida's claims. In a public statement titled "Our commitment to AP African American Studies, the scholars, and the field," the College Board admitted to a series of mistakes: The board should have instantly denounced Florida's meddling in order to dispel the mistaken impression that the revisions had anything to do with the state's "vitriol" and "slander," and it should have made clear that the framework was only an "outline," not a course, and that contemporary topics such as reparations were intended to be "optional." The College Board flatly denied that it had engaged in negotiations with Florida, much less that it had taken the state's concerns into account.[10]

But the middle ground that the College Board hoped to occupy no longer existed. Now more than a thousand signatories released another furious open letter, this one accusing the College Board of craven surrender to red-state pressure and demanding that the organization restore the original course framework.[11] At this point everybody piled on. Henry Louis Gates, the presiding elder of African American Studies, who had agreed to serve as a consultant to the project, wrote an op-ed in the *New York Times* pillorying Governor DeSantis.[12] A *Los Angeles Times* columnist accused the College Board of both cowardice and duplicitousness.[13] Stanley Kurtz ridiculed the board's insistence that the bowdlerized revision had nothing to do with Florida.[14] In April, the College Board announced that it was going back to the drawing board—again. "Regrettably," the organization noted, the dual goals of access to a new discipline and access for as many students as possible had "come into conflict."[15] A source involved with the controversy described the situation more bluntly as "a shitstorm."

In December, the College Board released its "Operational Course Framework." Queer studies was gone, Black Lives Matter was optional, but "intersectionality" was back in. "Afrocentricity" had become half of a larger unit, but Molefi Kete Asante was gone. As with the 2014 draft of

AP U.S. History, the final outcome seemed admirable and would prove to be widely acceptable. But as had been the case with the Virginia standards, the sheer savagery of the debate left the impression that it was possible to reach a broadly accepted version of history only after something like civil war.[16]

I contacted many of the scholars and educators who had contributed to the course in order to make sense of their deliberations. Had they, in fact, regarded Molefi Kete Asante and James Cone and the like as irrebuttable? Did they think of Black conservatives as not truly, or at least representationally, Black? Did they, in short, live in a world as intellectually hermetic as the authors of the "1776 Report"? Unfortunately, none of them even responded to calls and emails. Henry Louis Gates, a worldly figure of decidedly moderate temper, promised on several occasions to talk to me but apparently changed his mind. The issue had become radioactive.

I did find a revealing assertion in the second of the open letters. "African American Studies," wrote the authors, who themselves represented the field, "is the study of the persistence of anti-Blackness and the connections between historical and contemporary efforts to resist structural racism." Unlike any other subject for which the College Board designed an AP course, African American Studies was not only a domain but also a *claim* about that domain. If that was so, then it shifted the ground of the debate from the malicious argument that the course as first designed lacked significant educational value to a perfectly legitimate one over the merits of the antiracism argument. Eighty years earlier, the Rugg curriculum had come to grief because many Americans did not accept its critique of capitalism. Why, now, should states adopt an African American Studies course whose view of race they did not accept?

I did have a chance to see the real, existing African American Studies class, as opposed to the donnybrook over the course framework, in the lushly multicultural setting of the Academy of American Studies in Queens. Teachers across the country had been piloting the course starting in the fall of 2022. Alisa Dorfman was thus in her second year when I sat in on her class in the fall of 2023. (Mrs. Dorfman was the one and only teacher at the academy who allowed me to use her name.) Her students had read a series of documents on the *Dred Scott* case. Mrs. Dorfman had written several questions to frame the day's discussion: "How can we use historiography to understand the Dred Scott case? How have the 'facts' of the Dred Scott case changed over time? Why did I put 'facts' in quotes?" The subject of the day was not only Dred Scott but "history," understood not simply as a chronological record but as the means by which societies distill meanings from events. How did the understanding of the events summarized as "Dred Scott"—that is, the ownership of human chattel—change over time?

The readings consisted of excerpts from history textbooks from the 1880s to the present. I sat at a cluster of tables with four students. One observed that the more recent passages were more "perspective-based" than "fact-based." Another noted that only in the more recent passages "have we learned about Dred Scott as a person." Another was struck by the fact that both the first and last excerpts discussed the effects of the case on society, while those from 1905 and 1930, "during the Jim Crow era," did not. The students now re-formed into Harkness Discussion Circles, a favorite exercise at Academy of American Studies, to discuss the case itself. Mary (I will use their first names here) said that seven of the nine U.S. Supreme Court justices were slave-owners and thus were biased in favor of slavery. Kenzy had a question: "I'm curious about the Supreme Court members. What happened to them after the Civil War when slavery was outlawed?" Alice wondered what the repercussions of the decision had been for the justices. Mary noticed that the historical accounts they had read had furnished the background of Dred Scott's enslaver but not of Dred Scott himself—as if he had no background. She had also been struck by the claim of the Jim Crow–era texts that Scott had petitioned the Court at the behest of abolitionists, which "takes the credit away from him and gives it to people who probably weren't even involved." Francesca felt that we should slightly palliate the guilt of the justices. "I wouldn't put one hundred percent of the blame on them, because that's the way everyone was raised then."

I had only seen one class in one school. But if civic education means not simply instilling love of country but helping young people grapple with the complexities and shortcomings and halting progress of our nation, above all on the endlessly vexed question of race, AP African American Studies felt like a deeply worthwhile addition to the civic curriculum.

Florida, being Florida, had its very own version of African American Studies. HB 7, the "Stop Woke Act," included a list of required subjects of instruction, among them "flag education," "the true effect of all alcoholic and intoxicating liquors and beverages and narcotics," U.S. history and government, and "the history of African Americans." The accompanying language included no reference to Jim Crow or to the history of racial violence but did order educators "to celebrate the inspirational stories of African Americans who prospered even in the most difficult circumstances."[17]

Florida had established an African American History Task Force in 1994, but Commissioner Diaz convened a new committee to devise the standards. The group included ten Florida teachers and two new figures, both Black conservatives. One, William Allen, was a retired professor of political science, a member of the U.S. Commission on Civil Rights under Ronald Reagan, and, piquantly, the father of the Harvard political scientist and civics scholar Danielle Allen. The other, Frances Presley Rice, was an educational consultant and former head of something called the National Black Republican Association, based in Sarasota. According to news reports and to Cathy Boehme, chief lobbyist for the Florida Education Association, the ten educators largely agreed among themselves about content, while Allen and Rice pointedly reminded them of the language of HB 7 and of Governor DeSantis's refusal to countenance liberal interpretations of slavery and race. It must have been extremely odd for this diverse group of educators to be admonished by two Black figures not to present Black history in a way that would seem unfair to whites.

The reaction to the publication of the standards in the summer of 2023 constituted a mirror image of the initial rollout of the AP African American Studies framework. Most critics, including Vice President Kamala Harris, seized on a "benchmark clarification" in the middle school standards that stipulated "Instruction includes how slaves developed skills which, in some instances, could be applied for their personal benefit." This was, of course, true, but seemed a bizarre development to single out when slave-masters went to such great and often brutal lengths to prevent slaves from gaining the one skill that would have endangered the slave system: literacy. Committee members later said that Allen had insisted on including that passage, while Presley Rice was responsible for the benchmark that students learn about "violence perpetrated against and by African Americans" during the Jim Crow era, thus equally blaming whites who carried out massacres and Blacks who resisted them.[18]

The standards bore a distinct resemblance to elements of both the Civic Seal of Excellence course and the "1776 Report." The students were to be inoculated against the horrors of American slavery by first learning about the universality of the practice, including under "Sumerian law," two millennia before 1619. Students were to compare the living conditions of slaves in the colonies with those in Central and South America—presumably in order to learn that it was even worse to be a slave in Brazil than in Virginia. They were to learn about the efforts of the Framers, including George Washington, to end slavery. They would study, at great length, the heroic sacrifice of Black troops in major and minor American wars, though not about the violence perpetrated against returning Black soldiers. Included in a list of "political figures who shaped the modern Civil Rights efforts" were President Dwight D. Eisenhower and Senator Everett Dirksen—Republicans whose role in that effort was marginal at best—and two conservative Black scholars, Shelby Steele and Thomas Sowell, who may well have offered important correctives to the liberal consensus but did not shape civil rights efforts one way or another.[19]

As of the spring of 2025, three states, all in the South—Florida, South Carolina, and Arkansas—refuse to offer AP African American Studies. More were likely to join them. The course was being taught in seven hundred schools in forty states, numbers also bound to grow rapidly. If civic education in America necessarily includes education about the history of slavery and race, parts of the South had, in effect, seceded from the effort to foster a shared narrative on the subject. Jim Crow was gone, but not its long and dark shadow.

14

Culturally Responsive Teaching

In the early spring of 2024, I returned to Waubonsie Valley High School, the sprawling school in DuPage County with a planetarium and polished student newscasters and teams in just about everything. I had originally visited the Chicago suburbs to see a possible model of civic education, but instead I had come to view the schools there as the embodiment of the pervasive problems of teaching and learning. Was that fair? And if it was, I needed to learn about the source of the problem. Waubonsie was a high school. What was happening at the level of elementary and middle schools? And finally, how were things going with Carl Armstrong's "rewilding" project, which had qualified Waubonsie for the Illinois Democracy Network?

As it happened, the Botany class met first period; when I arrived, most of the kids were in the greenhouse caring for their plants—a pear tree and a cherry tree, butterfly milkweed, cordgrass that likes moisture and so would be planted along the borders of the Waubonsie Creek. All this the students explained to me with clarity and enthusiasm as they went about their watering. They would be doing the planting the following month. The project showed the pleasure that students can get from *doing*, and the way that doing something enjoyable can, in turn, lead to knowledge—a Deweyan moral. And rewilding was surely a civic activity: taking responsibility for the physical environment helped the students see themselves as active citizens making the world a slightly better place through their own efforts. It did not, of course, offer insights into life in a political community as the Legislative Simulation did.

It was much harder to say what students gained when "active learning" had no clear outcome, civic or academic. Later that day, I sat in on a ninth-grade class in Human Geography, a multidisciplinary subject meant to teach students about the sources and development of culture. Arlen McCann's class was doing what is known as a "four-corners exercise." Students were to sort themselves into four groups depending on whether they strongly or modestly agreed or disagreed with an assertion. Today's subjects included "If you're old enough to drive a car, should you be allowed to do any adult job?" and an allied proposal to weaken Illinois's child labor laws.

Students got up from their seats to stand in one of the room's corners and then explained their views. None of them referred to any of the readings they had done, much less to any particular domain of knowledge. (And none of them thought that students should work less in order to focus more on school or even sports or clubs. Work was a given.) Most of the remarks were personal: "When it's late at night, I can't focus on anything." Mr. McCann played honest broker from the middle of the classroom, summarizing the remarks so as to make them sound more pertinent than they had been. Adam Dyche, the Social Studies chairman—and also a Human Geography teacher—believed that the kids would learn if teachers brought the subject around to their personal interests. Mr. McCann's students were talking, but that wasn't the same thing as learning. I asked what, exactly, they had been working on. "A very broad unit," said Mr. McCann—agriculture, economics, labor. That certainly did sound broad.

I returned to the double-period Society class that fused American history and literature and operated by theme rather than chronology. The class had reached the unit on Equality. Kristan Crawford, who taught the history portion of the curriculum, had been talking to them about Reconstruction as background for a discussion of the civil rights movement. They were to begin working on a project in which each group of students would research one marginalized group and make a presentation to the class focusing on how the group had gained agency rather than waiting for the majority to accord them rights. This was, of course, the kind of exercise that would raise eyebrows, and hackles, in Florida, but not in Illinois.

While the students formed into groups of four or five and talked among themselves, Miss Crawford took up the thread from our previous meeting, in September. She and her colleague Kelly Rose had, she said, been regularly re-living our conversation—a bad sign, I thought. She had begun reading E. D. Hirsch's *Cultural Literacy*, which had afforded her a new intellectual framework for her sense of despair about Waubonsie's academic culture. In order to get the kids thinking about the idea of causality, she had given them a list of questions such as, "How is present-day education different from education at the turn of the century?," and then asked them to use that template to devise questions of their own. They had been flummoxed; half the kids hadn't even been able to come up with a question. Miss Crawford's explanation was distinctly Hirschian. "The kids have no background knowledge," she said. "They don't know who Uncle Sam is. They don't know anything about the Bible, which is really a problem for the English teachers. Even ten years ago I would have been able to engage my students with this material. Now there's nothing."

Miss Crawford invited me to roam around. I asked a group of boys if they knew anything about the Thirteenth, Fourteenth, and Fifteenth Amendments. "We 'know,' " said one, putting air quotes around the word; "but we don't know." What about Reconstruction? "It was . . . reconstructing," said another boy. Miss Crawford came over and sat with us; I had the impression that she felt both vindicated and miserable. "What was our anchor text for Reconstruction?," she asked. Blank looks. "The *Gettysburg Address.*" Miss Crawford began reciting. "Why did Lincoln call it 'a new birth of freedom?' " Blank. One boy, perhaps feeling sorry for his beleaguered teacher, asked, "Is the Black Codes the same as the Thirteenth Amendment?"

I moved to a group of girls and asked whether they had learned about the Reconstruction amendments. "We dabbled," said one. They explained that they had done all the wars together and things had gotten jumbled up. Miss Crawford beckoned me over. "I'm listening to their answers," she said. "And I'm devastated. I promise you, I'm not that bad a teacher. I was talking to them yesterday about the Thirteenth Amendment." She and her colleague, Miss Battaglia, had urged the students to take notes, but few did. Waubonsie had begun allowing students to take social studies classes—but not math and science—over the summer, perhaps online. Miss Crawford wondered whether some of the better students had decided "to take the easy A" in the summer class so that they could take Band instead of Society or a class in history in the regular school year. She felt that this perfectly expressed the school's, and her department's, order of priorities. (Adam Dyche confirmed that students are now permitted to take one and a half of the required two and a half credits over the summer online—which, he sadly agreed, seemed to reflect the district's priorities.)

Chris Wolak's Sociology class was talking about Erving Goffman's concept of the "total institution." Mr. Wolak was the relaxed freethinker with the battered "soapbox" in the middle of class. He had two self-mocking bumper stickers on the wall: "Vote Democrat. It's Easier Than Working" and "Vote Republican. It's Easier Than Thinking." Mr. Wolak asked whether Waubonsie had the kind of all-encompassing culture and structure of rules that constituted a total institution. Perhaps because I had just witnessed ninety minutes of educational futility, this felt like a very fruitful question. And when Mr. Wolak suddenly turned to me and asked if I'd like to tell the class about my book project and take questions from them, I took up the challenge.

I talked about the difference between classical schools, which put up thick walls between themselves and the external culture, and more typical public schools, which regarded permeability as itself a virtue. One was plainly closer to a "total institution" than the other, but which was better? The kids weren't sure. One girl said that the ubiquity of social media ensured that the enveloping culture was never actually outside; it was here, with them. We talked about reading. I asked how many kids read books at home for pleasure. Five or six out of the twenty-odd students raised their hands. I asked what they were reading. One was reading a Stephen King novel, one a mystery novel whose author and title she didn't know because she tended to pick them up at random, and one a "slice-of-life" novel, by which she meant a realistic story about a teenage girl like herself. Given that, as an elective, Sociology would attract Waubonsie's more intellectually engaged students, this was not a very encouraging tally.

Kelly Rose's AP European History class remained a high-minded refuge. The subject of the day was the interwar years, but before she embarked on the history, Miss Rose wanted to discuss something harder to grasp but more fundamental. How, she asked, did the understanding of the individual change in the aftermath of World War I, "forcing questions that society had to answer in order to sustain liberal democracy?" She showed images of Michelangelo's *David* and Alberto Giacometti's *City Square*, with its expressionless, etiolated figures isolated in space. What, she asked, would you infer about the different understandings of the individual implied by the two works? One girl said of the Giacometti, "The individual became unimportant because everybody had committed the same atrocities in the war. You can't tell them apart." Then Miss Rose put up the *Mona Lisa* and Edvard Munch's *Scream*. The kids were horrified. "My goal," she told them, "is to get you pieces of art that you can remember and you can use." She showed them Jean-Françoise Millet's *Des glaneuses* (*The Gleaners*) and René Magritte's *Ceci n'est pas une pipe* (*This Is Not a Pipe*). "Which one has a firmer grasp on objective reality?," she asked. The kids couldn't decide whether they were looking at a pipe, a picture of a pipe, or something else altogether—a thought experiment. "Magritte says, 'You're all right,'" Miss Rose explained. They talked at length about Emil Nolde's *Prophet*, a ravaged figure who both was and wasn't Jesus.

"None of you want to see modern art on the test," Miss Rose joked, "because you all like what? Certainty." But modern art expressed a disoriented, ambivalent modern sensibility. She asked them about the questions society now had to answer; and she had plenty of takers. Among them were, "Should I give up my individual rights for security and protection?" "Am I to blame?" "Should science be used to create weapons?" Then Miss Rose worked in the Treaty of Versailles and Keynesian economics. Her class decisively proved—lest it need proving—that an intense immersion in names, dates, places, and events enabled, rather than precluded, introspection and critical inquiry. Could that somehow be true only of the school's stars and not of its average students?

Toward the end of the day, I sat in on an eleventh-grade U.S. History class for students who had decided not to take Society. Mike DiTella was also talking about the civil rights movement. He explained that both Blacks who had gotten good manufacturing jobs during World War II and those who had gone off to fight found that their situation reverted to the status quo ante the moment the war ended. The combination of frustrated expectations and the new legal climate created by decisions such as *Brown v. Board of Education* had forged the irresistible momentum for the early civil rights struggle. Mr. DiTella kept splicing questions into his narrative, but the class was mostly silent.

Like Miss Crawford and others, Mr. DiTella was a thoughtful and dedicated teacher who felt a void at the heart of his work. He made a point of assigning primary texts, but the kids usually found they could skip the reading and cull answers from Google. He had tried to bring in current events to snag his students' interest, but even a unit on protest politics that he had improvised right after the George Floyd protests hadn't produced much of a spark. Mr. DiTella opened a new tab on his computer to show me something: even in his Military History elective, a big draw especially with boys, only half the students had even handed in a short assignment on time; a third of the students hadn't even read the principal assignment. "And what's cooler than the Vikings?," he asked plaintively.

One girl in class was lying on her stomach in between the aisles, facing the back of the room; Mr. DiTella had reached an agreement whereby she would agree to do the work if he would let her lie on the floor. A girl in Mr. Wolak's class had been almost ostentatiously eating her lunch. Thinking of my conversation with those kids, I asked Mr. DiTella about thin and thick walls. He instantly picked up on my metaphor. "As soon as I try to put up those walls," he said, "I realize I can't do it on my own. I need buy-in from families. We have to change the whole culture; but how are we going to do that?" How could he enforce a respect for books and learning or for the classroom itself? How could he keep social media at bay?

A few days ago, Mr. DiTella said, he had watched his daughter, a high school student so diligent that she was considered almost freakish by her friends, scroll raptly through her TikTok or perhaps Instagram feed. Her rapid-fire reaction had gone something like this: laugh-pause-laugh-laugh-pause-pause-laugh. "Each one is a dopamine hit," Mr. DiTella recalled thinking. "How can school compete with that?" I had long since learned that all but the most scholarly students got their news almost exclusively from TikTok or Instagram, but that was far from the greatest danger posed by social media. Students who spent five or six or seven hours a day with their phones could hardly be expected to muster the attention span to read a book. The informal survey I took in Mr. Wolak's class corresponds to a national norm: a study published by the American Psychological Association found that while in the late 1970s, 60 percent of twelfth-graders reported reading a book or a magazine every day, the figure had plummeted to 16 percent by 2016. It's almost certainly fallen further since then.[1]

Educators used to worry about the effects of television, but a television couldn't be carried in your pocket. And TV was a passive experience that dulled rather than excited the viewer. As the social psychologist Jonathan Haidt has written, social media, with its incessant ping notifications and its endless stream of "high-pleasure, low-effort digital experiences," disables the capacity for sustained attention. And the experience is intensely self-reinforcing. "When the child is not engaged in digital activity," Haidt observes, "the brain doesn't have enough dopamine, and the child experiences withdrawal symptoms."[2]

I had heard teachers complain about the deleterious effects of social media since September, but the devastating consequences hadn't fully come home to me until that day, perhaps because the effects of the smartphone were all-pervasive even as the object itself was barely visible. Some schools and school systems had begun to ask students to leave their phones in their lockers or to prohibit their use during the school day. When I had asked Miss Crawford if Waubonsie had a rule about phone use, she had laughed bitterly. "*Rule*? Are you kidding me?" Teachers were allowed to set their own rules, and many classrooms had a kind of shoe tree with thirty-six pockets for phones at the front of class. I saw very few phones in them. Nothing short of total prohibition appears to make a dent: a study by a mental health organization found that 97 percent of students use their phones during the school day, with the most popular functions being social media, YouTube, and gaming.[3] It was simply understood, and accepted, that students no longer had the attention span to read whole books. Like most schools, Waubonsie had bowed before that reality; that was why Miss Rose and Miss Crawford had been so astounded when I had told them in September about classical schools where students still read difficult novels.

So much of the best and most humane writing about the schools, from John Dewey to Charles Silberman and John Goodlad, has implored the schools to become more continuous with the life of the child, to dismantle the barriers that stand between the school and the rest of life. Only private schools, and above all religious schools, which regarded themselves as sanctuaries from a secular culture, consciously sought to fortify those barriers. Yet the cognitive forces shaping young people have become so pernicious that schools that are unable or unwilling to build those walls may simply lose the battle for students' attention. A growing number of schools, school districts, and even states have begun to ban or severely restrict the use of phones. That's a good start. Perhaps next they can begin converting their "media centers" back to libraries.

Back in September 2023, Mary Ellen Daneels of the Democracy Network had arranged for me to spend a day at Turner Elementary School, a feeder school for West Chicago High School. She had mentioned that the principal, Maurice McDavid, had played an important role in writing the new state standard on culturally responsive teaching. Mr. McDavid turned out to be an impressive figure, big and baritone and formidable, yet firm and gentle with his charges. When I asked about culturally responsive teaching, he explained that he had learned that "culture plays a role in how our brains are set up to receive information." For children of color, he said, "oral and auditory capacities need to be lifted up as opposed to the idea of just responding with a written essay." Such children came from cultures in which "you'd gather around the fire to hear the story being told." I found this cultural and cognitive relativism extremely dismaying—a progressive and supposedly liberatory version of what George W. Bush used to ridicule as "the soft bigotry of low expectations." I asked Mr. McDavid whether he thought that children of color—Black, Hispanic, Asian—learned differently from whites. He did, but he added that because "some research is now showing that orality benefits all learners," nothing was lost by shifting away from the traditional focus on reading and writing. The only thing lost, of course, was reading and writing.

Mr. McDavid suggested I read Zaretta Hammond's *Culturally Responsive Teaching and the Brain*, a central text in the field. I did, and I found that he had faithfully represented her views. "American culture," Hammond writes, is "individualistic," while people of color—all of them, it seems—"lean more towards collectivism." Though descendants of these formerly oral cultures now live in a world of reading and writing, many still depend on their oral traditions at home, so "learning will be more effective if processed using the common cultural learning aids." The Gullah people of South Carolina, for example, utilize a storytelling chant called Crick Crack; a culturally responsive teacher would thus develop a back-and-forth chant to cue children that something important is coming.[4]

This kind of cultural and racial essentialism stands perilously close to the overt racism that once relegated Black students to vocational school and the nonacademic track. Though the premise of culturally relevant teaching—another term known by the shorthand CRT, oddly enough—would shock many Black parents who believe that their children can and will succeed in school, it would utterly bewilder Asian parents who regard school—in its current form—as the royal road to success.[5] I don't know how widespread this pedagogy is; the younger high school teachers I spoke to in Illinois said that they had been taught in ed school to incorporate it into their practice, though I hadn't seen it actually deployed in a classroom.

Turner's student population is overwhelmingly Hispanic and disadvantaged. In practice, it seemed, culturally relevant teaching chiefly shaped the school's commitment to bilingualism. Teachers were instructed to remind students to speak in Spanish for classes conducted in that language even when the kids said that they could express a particular thought more easily in English. Like many schools with large Hispanic populations, Turner is committed to biliteracy: Mr. McDavid wanted students to retain their original language as an academic and not merely household instrument. He didn't think this would retard the process of gaining academic fluency in English. That said, only 12 percent of Turner's students in the third through the fifth grades scored at or above proficient in English Language Arts in 2019, the most recent year for which test results were available; that put Turner below the district and well below the state. (Students slightly outpaced the district in Math.)

Mr. McDavid suggested I attend a fifth-grade Science class where I would see the principles of culturally relevant teaching actually put into effect. The teacher, Callum Casey, asked the children to give him the names of scientists. Einstein, they cried out; and, with some prompting, Oppenheimer, Newton, Tesla. "What do you notice about them?," he asked. "What do they all have in common?"

They're smart.
Yes.
They create things.
Yes. What about them as *people*?
They're all men.

"What else?" Mr. Casey gave up hinting, because the kids weren't taking the hint.

Are any of them people of color? Are they Black? Are they Hispanic?
No. They're European.
Why do you think we don't know about scientists who are people of color? What is the implication of *not* studying scientists of color? Maybe you want to do science when you grow up. How many of you see yourselves represented in the scientific community? Do you? Yes or No? It could be either way.

The kids plainly weren't sure which way it should be: few of these immigrant children were likely to have thought about their membership either in the scientific community or in the category of people of color. But they quickly caught their teacher's drift. When he asked what race they pictured when they imagined a scientist, they all cried "White!" Mr. Casey said he was going to "change the perspective, because all of you are capable of becoming scientists." He told them the story of the great Indian mathematician Satyendra Nath Bose, who never won a Nobel Prize despite immense contributions to the field. "Why is that?" "Because he was Indian?" Exactly, said Mr. Casey. "We are so scared of talking about those things. That's why we need to be antiracist. And if we want to be antiracist, we have to study the history of racism." Mr. Casey was starting these kids early on the dogma that the Washburn students only learned in high school.

The kids broke into groups to discuss the lesson among themselves. I sat with a group of five boys and girls. I asked whether any of them wanted to be scientists when they grew up. Several said yes. I asked whether they felt that racism might stop them. All shook their heads vigorously. Why not? Because, one boy said, "'my parents always say that we should follow our dreams." Mr. Casey's lesson about structural racism had apparently failed to dent their strivers' ethos. But they were only ten or eleven years old; there was still time.

I had hoped that in the spring I would be able to visit a range of middle and elementary schools in DuPage County, but administrators in several districts declined my requests. I was, however, invited to visit Georgetown Elementary, in the Indian Prairie school district, which serves both Waubonsie Valley and Metea Valley. Georgetown is more diverse than Turner—48 percent Hispanic, 26 percent white, 14 percent Black, 5 percent Asian (as of 2019). My host there, Dr. Rachael Mahmoud, a scholar of curriculum as well as a social studies teacher, explained that at Georgetown, Social Studies alternated with Science in three- to four-week blocks. On average, she said, students get all of twenty-five minutes of Social Studies or Science a day, along with ninety minutes of Math, two hours of English Language Arts, fifty minutes of "special"—gym, art, or music—and fifteen minutes of "social-emotional learning," or SEL. Like many elementary schools, Georgetown is devoted to "the basics." Dr. Mahmoud had, however, scheduled my visit during the Social Studies block.

In any case, some improvising appeared to be permitted, as first-period SEL was in fact devoted to another vogue topic, "financial literacy." This is one of the very few subjects that both red and blue states are convinced students need to learn; in recent years, it has been mandated all over the country. The students learned about credit cards, checks, deposits, accounts. I then moved to Christina Min's third-grade Civics class, where an atmosphere of upright citizenship reigned that would have disarmed the fiercest culture warrior. The students learned about, and talked about, "public services"—policemen, firemen, parks, schools, hospitals, transportation. The class used a textbook called *Your Community and Beyond*, from the Social Studies Alive! series. The children got cards that assigned them to one of the services. Instructed to write about why their service was important and how important it was, every group decided that its service was a very important one. The children read their explanations to the others in their group. I sat with the police contingent. Why are police important? "They put away bad guys!" Only one of the children said that she had ever had an encounter with the police: her father had been stopped for speeding but let off with a stern warning. They gave a presentation to the whole class. The police, one girl explained, "help people in need. They put bad guys in jail *for good*." I wondered whether Miss Min was falling short on culturally relevant teaching or simply hadn't gotten the news that the police were an occupying force in communities of color.

Laura Gonzalez's second-grade History class would have been equally disappointing to conservatives hunting for signs of blue-state wokitude. The kids sat on a rug decorated with multicolored maps of the United States and the world. They, too, used the Social Studies Alive! series, where they had come to a unit on history. The lesson plan was organized around a compelling question: "How can I be a historian?" The lesson had been paired with what turned out to be a quite sophisticated video. The narrator explained that "the past can't be studied by setting up artificial conditions like in a lab," but that the student could apply "scientific disciplines" such as geography, archaeology, and chronology itself. The first exercise for the students was to gather visual evidence. The narrator showed pictures of a streetscape from around 1900. Were the buildings old or new? What specific details served as evidence? How can buildings tell us about the past? The kids talked about the windows and doors and sidewalks. In ensuing days they were to discover the tools they could use to learn about "the native American groups that lived in your area" and about their families and neighborhoods. It was a meta-lesson, concerned not with the history of any group or place but with the means by which one learned about all history.

I ended the day with Dr. Mahmoud, an activist who runs Georgetown's Social Justice Club and lines her classroom with pictures of Black heroes. Dr. Mahmoud sees herself as the protector of the school's Muslim students, not only from other students but also from insensitive teachers. Nevertheless, she is amused by the way her own mixed ethnicity—Jewish mother, Hindu father, Pakistani Muslim husband—upends attempts to pigeonhole her. She's a DEI person who is diverse-in-herself. So I was surprised that her fifth-grade Social Studies class began in a traditional mode of Founder-veneration. "Why was George Washington mad?," she asked her kids.

> Because he had to pay tea tax on top of other taxes.
> Where did the colonists get tea?
> They smuggled it from other countries.

Dr. Mahmoud established that King George III needed money to pay off war debts, that the Sons of Liberty urged resistance, that shots were fired. ("Why?" "For throwing snowballs!") She showed them a picture of the Declaration of Independence. "Who were the delegates?" Here Dr. Mahmoud gave hints broad enough that the kids responded in culturally relevant fashion: rich white men. She had an important narrative to impart. The Constitution had at first conferred full citizenship on white male Christians such as the Framers but now did so for all Americans. How did that happen? Women and minority groups had fought for their rights.

Dr. Mahmoud's narrative, in short, was the perpetual and unending struggle toward the "more perfect Union" promised in the Preamble to the Constitution. She read to the students from a rhyming picture book, *Equality's Call*. "White men with property went to the polls / but the rest of the people were left off the rolls." She led the students in a recitation of the book's theme: "A right isn't a right until it's granted for all." I'm not sure that eleven-year-olds need to be fed their civic education in the form of rhythmic chants, but as formulations go, this one was pretty unexceptionable. At the very heart of what I earlier described as the mainstream narrative of American history is the idea of a perpetually widening circle of inclusion that brings the full measure of citizenship to formerly marginalized groups.

The ultimate goal of Dr. Mahmoud's class, which met for two periods, was to learn enough about the rudiments of the Constitution that the students could write one for their own school. Dr. Mahmoud explained that the Constitution had seven articles, and then started with Article I, on the legislative branch. How should the Georgetown Elementary School pass legislation? What would be fair? The group I had joined finally settled on a two-thirds vote among all students. Brooklyn, the leader of another group, objected: "Kids should have a say, but then it passes through the principal." What about the executive? Should each grade have a president? One student said, "Why should each class have a president when we already have a school president?" But that was a fifth-grader. Could fifth-graders represent kindergarteners? Did the little kids deserve a voice? I overheard Gibril, one of the big talkers of the class, explain to a friend why they didn't: "Because this is a dictatorship." The class drew up the first three articles before the period came to an end.

Dr. Mahmoud explained to me afterward that she didn't like the anodyne textbook that all the Social Studies classes used. "They center the dominant group," she said. "They bring up one Indian who fought in the Revolutionary War, but they don't say anything about the Civil War. Does that mean they're all gone by then?" She was, on the other hand, pleased that the books had enough pictures of Blacks and Indians that children from those groups would not feel marginalized. So she did, indeed, hold the identitarian view that divides history into victim and victimizer and judges accounts by the weight they give to one or the other. That said, Dr. Mahmoud told her fifth-graders that her own eighth-grade teacher, Mr. Hood, had made her memorize the Preamble, which she then proceeded to recite. She wanted them to know what was in each of the seven articles of the Constitution, and she wanted them to make it their own. And she had a good word for George Washington.

Perhaps Dr. Mahmoud would have liked the texts she and her colleagues worked with to be centering the marginalized more than they did. Yet her approach to teaching seemed far more balanced and fair-minded than that of Mr. Casey, the science teacher at Turner Elementary who had so centered the marginalized as to squeeze everything else off the stage. I was more troubled by the marginalization of social studies, in whatever form. If anything risked disabling these students it was the obsession with "the basics," the reluctance to recognize, as Peter Brown in Oklahoma City had implored his superiors to do, that history and literature, taught well, offered the royal route to the land of books and reading.

15

Mrs. Hopfer's History Catechism

The question whether school can change the trajectory of children from high-poverty neighborhoods is very much distinct from the questions that I had been asking about civic education. But over the course of my year in school, I had learned how very much these two matters overlap. So many of the students I had seen in suburban Illinois, in Oklahoma City, and in Minneapolis were either immigrants or Black students from inner-city neighborhoods, and the high rates of failure they endured in the schools made a mockery of our hopes for civic revival. So many of the teachers I had talked to had despaired of raising the academic level of these students so that they could meaningfully engage with original documents in American history or difficult texts of any kind. Yet the educators I had met at the Great Hearts symposium insisted that they had cracked that code. Was that really true? Could a classical education transform the lives not just of brilliant exceptions such as Roosevelt Montás but of ordinary disadvantaged kids? Both of the classical schools I had visited served a largely white, middle-class population; I wanted to spend time at a school that worked with a less privileged student body.

At the end of April, I returned to the Dallas area in order to go to the Founders Classical Academy of Mesquite, which serves a population that is almost 100 percent Hispanic. Though Lewisville, with its boxy brick buildings and scruffy playing field, is hardly prepossessing, Mesquite had been saddled with by far the most dismal physical plant I had seen in my year of visiting schools. Behind a small converted church building off a highway stretched an open field covered with fifteen trailers subdivided into classrooms—save for the ones that house toilets and the lunchroom. In 2018, the Founders network had closed a troubled school that served "a very rough neighborhood," according to Jesse Bass, Mesquite's principal. Students and teachers from both that school and Mesquite had been moved into this temporary facility. I was later told that Founders is hoping to build or buy a new school; having the most disadvantaged students in the network occupy what resembles an army barracks is not a particularly good look.

I started the morning in Troy Hughes's ninth-grade Western Civilization class. Hughes counted himself lucky that his trailer room had two windows. I could see immediately that some of the austere standards that applied at Veritas Prep or Lewisville had been relaxed here. Mr. Hughes wore a blue T-shirt. The kids wore a uniform—khaki pants for the boys, skirts for the girls—but were permitted to choose their own sweatshirt on the very reasonable grounds that they might have to endure a long cold or wet walk from class to the bathroom trailer. The subject of Western Civilization 1 was the ancient world, but the students were conducting a mock legislative session in which they were debating a voucher program that would pay for parents to send their children to private school. Mr. Hughes's idea was to illustrate the workings of the Roman Senate; the students had elected a princeps, a tribune, and a censor, who together ran the exercise. Such was the classical gloss on daily events that when a boy arrived late, Mr. Hughes joked, "You had difficulty getting to Rome this morning on your chariot?"

The debate was fairly feeble; the kids didn't seem to know the arguments on either side. Then Mr. Hughes had them take out their text and read a short essay by Marcus Aurelius on the virtues of his father, Antoninus Pius. Perhaps thinking of my experiences elsewhere, I asked Isaac, the boy next to me, whether he had found the passage difficult. He looked at me with barely disguised sarcasm. "Yeah, I know how to read and write," he said. His grandparents had taught him to read at age four.

Grace, sitting in front of us, piped up that she had learned at three. Her parents had homeschooled all six of their kids; she had wound up teaching her little brother. Grace hadn't recognized the word "assiduity," so Mr. Hughes had given her a dictionary. This inspired Mr. Hughes to say, "There are three words in English that start 'dw.' What are they?" One kid shouted "dwarf!" Another said "dwell!" Grace then flipped to "dw" to come up with "dwindle." She was fluent in the archaic skill of dictionary navigation.

These ninth-graders had language abilities that put them far above kids I had encountered in West Chicago High School or in Oklahoma City. While Mesquite hadn't selected them, their parents had selected Mesquite; the kind of parents who care very much about their children's schooling are also the kind who teach them to read or homeschool them and hound them to do their homework. That gives charter schools such as Mesquite a built-in advantage. Nevertheless, Mr. Hughes told me something remarkable. "Of the twenty kids in this class," he said, "maybe two don't have a special designation." By that he meant that they were English-language learners or in special education. That was true of most of the kids at Mesquite. Mr. Hughes attributed their language skills to the fact that they had been learning Latin since third grade, as well as to their classes in Logic and Rhetoric. Like all the schools in the Founders network, Mesquite did not offer bilingual education; students could receive special help in English, but all classes involved total immersion. The Founders philosophy was the exact opposite of the bilingualism espoused by the culturally relevant teaching pedagogy that I had seen in practice at Turner Elementary in Illinois.

When I moved over to Sheryl Hopfer's eighth-grade U.S. History class, I understood why Mr. Hughes had told me that he was grateful his trailer room had two windows. Mrs. Hopfer had no windows at all, though her ceiling was covered with painted panels showing blue sky and puffy clouds. The class began with a chanted recitation of what Mrs. Hopfer calls the "History Catechism." "What are you?" "I am a king/queen because I rule myself." "How should we then live?" "The purpose of life is not to be happy. It is to be useful, to be honorable, to be compassionate, to have it make some difference that you have lived and lived well

(Ralph Waldo Emerson)." The chant included Emerson's name, though not the parentheses. And so through Frederick Douglass, Livy and Aristotle, George Washington and Alexis de Tocqueville, "the touchstone dates of American History," and the first eighteen presidents. If the class hadn't ended at Reconstruction, I imagine the kids would have done all forty-six. Some students recited from memory, while others consulted the printed list.

The subject of the day was the Gettysburg Address. Mrs. Hopfer began by vividly evoking the battlefield as Lincoln would have seen it, with bones sticking out of the earth and the pervasive stench of death. Mrs. Hopfer was getting her master's degree in American History online through the Gilder Lehrman Institute; she told me almost rapturously that she had been able to ask a question about Frederick Douglass of David Blight, Douglass's great biographer. She went through the address line by line. "Who are 'our fathers'?"

George Washington!
Who else?
Thomas Jefferson!
Who else?
Patrick Henry!
Why would he say 'fourscore and seven' instead of 'eighty-seven'?
When you say 'fourscore and seven' it makes it seem so *long.*
So it goes back to the Declaration of Independence, written by . . .
Thomas Jefferson!
Inspired by . . .
John Locke!

"So they weren't a monarchy. What were they?" Here a silence intervened; one student finally said, "a democracy."

Mrs. Hopfer tried to get the kids to hear the beauty and richness of the language, but they read the archaic words woodenly; figurative, metaphorical speech may have been beyond their current grasp. She wanted, above all, to help them see, as Roosevelt Montás had seen, that Lincoln was reaching across time and space, that he was not just an old man from another era. Who, she asked, was Lincoln addressing when he said that it was for "us" to be dedicated to "the great task" of rebuilding the nation? "Everyone." Yes, said Mrs. Hopfer, including ourselves. "It's like the Founding Fathers had a baton and they passed it on to the next generation. And then he passed it on to us. A lot of people say our country has never been as disunited as it is now. So there are lessons to be learned from that time." Though Mesquite does not teach civics, that was perhaps as distilled, and inspiring, a civics lesson as I had heard anywhere.

Mesquite could not be confused with Lewisville or Veritas Prep. In recent years, the school's population had dropped from six hundred fifty to five hundred as students left for other charter schools. I had been struck by how depopulated some classes seemed to be; I later found that 30 percent of Mesquite's students are listed as "chronic absentees," meaning that they miss 10 percent or more of school days. Students score below the state or district average in reading and math, though by eighth grade they catch up with the state (though not the district) on reading, despite the high number of second-language learners. The kids sometimes acted out. When I dropped by the principal's office in midafternoon, Mr. Bass told me that he had been dealing with the police. "A kid said something he shouldn't have said." "What?," I asked. "I'm not saying," said Mr. Bass.

Yet when I sat in on Margaret Carlson's Paideia class at the end of the day, I found that the kids were talking about *The Brothers Karamazov*—a steeper climb for these students than Dante was for those at Veritas. And these were tenth-graders. They had been reading Dostoyevsky since December; before that, they had studied Aristotle's *Ethics*. They were studying the famous speech by the prosecutor, Ippolit Kirillovich. They listened to an audiobook version of what they had already read. Plainly it was difficult; many of the kids had trouble making sense of the story. The discussion remained at the level of plot. Yet they had all written down quotes they liked in their "commonplace book." They talked about the passions that had driven Dmitri Karamazov to commit murder. Was it hate? Love? Both? One girl said, so quietly that I could just barely hear her, that she thought that Dmitri really did pose a threat to Russia, as Kirillovich insisted. The class ended early. When I went up to talk to Ms. Carlson, several kids immediately broke out a chess set.

I can hardly say for sure whether Mesquite answered the question I had asked the teachers at West Chicago the previous fall about offering a meaningful civic identity to their Hispanic students. It may well be that the Legislative Simulation gave them insight into, and even faith in, our democratic system that the purely text-based education at Mesquite did not. Maybe the simulation was building civic dispositions in a way that was foreign to the classical approach. Yet West Chicago was not providing many of its students what Roosevelt Montás had called a liberal education and perhaps wasn't convinced that it could; Mesquite believed that it could and was trying very hard to succeed. The students there lived in a world of books, as the students in Lewisville and Veritas Prep did. They were expected to know things, and did. That felt like a more profound preparation for civic life.

I had also planned to return to Lewisville. I had begun my school odyssey there; I wanted to see how I felt about the school in light of all the other places I had seen since. And I wanted to test my concern that the high school teachers, with their advanced degrees, were operating at a level well above their students. What had Lewisville graduates *gotten*? Jason Caros once again invited me to visit any class that interested me, though he did point out that Daniel Bishop's sixth-grade English class was preparing for Triumph, the annual Roman pageant. That's where I began.

A plywood arch bearing the words "Caius Caesar: Preparing for Triumph" had been fastened to Mr. Bishop's door. There was a brief discussion of togas and other preparations. Then Mr. Bishop got down to business, telling the kids to stand up and recite Shakespeare's Sonnet 65. And to my amazement, these twelve-year-olds began to recite one of the English language's greatest poems: "Since brass, nor stone, nor earth, nor boundless sea . . ." I had been proud of memorizing that poem—in eleventh grade! When I asked Mr. Bishop later if the kids hadn't had trouble both with the difficult language and complex logic of the sonnet, he said that he had explained to them that an Elizabethan sonnet poses a problem in twelve lines and a solution in two, and then left them to scratch their heads in groups of two. Most, he said, had been able to deduce the problem—mortality—though only a few had been able to puzzle out Shakespeare's solution: that "in black ink my love shall still shine bright."

Now it was time for *oratio*—oral presentation. The class was reading *The Count of Monte Cristo*. A girl volunteered to get up and summarize the chapter. When she came to the chief themes, she spoke of "false identity"—people misrepresenting who they really were. The floor was then open for questions. "What's a benefactor?," one kid asked. Mr. Bishop explained, adding, by the bye, that in Dante's *Inferno* the lowest circle of Hell was reserved for those who had betrayed their benefactor. Count Morcerf, he pointed out, had a strange name, which could be translated as "dead deer." He asked, "Are there dead deers in mythology that are significant?" Everyone seemed to know the story of Artemis, who turned Actaeon into a stag and allowed him to be torn apart by his own hunting dogs. Here was the classical model in miniature: memorization, great books, cultural knowledge, mythology, public speaking. The vibe was eager.

In his senior Moral Philosophy class, John Tutuska, a devotee of twentieth-century pedagogical technology, played a semi-audible recording of a story, from a series called Unsung Heroes, about a woman who felt ashamed of her shabby treatment of a panhandler and then approached him to ask forgiveness. "Who apologizes to a stranger?," he asked. "There's no incentive besides your conscience," a student pointed out. They talked about the courage the woman needed to summon in order to approach someone who might well prove hostile, even dangerous. The panhandler had grasped her hand, looked her in the eye, thanked her. A eudaimonistic moment, rendered in low-tech.

In tenth-grade Medieval History, Jonathan Rogers, the Lewisville classicist, told the story of the Knights Templar, founded by five penniless knights stuck in the Middle East with two horses between them. They had established a security business escorting pilgrims to Jerusalem. The class largely took the form of lecture; Mr. Rogers even dispensed with visual aids until the end of class, when he pulled down a map over the blackboard. But it didn't seem to matter: he had an easy, bantering rapport with the students and enjoyed such respect from them that they had competed to be chosen to hand out the documents for the day. Everyone listened and took notes. "This is one of the ways that the Middle Ages was really weird," Mr. Rogers went on. Rich Europeans heard about the impoverished knights, now calling themselves an "order" of monks, and made themselves right with God by donating money. Soon the Knights Templar had recruiting centers all over Europe and began issuing letters of credit to pilgrims. The Crusades ended, and the Knights Templar became a European bank. King Philip of France fell into debt and rather than paying up, accused the Knights of debauchery and Satanism. He dissolved the order and burned its leader at the stake. "And that," said Mr. Rogers, "is where many of today's conspiracy theories come from." The Illuminati. *The Da Vinci Code.*

Mr. Rogers was the very exemplar of narrative history—names, dates, places, esoterica, dead white males in glory. He talked, and the students listened. Was that effective pedagogy? Were they taking in what he was saying? I had the sense that they were because they listened so raptly. Mr. Rogers was open to participation, though he wasn't seeking it. In a ninth-grade class on Roman history, he asserted that people's wish to live under a fair government was "one of the most underrated factors in history." A student raised his hand to ask about the protests over Israel's war in Gaza then rocking college campuses. "I can't talk about that," Mr. Rogers said, "but you can, so go for it." The student responded, though no one else in class seemed eager to pursue the subject.

Rigorous nonpartisanship was easier to maintain when your subject was ancient or medieval history. The closer you got to current affairs, the greater became the temptation to proselytize. For his junior Government class, Brad Dietzen, the Hillsdale alum, assigned a reading from a unit titled "The Progressive Rejection of the Founding." Why, Mr. Dietzen asked, did the progressives feel impelled to build a "fourth branch of government"—the administrative state? The progressives believed in the enlightened leader, like Plato's philosopher-king. They revered the Founders, but they thought America faced new problems that the Constitution hadn't envisioned. "I would argue," said Mr. Dietzen, "that there were valid criticisms that the progressives put forth, but I would argue more so that it came from a perversion of what the Founders thought." They believed in history rather than natural law. A student asked,

"Isn't it dangerous to follow history when history may be bad?" "That," Mr. Dietzen replied with a note of triumph, "is why it's an expert's job to guide society." Here was the "1776 Report" in a nutshell.

We were reaching the end of the year, and John Woods's U.S. History class had arrived at the second half of the twentieth century. That morning they were finishing up a unit on Communism. They had read the foreword to *Witness,* the 1952 memoir by anti-Communist intellectual Whittaker Chambers. It was not, however, Chambers's ideology that Dr. Woods wanted to highlight. "He writes that he came close to suicide," Dr. Woods pointed out. "Why didn't he?" He had thought about the beauty of the natural world, which had brought him back to his religious faith. "He writes that faith is the problem of the age—not politics or economics. Does this remind you of Solzhenitsyn or Wiesel?" They had read both earlier. A student replied, "Solzhenitsyn said that the Communist Party shatters the soul." Yes, Dr. Woods rejoined, "there's an existential part of their suffering." Faith was the problem of the age—that's how Jason Caros's intellectual hero Russell Kirk would have put it.

I was wondering how Woods would handle the civil rights movement. He had assigned several texts: the 1960 founding statement of the Student Nonviolent Coordinating Committee, an oral history in which Fannie Lou Hamer described her effort to register to vote in Mississippi, Martin Luther King, Jr.'s "Letter from Birmingham Jail," John Lewis's speech at the March on Washington, and Malcom X's 1963 "Message to the Grassroots." Though a happy camper so far as I could tell, Dr. Woods was also more inclined than any of the other teachers I had met to question whether he and his colleagues were reaching their students at the deepest level. Here was a chance to see.

Woods had asked the students to write brief paragraphs on several of the texts and also to think about "commonalities" between civil rights workers and antitotalitarians such as Solzhenitsyn, Chambers, and Elie Wiesel. First they discussed Hamer. Dr. Woods asked, "To what extent do you think it's right to put your children's lives at risk"—as she had done—"in order to achieve change?" This sparked a general discussion. "If you get long-term freedom in the end," said one student, "then I feel that it's justified. She's willing to fight so that her kids have a better life than she had." Another said, "She's sacrificing herself for the common good. And sometimes that's necessary." Dr. Woods pointed out that Hamer was not "the source of the harm that's coming to her children." The underlying civics lesson was that a commitment to truth can exact a terrible price.

The heart of the day's lesson was a comparison of King and Malcolm X. "Malcolm advocates violence to respond to an authentically violent situation," Dr. Woods pointed out. "Isn't violence necessary in a situation like that?"

"In one sense, yes," said Rebekah. "But I think it leaves you a lot more damaged. It's almost doing the same thing that other people are doing to him."

"Why is violence wrong in this case," Dr. Woods asked, "when it's not in, say, the American Revolution?"

A student tried to answer: "The situation you're fighting is basically against a culture. You're not fighting an oppressive government. Your response would wind up reinforcing the culture."

"So there has to be a reasonable chance of success," Dr. Woods summarized.

Rebekah spoke again; she was troubled by Malcolm's language. "He uses metaphors like 'the Mayflower' to mean all Americans, as if all non-black Americans are white and privileged. He defines white people as the enemy."

Dr. Woods kept challenging. "His perspective is that 'we're not allowed to be Americans. We tried for a long time, and we haven't been accepted. Martin Luther King still believes that we can be accepted.'"

"If I were in that situation," said another student, "I would feel that way too. But Martin Luther King has somehow been able to move past that."

Dr. Woods said, "As we've said many times in our discussion of totalitarianism, love is more powerful." After he returned from his trip to Mecca, he pointed out, Malcolm shed his racialist worldview and embraced religious faith. The class ended on this hopeful note.

Afterward, Rebekah, who had made many thoughtful contributions, came up to Dr. Woods looking slightly flushed with excitement. "That was a great conversation," she said. "It made me really happy."

It had made me happy, too. I hadn't heard that many great conversations on my first visit to Lewisville, but I had this time around—and not just from the students in Dr. Woods or Mr. Bishop's class. The sophomores in Dr. Terranova's English class, formed into a square for "Socratic seminar," had conducted a vigorous discussion of the theme of sacrifice in Dickens's *Tale of Two Cities*. I had also heard stirring debate in West Chicago's Legislative Simulation, and delightful and well-informed skits on the Founders at the Academy of American Studies, and a clarifying discussion of the nature of rules in Miss Brewer's eighth-grade class at Belle Isle in Oklahoma City. Miss Rose at Waubonsie Valley had shown me what great teaching looked like. Yet those moments had been rare. A disproportionate number of the inspiring conversations I had heard over the previous year had taken place in classical schools.

That was, at least, a seeming paradox. The child-centered pedagogy that has dominated schooling, or at least school doctrine, for much of the past century, seeks to foster inquiry, critical thinking, open discussion, and debate. Classical schooling is text-centered; it rests upon respect for the instructor and for the "beautiful content" the student is to master; its soul dwells more in the past than in the present. Yet it was in classical schools, rather than mainstream ones, that I had most often heard the kind of reflective discussion that civic education seeks to foster. That discussion, it's true, focused on ancient texts rather than current events. But does that really matter? If you can speak thoughtfully about *The Nicomachean Ethics* or *The Brothers Karamazov*, you can do so about the fairness of our tax system. If you can't make sense of the Declaration of Independence because the words are too hard, you will soon get lost in the thicket of public policy or even a newspaper editorial. The democratic dispositions that students acquire will be hollow in the absence of language and of knowledge. There, and not elsewhere, is the frontier of civic education.

16

What Is to Be Done?

Readers old enough to recall America's bicentennial celebration may not remember much beyond the "tall ships"—the international fleet of tall-masted ships that gathered in New York Harbor and then sailed on to Boston. In 1976, the nation was trying to put Vietnam and Watergate behind itself under the anodyne leadership of President Gerald Ford. Queen Elizabeth and Prince Phillip came on their own yacht. Johnny Cash served as grand marshal of the parade in Washington, D.C. Local events involved parades and fireworks and historical reenactments. The Bicentennial came, and it went.

You may be reading this book in the year of the Semiquincentennial. As we are no longer the country that we were in 1976, so we are no longer able to celebrate our birth with anything like the complacency we felt then. President Trump has made American history a battleground of irreconcilable visions—the "patriotic" against the "woke." He will use the occasion of the two hundred fiftieth anniversary of our founding to openly wage that war. He has appointed a "Task Force 250" to stage-manage the celebrations, whose centerpiece is to be a National Garden of American Heroes with statues of two hundred fifty specified Americans.[1] Frederick Douglass and Sacagawea make the cut, but so, too, do William F. Buckley, Jr., Barry Goldwater, Charlton Heston, Milton

Friedman, Jeane Kirkpatrick, and others regarded as heroic only on one end of the ideological spectrum.[2]

While Donald Trump uses all the powers of the executive office to hold his jamboree of American glory, America250, a bipartisan organization established by Congress in 2016 will be engaging in orthodox civics activities. Planned events include a contest in which children in grades 3 through 12 will submit essays or artwork answering the question "What does America mean to you?" as well as a program called "America Gives" described as "the largest-ever national service program in American history."[3] Civic and academic organizations will be staging events of their own designed to counteract the one-sided narrative advanced by the White House. The left-leaning iCivics will be teaming up with the right-leaning Bill of Rights Institute to encourage teachers to incorporate themes from the Declaration into their curriculum. In early 2025, the American Historical Association, iCivics, several leading historians, and high school teachers staged a discussion to highlight the role of schools and teachers in using the anniversary to educate students about the American story. David Blight, the biographer of Frederick Douglass, used the occasion to implore his fellow historians to stand by their nuanced accounts of slavery and race.[4] The two hundred fiftieth anniversary celebration is almost guaranteed to highlight and reinforce our profound divisions over the American story rather than to heal them.

Donald Trump will do enormous damage to our civic culture no matter how the Semiquincentennial plays out. He will make people crazier, and angrier, than they already are. He'll drive the wedge even deeper between his supporters and his opponents; he'll bring science, reason, and the entire empire of fact into yet greater disrepute; his preening and cruel version of manhood will offer a pretext for boys to behave like jerks; he'll convince yet more Americans that other countries are out to steal our lunch; and he will further legitimize hostility to immigrants, the poor, and gay and trans people.

I have argued in this book that schools can help save democracy by giving students a solid foundation of linguistic skills, historical knowledge, and habits of reflection. But I recognize that the surrounding culture shapes the schools more than the other way around. Humane schools are not likely to flourish in a coarse society with a short attention span and a hair-trigger temper. Nevertheless, the influence runs in both directions. Plato believed that, over time, good schools made good leaders; Thomas Jefferson, who believed in the ordinary man as Plato did not, argued that good schools shaped good citizens. As Horace Mann observed, school is the only social institution that operates on all citizens and does so from early childhood to the edge of adulthood. School is a powerful civic force whether we wish it to be or not. We should neither expect too much nor ask too little.

Unlike the dogmatists of the Left and Right, I do not believe that our wildly heterogeneous society can be shoehorned into a single kind of school or curriculum. I might wish that everyone shared my center-left view of American history, but I recognize that they don't. That is why I admire the Educating for American Democracy Roadmap, even though I would prefer an explicit curriculum to an inquiry-driven one. I very much hope that classical education spreads into the blue world and takes on new forms there. But I understand that that rule-bound culture, that respect for elders and for authority, is not for everyone. It is far beyond the powers even of Donald Trump to strap our giant, sprawling school system into a Procrustean Bed.

But if we will not have one school or one curriculum, we need to have models to emulate and mistakes to avoid. Some of those models pertain directly to civic education, but others to the pedagogical foundations of schooling. I am, for example, convinced that we must restore the centrality of books—of words and language, of facts and knowledge, of the depth of experience that comes only with learning from an early age to navigate challenging texts. Anything that gets in the way of that, whether "culturally responsive teaching" or "financial literacy" or "test prep" or "critical thinking skills" is to that degree a distraction. "Linguistic empowerment," as Danielle Allen writes, is the foundation of civic education. And there is no shortcut to that empowerment. I am, I suppose, prescribing one pedagogy for all—some version of E. D. Hirsch's Core Knowledge. I am, like Jason Caros, a Hirschian. I know that Hirsch and the pedagogy of learning particular things are regarded as conservative. But the fact that conservatives like it doesn't make it wrong. Such a drastic change in pedagogy would, however, require an equally drastic change in the way that we recruit and train teachers. There is no other way.

If we are to have more books, we will have less technology. That doesn't mean seventh-graders have to read *A Raisin in the Sun* in a tattered paperback rather than a PDF; a book is a book in whatever format. But screens have come to serve as babysitting and pacifying devices. We know students don't like to read, so we show them a video instead. We show them cartoon characters in colonial dress. We show them plenty of news clips from the CNN archive. But the steady stream of cute or even engrossing images undermines the patience and self-discipline required for reading, writing, and thinking. Social media already corrodes those faculties when students aren't at school. That's why phones must be banned absolutely from the classroom, if not from the school itself.

The teaching of history should be historical—that is, chronological. The classes that I saw in Illinois that combined history and literature did a disservice to both. Chronological study does not mean "one damn thing after another"; larger meanings arise from our study of the small particulars of history. Advanced Placement history classes are rigorously chronological but, as Miss Rose's students know, scarcely a mere record of names and dates and places. You cannot make sense of the past or draw many meaningful lessons about the present unless you know what came before what. Also, another word for historical events is "stories." Students like stories—even stories about bizarre folk such as the Knights Templar. Sociology doesn't have good stories. That doesn't mean students shouldn't study sociology or economics. But they need the chronological framework first. And there's no reason not to begin in the later grades of elementary school.

But students also need experiences. Conservatives have gotten so hysterical over the phantasm of "action civics" that they cannot see the tremendous civic value of exercises that bring students out of the classroom and even out of the schoolhouse. Students like to *do*; and civic life involves not just knowing but also doing. Exercises such as the Legislative Simulation are simulacra of civic life—not because students will grow up to be legislators, but because they will have to learn how to talk about and argue about public issues, and they will have to learn how to get along with people with whom they disagree. They need to be equipped with what Danielle Allen calls the "participatory readiness" for future civic roles. One of the ancillary benefits of West Chicago's program is that in the highly stratified world of the big public school, students from all strata participated. Perhaps one of the elements of adult life that the exercise simulated was the way in which people live simultaneously in the highly unequal world of the capitalist marketplace and in the formally equal world of democratic citizenship. That is a lesson worth reinforcing.

While I feel resigned to the intense polarization that turns so many debates over state history standards into a wild donnybrook, the effect is only to deepen that polarization. Each side seems to make the other more dogmatic. If Florida compels teachers to tell their students that America is God's gift to the nations, Minnesota counters that ours is a tale of oppression and resistance. Both narratives, as I say in an earlier chapter, flatten history to make it fit current politics. Donald Trump plans to solve this problem by threatening blue-state schools until they sound like Florida. America's deep-seated tradition of educational localism may frustrate his designs. Even if it does, some combination of the chastening effect of the election and declining enthusiasm for identity politics on the left may diminish the appeal of the 1619 ideology. Nothing, alas, is likely to take the wind out of the sails of the rival orthodoxy of 1776.

I believe, as I have written throughout this book, that our schools must feel different from the surrounding society in some important ways—more respectful of knowledge, of reflection, of difference of opinion. I recognize that the walls of any public institution, including schools, can only be just so thick. Their very publicness means that they will be pervaded by the values and habits of the larger culture. And yet if schools merely reproduce that culture, they can offer this or that admirable civic program, but they will not produce young people who are more prepared to sustain our democracy than we are today. Can we ask our schools to help shape an ethos that seems to be vanishing from the larger culture?

The Founders believed, like the classical writers they so admired, that a republic ultimately rests on the virtue of citizens. We no longer think that way. The great American historian Gordon Wood argues in *The Idea of America* that the preoccupation with personal virtue began to fade as America became more democratic in the age of Andrew Jackson; politics came to be seen as a clash of interests rather than the "disinterested" search for the public good.[5] The language of virtue that I encountered in classical schools constitutes a self-conscious effort to resurrect an older view both of schooling and of our own natures. We are far more comfortable speaking of "values," which is to say, personal choices that reflect our own preferences, than of virtues.

Yet I wonder whether we will continue to be defined by unremitting individualism. Perhaps one element in the compound of rage and frustration that restored Donald Trump to office is a sense of isolation that comes of a society where almost everything is reduced to market competition. A quarter of a century ago, Michael Schudson could write in *The Good Citizen,* a history of American civic identity, that the modern idea of citizenship as maximum personal freedom had deepened our democratic egalitarianism in a way that more than compensated for the loss of an older sense of communal identity and collective purpose.[6] I don't think that can be said today; we have lost far more than we have gained. We may have more to learn from communitarian thinkers such as Michael Sandel and Alasdair MacIntyre, who do not accept the model of the individual as autonomous agent. Rather, Sandel argues, we are "encumbered selves" who exist in relation to our families, neighborhoods, friends, nations. The good that we seek is not merely what maximizes our freedom but what is good for the community of which we are a part. We must, Sandel argues, cultivate civic virtue if we are to find our way to a language and ethos of the common good.[7] I do not think that is so very far from Danielle Allen's model of the "civic friendship" that enables each of us to accept the full selfhood of others and to substitute mutual "purposes" for selfish "interests."

We may have reached the limit of individualism. While the Founders may have been wrong in believing that democracies depend on the virtue of citizens, they may have been right in thinking that democracy cannot survive unless citizens are willing to look to a greater good beyond themselves. I suspect that in years to come, more parents will seek out schools that have an overtly communitarian or ethical culture.

They may not call themselves "classical schools" or even claim that they are furnishing a "liberal education," but they will nevertheless offer an alternative to the consumerist, vocational, instrumental culture of today's public education. I dearly hope that such schools will take their place in a larger revival of our civic spirit.

ACKNOWLEDGMENTS

At a time when many schools are terrified of bad publicity, I'm very grateful to the school leaders who either invited me without hesitation to visit their buildings or helped me get access to other schools: Jason Caros of the Founders Classical Academy in Lewisville, Texas; Mary Ellen Daneels of the Illinois Democracy Network; Peter Brown of the Oklahoma City Public Schools; Dr. Emily Palmer of Washburn High School and Vernon Rowe of Northeast Middle School, both in Minneapolis; Jake Tawney of the Great Hearts Institute. They had the confidence to let me draw my own conclusions. I often turned for help and counsel to Emma Humphries and Louise Dubé of iCivics and to Jim Basker at the Gilder Lehrman Institute.

I was saved from many errors, and guided on to a better path, by the friends and loved ones who read portions of the book: my wife, Elizabeth Easton; my friend Roosevelt Montás; and the members of my writers' group: David Greenberg, Claire Potter, Jim Goodman, Clay Risen, Ted Widmer, Kati Marton, Natalia Petrzela, Mike Massing, Matt Connelly, and the late Jim Ledbetter.

I am indebted, as always, to my agent, Andrew Wylie, and to my friend and editor John Glusman and his team.

NOTES

Introduction: Why Civics Matters

1 Horace Mann, *Lectures on Education* (Boston: William B. Fowle and N. Capen, 1845), 55–56.

2 Mann, *Lectures*, 187.

3 Mary Tyler Peabody Mann, *Life of Horace Mann* (Boston: Walker, Fuller & Co., 1865), 142.

4 R. Freeman Butts, The Civic Mission in Education Reform: Perspectives for the Public and the Profession (Stanford, CA: Hoover Institute Press, 1989), 70.

5 Jonathan Rauch, *The Constitution of Knowledge: A Defense of Truth* (Washington, DC: Brookings Institution, 2021).

6 Alexis de Tocqueville, *Democracy in America* (New York: Vintage Press, 1990), 1:191ff.

7 On newspapers, see Danny Hayes and Jennifer L. Lawless, *The News Hole: The Decline of Local Journalism and Political Engagement* (Cambridge: Cambridge University Press, 2021); on civic associations, Robert Putnam, *Bowling Alone: The Collapse and Revival of American* Community (New York: Simon & Schuster, 2000).

8 John Fensterwald, "Latest National Test Results Underscore Declining Knowledge of U.S. History and Civics," EdSource, May 3, 2023.

9 National Assessment of Educational Progress (NAEP), "The Nation's Report Card."

10 "National Survey Finds Just 1 in 3 Americans Would Pass the Citizenship Test," Institute for Citizens and Scholars, October 3, 2018.

11 Jeremy A. Stern, Alison E. Brody, et al., "The State of State Standards for Civics and U.S. History in 2021," Thomas B. Fordham Institute, June 23, 2021.

12 Diane Ravitch and Chester Finn, Jr., *What Do Our Seventeen-Year-Olds Know? A*

Report on the First National Assessment of History and Literature (New York: Harper & Row, 1987), 54.

13 Peter Wood, "Why We Need a Civics Alliance," National Association of Scholars blog, March 22, 2021.

14 Danielle Allen, *Justice by Means of Equality* (Chicago: University of Chicago Press, 2023), 199; Danielle Allen, *Education and Equality* (Chicago: University of Chicago Press, 2016), 35.

15 Cited in James Davison Hunter, *The Death of Character: Moral Education in an Age Without Good or Evil* (New York: Basic Books, 2000), 6.

16 Michael A. Rebell, *Flunking Democracy: Schools, Courts and Civic Participation* (Chicago: University of Chicago Press, 2018), 17.

17 See, for example, Stephen J. Thornton, "The Social Studies Near Century's End: Reconstructing Patterns of Curriculum and Instruction," *Review of Research in Education* 20, no. 1 (1994): 223–54.

18 For the first, see Meira Levinson, *No Citizen Left Behind* (Cambridge, MA: Harvard University Press, 2012). For the second, see Keith C. Barton and Linda S. Levstik, *Teaching History for the Common Good* (Mahwah, NJ: Lawrence Erlbaum, 2004).

19 See Diane Ravitch, *The Troubled Crusade: American Education, 1945–1980* (New York: Basic Books, 1983).

1: Civics Without Knowledge

1 Jeremy A. Stern, Alison E. Brody, et al., "The State of State Standards for Civics and U.S. History in 2021," Thomas B. Fordham Institute, June 23, 2021.

2 "Illinois Social Studics Standards," ISBE College & Career Readiness, June 2017.

3 Stern, Brody, et al., "State of State Standards."

4 "The College, Career and Civic Life (C3) Framework for Social Studies State Standards," National Council for the Social Studies, 2013.

5 "AP U.S. History: Course and Exam Description," College Board, 2023.

6 "Illinois Learning Standards for Social Science," 2022 and "Illinois State Board of Education Notice of Proposed Amendments," 2021, Illinois State Board of Education.

7 This history is recounted in Jacob Berkman's "Implementation in Illinois: What States Can Learn from How Illinois Implemented its 2015 Civic Education Law," iCivics, 2021.

8 Meira Levinson, *No Citizen Left Behind* (Cambridge, MA: Harvard University Press, 2012), 87.

2: How History Became Social Studies, and Meat Became Meatloaf

1 Lawrence A. Cremin, *The Transformation of the School: Progressivism in American Education, 1875–1957* (New York: Knopf, 1969), 5.

2 *The Study of History in Schools: Report to the American Historical Association by the Committee of Seven* (New York: Macmillan, 1906).

3 Ronald W. Evans, *Social Studies Wars: What Should We Teach the Children?* (New York: Teachers College Press, 2004), 5.

4 Lawrence Cremin, *American Education: The National Experience, 1783–1876* (New York: Harper & Row, 1980), 73.

5 "Report of the Committee on Secondary School Studies Appointed at the Meeting of the National Educational Association July 9, 1892" (Washington, DC: Government Printing Office, 1893).

6 James Davison Hunter, *The Death of Character: Moral Education in an Age Without Good or Evil* (New York: Basic Books, 2000), 51.

7 *Study of History in Schools*, 7.

8 *Study of History in Schools*, 18–24.

9 *Study of History in Schools*, 116.

10 Hunter, *Death of Character*, 65–66.

11 John Dewey, *Democracy and Education: An Introduction to the Philosophy of Education* (Gorham, ME: Myers Education Press, 2018), 43, 57, 76.

12 "The Teaching of Community Civics," Bulletin no. 23, U.S. Bureau of Education, 1915.

13 "The Social Studies in Secondary Education," Bulletin no. 28, Bureau of Education, Department of the Interior, 1916.

14 Claudia Goldin, "Appendix to 'How America Graduated from High School, 1910 to 1960,'" Historical Paper no. 57, National Bureau of Economic Research, June 1994.

15 John Dewey, "The Child and the Curriculum," in *John Dewey on Education*, edited by Reginald Archambault (Chicago: University of Chicago Press, 1964), 347.

16 John Dewey, *Experience and Education* (New York: Collier Books, 1938), 18, 20, 23.

17 See, for example, Evans, *Social Studies Wars*, or David Labaree, *The Trouble with Ed Schools* (New Haven, CT: Yale University Press, 2006).

18 Derek Heater, A History of Education For Citizenship (London: Routledge Falmer, 2004); Heater, p. 117; Michael Schudson, *The Good Citizen: A History of American Civic Life* (New York: Free Press, 1998), 203.

19 John J. Patrick and John D. Hoge, "Teaching Government, Civics and Law," in *Handbook of Research on Social Studies Teaching and Learning*, edited by James Shaver (New York: Macmillan, 1991), 427–36.

20 Allan Nevins, "American History for Americans," *New York Times Magazine*, May 3, 1942.

21 *New York Times*, May 4, 1943; June 23, 1943.

22 Peter Novick, *That Noble Dream: The "Objectivity Question" and the American History Profession* (Cambridge: Cambridge University Press, 1988), 369.

23 Edgar B. Wesley, *The Report of the Committee on American History in Schools and Colleges of the American Historical Association* (New York: Macmillan, 1944).

24 Albert Lynd, "Quackery in the Public Schools," *Atlantic Monthly*, March 1950.

25 Arthur Bestor, *Educational Wastelands: The Retreat from Learning in Our Public Schools* (Urbana: University of Illinois Press, 1953), 118–19.

26 Labaree, *Trouble with Ed Schools*, 185.

27 Jonathan Kozol, *Death at an Early Age: The Destruction of the Hearts and Minds of Negro Children in the Boston Public Schools* (Boston: Houghton Mifflin, 1967).

28 Charles Silberman, *Crisis in the Classroom: The Remaking of American Education* (New York: Random House, 1970), 10, 208.
29 *New York Times*, August 15, 1969.
30 Stephen J. Thornton, "Continuity and Change in Social Studies Curriculum," in *Handbook of Research in Social Studies Education*, edited by Linda S. Levstik and Cynthia A. Tyson, chap. 2 (London: Routledge, 2008).
31 Diane Ravitch, *Left Back: A Century of Failed School Reforms* (New York: Simon & Schuster, 2000), 407.
32 Diane Ravitch, *National Standards in American Education: A Citizen's Guide* (Washington, DC: Brookings, 1995).
33 The National Commission on Excellence in Education, "A Nation at Risk: The Imperative for Educational Reform," April 26, 1983.
34 Diane Ravitch and Chester Finn, *What Do Our 17-Year-Olds Know? A Report on the First National Assessment of History and Literature* (New York: Harper & Row, 1987).

3: Beautiful Content: The Model of the Classical School

1 Karen Francisco and Carol Burris, "A Sharp Turn Right: A New Breed of Charter Schools Delivers the Conservative Agenda," Network for Public Education, June 2023.
2 Daniel Buck, "Should Elementary Schools Teach Reading Comprehension," Thomas B. Fordham Institute, May 5, 2024. Many more studies are available on the website of the Core Knowledge Foundation, under "Research Studies."
3 John Dewey, *Democracy and Education: An Introduction to the Philosophy of Education* (Gorham, ME: Myers Education Press, 2018), 145.
4 Cited in Roosevelt Montás, *Rescuing Socrates: How the Great Books Changed My Life and Why They Matter for a New Generation* (Princeton, NJ: Princeton University Press, 2021), 107.
5 James Davison Hunter, *The Death of Character: Moral Education in an Age Without Good or Evil* (New York: Basic Books, 2000), 147.
6 See, for example, Pete Hegseth with David Goodwin, *Battle for the American Mind: Uprooting a Century of Miseducation* (New York: Broadside Books, 2022).
7 See "Texas Public Schools Are Teaching Creationism," *Slate*, January 16, 2014.
8 "Fast Facts: Charter Schools," National Center for Education Statistics.
9 Cassidy Syftestad and Albert Cheng, "Classical Charter School Enrollment Skyrockets in Texas," Thomas B. Fordham Institute, June 8, 2023.
10 Russell Kirk, *The Roots of American Order* (Wilmington, DE: ISI Books, 1974).

4: 1619 v. 1776: The War Over the American Past

1 "The 1619 Project," *New York Times Magazine*, August 14, 2019.
2 Jonathan Zimmerman, *Whose America? Culture Wars in the Public Schools* (Chicago: University of Chicago Press, 2002), 31–35.
3 Donald Yacovone, *Teaching White Supremacy: America's Democratic Ordeal and the Forging of Our National Identity* (New York: Pantheon Books, 2022), 244–66.

4 C. Vann Woodward, *The Strange Career of Jim Crow* (New York: Oxford University Press, 1974), 82.

5 List available at College Board website, "Course Audit" under "AP United States History."

6 Mary Beth Norton, David M. Katzman, David W. Blight, Howard P. Chudacoff, Thomas G. Paterson, William M. Tuttle, Jr., and Paul D. Escott, *A People and a Nation: A History of the United States*, 6th ed. (Boston: Houghton Mifflin, 2001).

7 Norton et al., *People and a Nation*, 188 and 337.

8 Norton et al., *People and a Nation*, 357 and 578.

9 Howard Zinn, *A People's History of the United States* (New York: Harper Perennial, 2015), 59, 96, 189, 349, and 393.

10 David Greenberg, "Agit-Prof: Howard Zinn's Influential Mutilations of American History," *New Republic*, March 19, 2013.

11 Sean Wilentz, "American Slavery and 'The Relentless Unforeseen,'" *New York Review of Books*, November 19, 2019.

12 Tom Mackaman, "An Interview with Historian Gordon Wood on The New York Times' 1619 Project," World Socialist website, November 28, 2019.

13 Cited in Adam Serwer, "The Fight Over the 1619 Project Is Not About the Facts," *Atlantic Monthly*, December 23, 2019.

14 In a speech at Howard University, Johnson said, "You do not take a person who, for years, has been hobbled by chains and liberate him, bring him to the starting line of a race and then say, 'You are free to compete with all the others,' and still justly believe that you have been completely fair." Lyndon B. Johnson, "Commencement Address at Howard University: 'To Fulfill These Rights,'" American Presidency Project, June 4, 1965.

15 John McWhorter, "*John McWhorter*: We Cannot Allow '1619' to Dumb Down America in the Name of a Crusade," *Broad + Liberty*, May 24, 2020.

16 "1776 Unites' Bob Woodson and Ian Rowe Introduce New High School Curriculum Emphasizing the History and Future of African American Resiliency in the United States," AP News, September 16, 2020. See the 1776 Unites website for the complete curriculum: https://1776unites.org/.

17 Peter W. Woods, *1620: A Critical Response to The 1619 Project* (New York: Encounter Books, 2020), 7 and 16.

18 Nolan D. McCaskill and Natasha Korecki, "Trump Says He Can Heal National Divide, Then Trashes Protestors, Democrats," *Politico*, September 1, 2020.

19 Sam Dorman, "Chris Rufo Calls on Trump to End Critical Race Theory 'Cult Indoctrination' in Federal Government," Fox News, September 1, 2020.

20 Juan Perez, Jr., and Nicole Gaudiano, "Trump Blasts 1619 Project as DeVos Praises Alternative Black History Curriculum," *Politico*, September 17, 2020.

21 "Executive Order on Establishing the President's Advisory 1776 Commission," Trump White House Archives, November 2, 2020.

22 Emma Green, "The Christian Liberal Arts School at the Heart of the Culture Wars," *New Yorker*, April 3, 2023.

23 Danny Hakim, "How a Conservative Christian College Got Mixed Up in the 2020 Election Plot," *New York Times Magazine*, January 8, 2024.

24 "The 1776 Report," The President's Advisory 1776 Commission, Trump White House Archives, 2021.
25 Jonathan Eig, *King: A Life* (New York, Farrar, Straus & Giroux, 2023), 211.
26 Roger Kimball, "The January 6 Insurrection Hoax," *Imprimis*, September 2021.

5: *Hamilton* on the Stage and in the Classroom

1 Retrieved from "History U," The Gilder Lehrman Institute of American History and Roberta McCutcheon, "History Resources: Andrew Jackson and the Bank War," Gilder Lehrman Institute of American History.
2 "A Dive Into Democracy" lesson plans, iCivics Education.
3 "Brief the Chief," iCivics Education.
4 "Lessons," Bill of Rights Institute.
5 Scott Warren, *Generation Citizen: The Power of Youth in Our Politics* (Berkeley, CA: Counterpoint Press, 2019), 39.

6: The History Wars in a Purple State

1 Virginia Board of Education Business Meeting, August 17, 2022. YouTube, https://www.youtube.com/watch?v=LYT9-P5_gHc.
2 H.R. 2460 (102nd) America 2000 Excellence in Education Act, GovTrack.us.
3 *Washington Post*, March 29, 1995.
4 *Washington Post*, March 30, 1995; April 6, 1995; April 7, 1995; April 26, 1995; and April 27, 1995.
5 Peter Wood, "Why We Need a Civics Alliance," National Association of Scholars blog, March 22, 2021.
6 Stanley Kurtz, "The Partisanship Out of Civics Act," National Association of Scholars blog, February 15, 2021.
7 Morgan Matzen, "South Dakota Education Department to Change Social Studies Standards After Review," *Argus Leader* (Sioux Falls, SD), August 7, 2021.
8 Stanley Kurtz, "Noem Must Fix South Dakota Standards Fiasco," *National Review*, September 20, 2021.
9 Tyler O'Neil, "'Model for Rest of the Country': South Dakota History Standards Scrap Critical Race Theory, Build on Hillsdale Foundation," *Daily Signal*, May 9, 2023.
10 Alex Schemmel, "Va. Gubernatorial Candidate Says Parents Should Not Control What Schools Teach Their Kids," ABC 13 News, September 29, 2021.
11 "Final Report of The Virginia Commission on African American History Education in The Commonwealth," Secretary of Education, Commonwealth of Virginia, August 2020.
12 Jillian Balow, letter to Governor Glenn Youngkin and Secretary Aimee Guidera, Virginia Department of Education, February 23, 2022.
13 "The Guiding Principles for Virginia's 2022 History and Social Science Standards Revisions," Virginia Department of Education.
14 "The Guiding Principles for Virginia's 2022 History and Social Science Standards Revisions," Virginia Department of Education; and "Proposed History and Social Science Standards of Learning," Virginia Department of Education.

15 Ben Paviour, "Youngkin's Revised History Standards Draw from Broader Conservative Movement," *Virginia Public Media*, December 21, 2022.

16 Tweet from Red4EdVA, *X*, November 19, 2022, https://twitter.com/Red4EdVA/status/1594118165419724801.

17 "August 17, 2022 Draft History and Social Science Standards of Learning," Virginia Department of Education.

18 "VSSLC, VASCD, AHA, VCSS, NCSS, & VGA Respond to the January Draft History & Social Science Standards of Learning for Virginia Public Schools," National Council for the Social Studies.

19 "VSSLC, VASCD, and AHA Respond to VBOE's Request for Combined History and Social Science Standards," December 20, 2022, https://drive.google.com/file/d/17xMPq6-jCUljapJdfpc-3S1GmN7-Cha5/view.

20 "History and Social Science Standards of Learning for Virginia Public Schools," January 2023, Board of Education, Commonwealth of Virginia.

21 "2023 History and Social Sciences Standards of Learning for Kindergarten–Grade 12," Virginia Department of Education.

22 "Applause for New Virginia Social Studies Standards," Civics Alliance.

7: You Realize That Everyone Has Reasons for What They Think

1 Pete Hegseth with David Goodwin, *Battle for the American Mind: Uprooting a Century of Miseducation* (New York: Broadside Books, 2022), 47 and 102.

2 Meira Levinson, *No Citizen Left Behind* (Cambridge, MA: Harvard University Press, 2012), 97.

3 See, for example, Michael A. Rebell, *Flunking Democracy: Schools, Courts and Civic Participation* (Chicago: University of Chicago Press, 2018), 120.

4 Ian McMullen, *Civics Beyond Critics: Character Education in a Liberal Democracy* (Oxford: Oxford University Press, 2015), 13 and 22.

5 Amy Gutmann, *Democratic Education* (Princeton, NJ: Princeton University Press, 2001), 62.

6 Danielle Allen, *Talking to Strangers: Anxieties of Citizenship Since Brown v. Board of Education* (Chicago: University of Chicago Press, 2009), 127 and 137.

7 Danielle Allen, *Justice by Means of Democracy* (Chicago: University of Chicago Press, 2023), 199.

8 Danielle Allen, *Education and Equality* (Chicago: University of Chicago Press, 2016), 22 and 33.

9 Allen, *Education and Equality*, 47.

10 See "8th Grade Curriculum," Democratic Knowledge Project.

8: The One True Curriculum—or, Failing That, a "Roadmap"

1 Harold Rugg, *Our Country and Our People* (Boston: Ginn and Company, 1938), vii.

2 Elmer A. Winter, "Man and His Changing Society: The Textbooks of Harold Rugg," *History of Education Quarterly* 7, no. 4 (Winter 1967): 493–514.

3 Harold Rugg, *Building a Science of Society for the Schools* (New York State: n.p., 1934), 26–30.

4 Jonathan Zimmerman, *Whose America? Culture Wars in the Public Schools* (Chicago: University of Chicago Press, 2022), 73.
5 Rugg, *Our Country and Our People*, 198.
6 Zimmerman, *Whose America?*, 66 and 76.
7 Bradley Commission on History in Schools, "Building a History Curriculum: Guidelines for Teaching History in School," *History Teacher* 23, no. 1 (1989): 7–35.
8 Diane Ravitch, *Left Back: A Century of Failed School Reforms* (New York: Simon & Schuster, 2000), 429–31.
9 Diane Ravitch, *National Standards in American Education: A Citizen's Guide* (Washington, DC: Brookings Institution, 1995), 159.
10 Gary B. Nash, Charlotte Crabtree, and Ross E. Dunn, *History on Trial: Culture Wars and the Teaching of the Past* (New York: Vintage Books, 2000), 153–82.
11 Lynne Cheney, "The End of History," *Wall Street Journal*, October 20, 1994.
12 Ravitch, *Left Back*, 434.
13 Ravitch, *Left Back*, 436; Nash et al., *History on Trial*, 255.
14 "National Standards for History Basic Edition 1996," History Standards, UCLA History Public History Initiative.
15 "The Civic Mission of Schools," A Report from Carnegie Corporation of New York and CIRCLE: The Center for Information and Research on Civic Learning and Engagement, 2003.
16 "Educating for American Democracy: Excellence in History and Civics for All Learners," Educating for American Democracy, 2021.
17 "Roadmap to Educating for American Democracy," Educating for American Democracy, 2021.
18 "Educating for American Democracy: Pedagogy Companion to the Roadmap to Educating for American Democracy," Educating for American Democracy 2021.
19 Mark Bauerlein, "Always Be Founding," *City Journal*, May 7, 2021.
20 John Fonte, "No to Conservative Accommodationism," American Greatness, April 22, 2023.
21 James Stoner and Paul O. Carrese, "What's Un-American About Accommodationism?," *Law & Liberty*, May 8, 2023.

9: The New Vision Struggles to Be Born

1 "Oklahoma City Public Schools Statistical Profile, 2021–2022," Oklahoma City Public Schools.
2 Brianna Bailey, "Hear and Read Ryan Walters' Full Remarks About the Tulsa Race Massacre," *The Frontier*, July 7, 2023.
3 Tim Walker, "'No Accountability': Vouchers Wreak Havoc on States," *The Hill*, July 7, 2024.
4 Scott Warren, *Generation Citizen: The Power of Youth in Our Politics* (Berkeley, CA: Counterpoint Press, 2019), 39 and 25.
5 David Randall, "Oklahoma Education Agency Promotes Progressive Activism Masquerading as Civics," Oklahoma Council of Public Affairs, December 26, 2019.

6 Amy Curran and Scott Warden, "Partisan Takes won't Define Nonpartisan Action Civics," CSS Partners, January 13, 2020.
7 *New York Times*, June 27, 2024.
8 NPR, May 22, 2025.
9 *New York Times*, September 16, 2024.

10: In Florida, American History Is What the Governor Says It Is

1 "Florida's State Academic Standards—Social Studies, 2023," Florida Department of Education, https://www.fldoe.org/core/fileparse.php/20573/urlt/5-3.pdf.
2 Ana Ceballos and Sommer Brugal, "Some Teachers Alarmed by Florida Civics Training Approach on Religion, Slavery," *Tampa Bay Times*, June 28, 2022.
3 "Florida Civics Seal of Excellence Course," Florida Department of Education, Civics Literary Excellence Initiative.
4 "Educational Intimidation," PEN America, August 23, 2023.
5 Kim Bellware, "Florida Law Blasted After Permission Slip Sent to Hear Black Author's Book," *Washington Post*, February 15, 2025.
6 Kerry Sheridan, "What Parents Should Know About PragerU Kids Videos, Which Can Now Be Shown in Florida's Schools," NPR, August 9, 2023.
7 Elaine Povich, "Controversial PragerU Videos Gain Educational Foothold in a Handful of Starters," *Missouri Independent*, November 3, 2023.
8 Kerry Sheridan, "Why Was Dave Ramsey's Financial Literacy Textbook Approved in Florida? Questions Remain," NPR, September 28, 2023.
9 Nicholas Confessore, "How Ron DeSantis Joined the 'Ruling Class'—and Turned Against It," *New York Times*, August 20, 2023.
10 "Former BPS Board Member Tina Descovich Co-Founds 'Moms for Liberty'; Defends Parental Rights in Education," *Space Coast Daily*, February 9, 2021.
11 Jennifer D. Jenkins, "I'm a Florida School Board Member. This Is How Protestors Came After Me," *Washington Post*, October 20, 2021.
12 Jeffrey S. Solochek and Ana Ceballos, "At Moms for Liberty Event in Tampa, a Push to Win School Board Elections," *Tampa Bay Times*, July 15, 2022.
13 Kathryn Varn, "After Contentious Elections, Conservative Florida School Boards Boot Out Superintendents," *Tallahassee Democrat*, December 14, 2022.
14 Jeffrey S. Solochek and Ana Ceballos, "Jenkins 'Toying' with Idea of 2024 Run After Desantis Announces School Board Target List," *Tampa Bay Times*, July 15, 2022.
15 "Banned in the USA: Rising Books Bans Threaten Free Expression and Students' First Amendment Rights," PEN America, April 11, 2022.
16 "Banned in the USA: Narrating the Crisis," PEN America, April 16, 2024.
17 Nadra Nittle, "Even Dictionaries Aren't Safe from Censorship in This Florida District," The 19th News Network, January 12, 2024.
18 Jay P. Greene, Max Eden, and Madison Marino, "The Book Ban Mirage," Heritage Foundation.
19 Maia Kobabe, *Gender Queer: A Memoir* (Portland, OR: Oni-Lion Forge Publishing

Group, 2023); Rupi Kaur, *Milk and Honey* (Kansas City, MO: Andrews McMeel Publishing, 2015).

20 "What's in a Book?" Booklooks.org (the organization ceased operations on March 23, 2025).

21 "Surge in Book Challenges Press Kit," American Library Association.

22 Ryan Dailey, "Florida School Library Workgroup Roiled by Conflict with Moms for Liberty Members," *Orlando Weekly*, December 9, 2022.

23 "Library Media and Instructional Materials Training," Florida Department of Education.

11: In Minneapolis, There Is Only Racism and Antiracism

1 Stanley Kurtz, "The Blue-State Education Nightmare," *National Review*, April 17, 2023.

2 "Rhode Island Social Studies Standards, Kindergarten Through High School," Rhode Island Department of Education, March 2023; David Randall, "Taken for a RIDE: How Rhode Island's Social Studies Standards Short-Change Students," National Association of Scholars, January 28, 2023.

3 Wilfred M. McClay, "National Expert: Minnesota Standards Among the Nation's Worst," Center for the American Experiment, October 2022.

4 McClay, "National Expert."

5 "2021 Minnesota K-12 Social Studies Academic Standards," Minnesota Department of Education.

6 "National Experts Highly Critical of Minnesota Social Studies Standards," American Experiment Policy Briefing, February 2024.

7 Jason Reynolds and Ibram X. Kendi, *Stamped: Race, Antiracism, and You* (Boston: Little, Brown, 2001).

8 Claudia Rankine, *Citizen: An American Lyric* (Minneapolis, MN: Graywolf Press, 2014).

12: Great Books Can Set You Free

1 Roosevelt Montás, *Rescuing Socrates: How the Great Books Changed My Life and Why They Matter for a New Generation* (Princeton, NJ: Princeton University Press, 2021), 12.

2 Pete Hegseth with David Goodwin, *Battle for the American Mind* (New York: Broadside Books, 2022), 54 and 187.

13: The War Over African American Studies: Two Irreconcilable Narratives

1 "AP United States History: Course and Exam Description, Effective Fall 2014," College Board, https://time.com/wp-content/uploads/2015/02/ap-us-history-course-and-exam-description.pdf.

2 "What's in the New, New AP History Framework?," *Education Week*; Libby Nelson, "How Conservatives Forced Changes to AP US History to Make It More 'Pro-American,'" *Vox*, August 3, 2015.

3 John Fonte and Stanley Kurtz, "AP US History Bias Still Runs Deep," *National Review*, September 22, 2015; Frederick M. Hess and Max Eden, "Surprise—The New AP U.S. History Framework Is Scrupulously Fair-Minded," *National Review*, July 30, 2015.

4 The College Board appears to have removed the online version of this draft. A slightly later version, from May 2022, is available at https://dam.assets.ohio.gov/image/upload/transfercredit.ohio.gov/files/internal-comms/AP-African-American-Studies-Framework-HE.pdf.

5 Molefi Kete Asanta, *The Afrocentric Idea* (Philadelphia: Temple University Press, 1987). That same year, Martin Bernal also published the first of his three-volume study, *Black Athena*, making a similar case about the origins of Western culture.

6 James Cone, *A Black Theology of Liberation* (Philadelphia: Lippincott, 1970).

7 "The First A.P. African American Studies Class Is Coming This Fall," *New York Times*, August 31, 2022.

8 African American Studies Faculty in Higher Ed, "Open Letter in Defense of AP African American Studies," *Medium*, January 31, 2023.

9 Alex Schwerha, "DeSantis Administration Requests Additional Information on Now-Revised African American Studies Course," *Daily Caller*, February 8, 2023.

10 College Board, "Our commitment to AP African American Studies, the scholars, and the field," College Board Newsroom, February 11, 2023.

11 African American Studies Faculty in Higher Ed, "A Call to the College Board to Restore the Integrity of the AP African American Studies Course," *Medium*, February 16, 2023.

12 Henry Louis Gates, Jr., "Who's Afraid of Black History," *New York Times*, February 17, 2023.

13 Michael Hiltzik, "Caving to the Right on Black History, the College Board Gives a Course in Cowardice," *Los Angeles Times*, February 1, 2023.

14 Stanley Kurtz, "The College Board Goes to War with DeSantis," *National Review*, February 13, 2023.

15 College Board, "AP African American Studies Scholars to Make Changes to Course," College Board Newsroom, April 24, 2023.

16 "AP African American Studies Operational Course Framework, Project and Exam Overview," College Board, https://apcentral.collegeboard.org/media/pdf/ap-african-american-studies-course-framework.pdf.

17 House Bill 7, Florida House of Representatives, Session 2022.

18 Janelle Griffith, "Most of Florida Work Group Did Not Agree with Controversial Parts of State's New Standards for Black History, Members Say," NBC News, July 28, 2023.

19 "Florida's State Academic Standards—Social Studies, 2023," Florida Department of Education.

14: Culturally Responsive Teaching

1 Jean M. Twenge, Gabrielle N. Martin, and Brian H. Spitzberg, "Trends in U.S. Adolescents' Media Use, 1976–2016: The Rise of Digital Media, the Decline of TV, and the (Near) Demise of Print," *Psychology of Popular Media Culture* 8, no. 4 (2019): 329–45.

2 Jonathan Haidt, "End the Phone-Based Childhood Now," *The Atlantic*, March 13, 2024.

3 "Constant Companion: A Week in the Life of a Young Person's Smartphone Use," C. S. Mott Children's Hospital, 2023.

4 Zaretta Hammond, *Culturally Responsive Teaching and the Brain: Promoting Authentic Engagement and Rigor Among Culturally and Linguistically Diverse Students* (Thousand Oaks, CA: Corwin, 2014), 24, 28, 130.

5 For a far less bizarre work of advocacy on the subject, see Geneva Gay, *Culturally Responsive Teaching: Theory, Research and Practice* (New York: Teachers College Press, 2018).

16: What Is to Be Done?

1 See amended Executive Order 13934, "Celebrating America's 250th Birthday," January 29, 2025, The White House.

2 Executive Order 13934, "Executive Order on Building the National Garden of American Heroes," July 3, 2020, Trump White House archive.

3 America250. https://america250.org/.

4 "V. Defining a Distinctive Role for the Master's Level in History," American Historical Association, February 1, 2025.

5 Gordon Wood, *The Idea of America: Reflections on the Birth of the United States* (New York: Penguin Books, 2011).

6 Michael Schudson, *The Good Citizen: A History of American Civic Life* (New York: Free Press, 1998).

7 Michael Sandel, *Justice* (New York: Farrar, Straus & Giroux, 2009), 218 and 264.

INDEX

Abbott, Greg, 108
Abbott, Tony, 213–14
abolitionism, 39, 70, 74–75, 81, 173, 178, 199, 225
abortion, 130
Academy of American Studies, Queens, NY, 89–93, 95–104, 224–26, 253
Accelerated Christian Education, 59
Achievement Tests (College Board), 45–46
"action civics," 99–100, 110–11, 114, 150, 161, 163, 179, 193, 257
Adams, Herbert Baxter, 31
"administrative progressivism," 42–43, 57
Advanced Placement (AP)
  AP African American Studies, 14–15, 219–27
  AP European History, 15–16, 232
  AP Government, 91, 101–2
  AP U.S. History, 20, 102, 196, 219, 223–24
affirmative action, 74, 82, 85, 129, 204, 213
African American history, 21, 82, 118, 135, 219–20, 251–52
  AP African American Studies, 14–15, 219–27
  Black conservatism and, 76–77, 221, 224, 226
  Dred Scott case, 132, 160, 225
  Great Migration, 196
  Great Society, 76, 86, 95
  Harlem Renaissance, 104, 199, 201
  Jim Crow laws, 6, 69–70, 73, 195, 225, 226–27
  reparations, 74, 82, 233
  the "1776 Unites" project, 76–77
  the "1619 Project," 5, 9–10, 68–88, 95, 108, 109, 134, 143–45, 191, 204, 207, 212–13, 224
  slavery, 16, 68–88, 111, 118, 121, 128, 129, 147, 150, 173, 212–13, 225–27, 255
African Americans
  Black Lives Matter, 18, 199–200, 219, 223
  murder of George Floyd, 74, 77, 187–88, 191, 195, 197, 207, 219, 233
  perspectives of Black parents, 207, 236
  students in the schools visited, 13–15, 60
Afrocentric Idea, The (Asante), 221, 223–24
"age-appropriateness," 115, 136, 192
agency, 126, 128, 131, 229–30, 259
Ahlbum, Tatiana, 172
Alexander of Macedon, 91–92, 99
Allen, Danielle, 7, 127–32, 142–43, 146–47, 151, 166, 226, 256, 258, 259
Allen, George, 107–8, 117
Allen, William, 226–27
America 2000 presidential initiative, 106
America250 (organization), 255
"American Birthright" standards, 114–16, 167, 170
American culture
  civic culture, 1–3, 8, 41, 208, 255
  exceptionalism, 5, 7, 80, 82
  "melting pot" of, 25–26
  newspapers, 1, 4, 38–39, 41, 102, 172, 253
  pluralism of the, 143–47
  profound Americanness of Black culture, 221
  public libraries, 97, 202
  respect for diversity, 119, 139, 144–50, 256
  shared narratives, 68–69, 227
  social media, 4, 231–35, 257

American culture (*continued*)
the Sunbelt, 49, 60
television, 73, 234
See also culture wars; individualism; values
American Enterprise Institute, 220
American Federation of Teachers, 138–39, 191
American Historical Association (AHA), 31–37, 39–40, 109, 134, 255
American History, An (Muzzey), 69
American Institute for Economic Research, 172
American Legion, 38, 137
American Library Association, 182, 183
American Promise, The (textbook), 196
American Psychological Association, 234
"Americanization," 25–26
ancient Greece and Rome, 29–30, 171. *See also* classical education
anti-intellectualism, 36, 41–43, 46
antiracism, 74, 108, 113, 187–208, 224, 238
antisemitism, 116
Anton, Michael, 109
"application schools," 155, 159
Archway Veritas Elementary School, Phoenix, AZ, 215–16
Arendt, Hannah, 128, 131
Aristotle, 7, 55–66, 211–12
Ethics, 217, 247, 253
idea of "civic friendship," 127–28, 130, 149, 259
Arizona, 9, 59–60, 214
Archway Veritas Elementary School, Phoenix, 215–16
Great Hearts classical charter schools, Phoenix, AZ, 59–60, 209–18, 243
Trinity schools, Phoenix, AZ, 59–60
Arkansas, 48, 227
Armstrong, Carl, 12–14, 120, 228
Army-McCarthy hearings, 3
Arnn, Larry, 78–79
art education, 215, 216, 232
Asante, Molefi Kete, 221, 223–24
Ashoka of India, 91–92
Asian American history, 21, 117, 190, 209–10, 236
Asian American students, 13, 17, 24, 27, 60, 91, 97, 129–31, 236, 238
Ave Maria University, 172
Ayres, Ed, 120

"back to the basics" on education, 107, 167. *See also* classical education
"balanced literacy" pedagogy, 50
Baldwin, James, 221
Ballen, John, 149
Balow, Jillian, 106, 112–18, 120, 121
Barkley, Alben, 101–2
Barney Charter School Initiative, 60, 84, 86, 214
Basker, James, 90, 103
Bass, Jesse, 244, 247
Bassell, William, 92–93, 99, 103
Battaglia, Alyssa, 11–12, 14, 16, 231
Battle Cry of Freedom (McPherson), 85
Battle for the American Mind (Hegseth and Goodwin), 125, 214
Bauer, Susan Wise, 118
Bauerlein, Mark, 149–50, 167
Baumann, F. Cayla, 206
Baxendale, Helen, 213–14
Beard, Charles, 69, 70, 136
Beard, Mary, 69
"beautiful content," 48–67, 215, 253. *See also* classical education
Beavers, Michelle, 184
Bell, Derrick, 222
Belle Isle Middle School, Oklahoma City, OK, 155–56, 160, 166, 253
Bestor, Arthur, 41–42, 44, 45, 46
Beukema, Melissa, 196
Bible study, 30–31, 107, 166–67, 210, 214, 230
Biden, Joe, 77, 79–80, 87, 169, 170, 213–14
bilingualism, 236, 245
Bill of Rights, 27, 81
Bill of Rights Institute, 84, 93–95, 124, 150, 168–69, 172, 255
bipartisanship, 10, 80, 134–35, 142–43, 151, 255
Bishop, Daniel, 51, 248–49
Black Lives Matter, 18, 199–200, 219, 223
Blight, David, 71, 246, 255
Bloom, Allan, 52
"Blue-State Education Nightmare" (Kurtz), 190
Blum, John Morton, 70
Board of Education v. Pico (1982), 183
Bobb, David, 84, 95, 124, 150
Boehme, Cathy, 184, 226
Booklooks.org (website), 183
books. *See* reading
Born on the Water, 73
Bose, Satyendra Nath, 238
Boston Massacre, 17, 98
Boston public schools, 43
Bradley Commission on History in Schools, 138
Brandeis, Louis, 82
Brands, H. W., 71
Breitbart, Andrew, 108
Brevard County, FL, 170, 175, 179–86
Brewer, Nancy, 155–61, 164, 165, 253
Brighouse, Harry, 126
Brinkley, Alan, 71
Brinkmann, Lindsay, 175
Brothers Karamazov (Dostoevsky), 247, 253
Brown v. Board of Education (1954), 233
Brown, Christonya, 105
Brown, Peter, 153–67, 242
Buchanan, Karen, 53–54
Buckley, William F., Jr., 254
Burr, Aaron, 95, 98, 100

Bush, George H. W., 106, 138–39, 141
Bush, George W., 22, 64, 113, 142, 235–36
Bynum, Virginia, 75–76

C3 Framework, 19–20, 26, 110, 145–46
Calhoun, John, 73, 82, 86
California, 44, 138
Caltagirone, Nick, 17, 27, 133
"Campaign for the Civic Mission of Schools," 23
Campos, Mario, 165
capitalism, 68, 69–71, 137, 171, 192, 195, 224, 258
Carlson, Margaret, 247
Carmichael, Sheila Byrd, 115–18, 120
Carmichael, Stokely, 201
Carnegie Foundation, 22–23, 37, 93, 141, 142
Caros, Jason, 48–50, 52–53, 56–67, 127, 215, 248, 256
Carrese, Paul, 143–45, 147, 150–51
Casey, Callum, 237–38, 242
Cash, Johnny, 254
Catholic schools, 25, 48–49, 59
Cato Institute, 169
Ceci n'est pas une pipe (painting), 232
cell phone use, 58, 61, 117, 123, 210, 234–35, 257
Center for Information and Research on Civic Learning and Engagement (CIRCLE), Tufts University, 22, 142
Center of the American Experiment, 191–93
Cézanne, Paul, 215, 217
Chambers, Whittaker, 251
character development, 10, 43, 45, 57–62, 67, 126–27, 215–16
charter schools, 59–62, 102–3
  Barney Charter School Initiative, 60, 84, 86, 214
  classical charter schools, 48, 54–61
  enrollment at, 59, 154, 159, 197, 207, 245, 247
  Responsive Ed charter schools, MI, 59–60
Cheney, Lynne, 108, 138–39, 140, 144, 149–50
Chernow, Ron, 90
Chicago, IL. *See* Turner Elementary School
  West Chicago High School
children
  child labor laws, 229
  child-centered pedagogy, 37, 43, 53, 193, 253
  children of color, 91, 235–36
  continuity with the life of the child, 235
  graduation as educational milestone, 21, 23, 25, 39, 42, 46, 154, 248
  kindergarten, 50, 191–92, 216
  See also parents; students
Chisholm, John, 26, 27
Christianity
  Catholic schools, 25, 48–49, 59
  "Christianization," 125, 214
  classical schools, 48, 58–60, 214–16
  and the Founding Fathers, 151
  homeschooling, 59
  nationalism, 49, 58–59, 193
  as once-shared ethos, 57, 171
  Protestant, 16, 25, 30, 59
  Ten Commandments in schools, 159, 166
church and state, separation of, 31, 173
Churchill, Casey, 84
Citizen (Rankine), 203
citizenship, 1–8, 20–27, 30–36
  civic education's goals, 1–8, 22–24, 35, 79
  defining "good" citizenship, 34–35, 43–44, 47–49, 57
  happiness and, 66–67, 128
  immigration and, 132, 144–45, 165
  loyalty in the face of injustice, 43, 76
  modern ideas of, 259
  participation of an active citizenship, 66–67, 126–29, 144, 147–50, 228–29
City College of New York, 6
City Journal, 149
City on a Hill (Traub), 6
City Square (sculpture), 232
"civic dispositions," 7–8, 23, 66, 99, 124, 126–28, 132, 248, 253
civic education, 1–10, 254–60
  "action civics," 99–100, 110–11, 114, 150, 161, 163, 179, 193, 257
  Arendtian life of democratic action, 128, 131
  developing character, 10, 43, 45, 57–62, 67, 126–27, 215–16
  forging civic identities, 7, 26, 64, 68–69, 122, 125–26, 189–90, 248, 259
  fostering civic engagement, 13, 14, 22–23, 26–28, 100, 109–10, 124, 144, 162–63
  in the history of school reform, 1–3, 9–10, 22, 29–47, 193
  "national/social efficiency," 35–37, 42, 46
  the "New Civics," 109
  the orchestra as a "harmonious community," 24, 125
  preserving American civic culture, 1–3, 8, 41, 208, 255
  the problem of ignorance, 4–6, 39, 46–47, 190
  of the self, 36, 56–59, 67, 126–28, 148–49, 213–15, 218, 259
  varying goals of, 1–8, 13, 22–24, 35, 50, 56–58, 64, 79, 127, 135–36, 147, 213
  See also citizenship; values; virtues
"civic friendship," 127–28, 130, 149, 259
"Civic Mission of Schools, The" report, 22–23, 93, 141, 142

Civic Seal of Excellence course (FL), 169, 172–73, 227
Civics Alliance, 109–10, 114–16, 122, 163, 167, 170
Civics Language Perceptions Project, 13
"civics," 34. *See also* civic education
civil libertarians, 128, 137, 168–69
civil rights movement, 69 72, 82, 99, 118, 175, 200–202, 227–30, 233, 251
Civil War, 2, 6, 46, 69–75, 83–85, 99, 111, 118, 121, 199, 225, 241
Claremont Institute, 109, 172
classical education, 7–8, 29–30, 57, 91–93
  ancient world history in, 91–92
  for the benefit of progressive liberalism, 6–8, 212–14, 217–18, 231–32, 256–60
  classical origins of democracy, 7–8, 94–95, 128, 258–60
  Latin language, 216, 245
  moral philosophy, 63–65, 249
  natural law, 80–82, 171–72, 250–51
  "natural philosophy," 210–11
  virtue in classical philosophy, 7–8, 23–24, 57–58, 64, 66–67, 210–11, 258–60
classical schools, 10, 48–67, 78–79, 83–84, 93
  Barney Charter School Initiative, 60, 84, 86, 214
  centrality of reading in, 99–100, 209–18, 235, 253
  charter school movement and, 48, 54–61
  Christian, 48, 58–60, 214–16
  as critique of progressivism, 111
  direct classroom instruction and, 95
  a false flag in the culture wars, 212–15, 231–32
  Founders Classical Academy of Lewisville, TX, 48–54, 58, 60–67, 84–85, 99, 209–10, 215–16, 243–53
  Great Hearts network, Phoenix, AZ, 59–60, 209–18, 243
  private schools, 48–49, 214
  the 1776 Commission curriculum, 5, 9–10, 69, 73, 78–88, 146, 212–13, 227, 250–51, 258
classrooms
  case study methods, 24–25, 132
  direct classroom instruction, 95
  double-period classes, 156, 160, 229
  "four-corners exercise," 229
  Harkness Discussion Circles, 101, 225
  intrinsic problems of the classroom, 201
  seating arrangements, 188, 217–18
  Ten Commandments in schools, 159, 166
  value of classroom observation, 9–10, 110
climate change, 176, 178
Clinton, Bill, 140, 163
College Board, 20, 45, 91, 219–24
  Achievement Tests, 45–46
  AP African American Studies, 14–15, 219–27
  AP European History, 15–16, 232
  AP Government, 91, 101–2
  AP U.S. History, 20, 102, 196, 219, 223–24
  SAT scores, 45–46, 154, 219
"College, Career and Civic Life (C3) Framework for Social Studies State Standards," 19–20, 26, 110, 145–46
"color-blindness," 189, 222
Columbia University Teachers College, 42, 135
Committee of Seven, American Historical Association, 31–37
Committee of Ten, National Education Association, 29–33, 36, 42, 193
Common Core Learning Standards, 19, 103
Communist Manifesto (Marx), 63
competencies. *See* knowledge; skills; state standards
complexity, 36, 225–26
  in the "classroom," 89–90, 100–102, 194–95
  the cognitive demands of complex abstraction, 128–29, 145, 148–49
  tackling "inherently divisive" concepts, 112–13
Cone, James, 221, 224
conservatism, 7, 26–27, 45, 49, 55–56, 76, 59–61, 77–84, 99
  Black conservatism, 76–77, 221, 224, 226
  claims of depoliticizing the schools, 178–79
  cultural conservativism, 61–65, 80, 107–10, 116, 125
  in search of patriotic education, 5, 7–8, 29–32, 35–39, 78–79, 82–88, 108, 115–20, 254
  textbooks, 84–86
  See also Christianity
conspiracy theories, 2, 16, 169, 250
Constitution Day, 78, 173
Constitution of Knowledge: A Defense of Truth, The (Rauch), 4
Constitutional Convention, 75, 96, 156–57. *See also* U.S. Constitution
"constitutional democracy," 144
content, 8–9, 135
  "age-appropriateness," 115, 136, 192
  art education, 215, 216, 232

content-neutral skills, 9, 18–23, 51–52, 111–20, 255–56
"divisiveness" and neutrality in content, 108, 115, 146–49, 157, 161
music education, 165, 216, 238–39
restoring content to standards, 86–87, 111–13
See also curriculum; *specific disciplines*
Cook, Charles, 59
Core Knowledge curriculum, 51–52, 86, 120–21, 149, 211, 216, 256
Council for Basic Education, 140–41
Count of Monte Cristo, The (Dumas), 249
Covid-19, 108, 112, 170, 174, 179–81, 188, 196
Crabtree, Lynn, 139
Crawford, Kristan, 11–12, 14–16, 19, 229–31, 233–35
creationism, 59
Crenshaw, Kimberlé, 175, 222
Crisis in the Classroom (Silberman), 43–44
Crist, Charlie, 170–71
critical race theory (CRT), 56, 78, 108–15, 122, 159, 168, 174–75, 177, 184–85, 190, 222, 236
"critical thinking," 9, 126, 253, 256
Croly, Herbert, 82
Crucible, The (Miller), 11–12
Cruz, Ted, 79
Cultural Literacy (Hirsch), 51–52, 84, 230
"Cultural Marxist Paideia," 125
culturally responsive teaching, 21, 112, 228–42, 256
"Culturally Responsive Teaching and Leading Standards," 21
Culturally Responsive Teaching and the Brain (Hammond), 236
culture, 1–10. *See also* American culture
culture wars, 5, 10, 19, 117, 151
battles over state standards, 5, 9–10, 105–22
classical schools, a false flag in the, 212–15, 231–32
conservative view of the, 26–27
delusions on both sides about the, 190–93
earlier history textbook wars, 69–77
federal education standards, 106–7, 134–52, 157–58, 166–67, 256
history vs. social studies, 11–15, 18–19, 29–47, 51–52, 56, 84, 135–38, 242
liberal view of the, 49, 190
school libraries vs. media centers, 32, 87, 181–85, 235
Ten Commandments in schools, 159, 166
Curran, Amy, 162
curriculum
"back to the basics" on education, 107, 167
Core Knowledge curriculum, 51–52, 86, 120–21, 149, 211, 216, 256
differentiated (tracking), 27, 36, 42, 44, 130, 236
electives, 14, 44, 47, 57, 127, 188, 216, 232, 233
instructional materials providers, 10, 20, 74, 90–94, 108, 149, 159, 168–69, 172, 210
"Man and His Changing Society" curriculum, 135–39
"Passport to Social Studies" curriculum, 103
Rugg texts, 135–38, 224
the "1619 Project," 5, 9–10, 68–88, 95, 108, 109, 134, 143–45, 191, 204, 207, 212–13, 224
the 1776 Commission curriculum, 5, 9–10, 69, 73, 78–88, 146, 212–13, 227, 250–51, 258
See also classical schools; *specific subjects and topics*
cursive handwriting, 216
Curtis, Trey, 98

Dallas, TX, 60, 243
Daneels, Mary Ellen, 12–13, 21–22, 25, 28, 235
Dante, 217, 249
Dare to Be Real (organization), 206–7
David (sculpture), 232
Davis, Emily, 86
Davis, Rick, 199
Death at an Early Age (Kozol), 43
Death of Character: Moral Education in an Age Without Good or Evil (Hunter), 57–58, 67
Declaration of Independence, 11–12, 38, 75, 81–82, 171, 240, 246, 253, 255
DEI, 114, 167, 190, 240
democracy, 1–8
cognitive demands of democratic participation, 126–29
democratic citizenship, 7, 104, 124, 142, 183–84, 258
"democratic eudaemonia," 128
the future of liberal democracy, 6–8
representation in a democratic system, 101–2, 144–45
student mock elections, 22, 28, 171, 205
Democracy and Education (Dewey), 33
Democracy in America (Tocqueville), 4
Democracy Network, 12–13, 18, 23–24, 64, 66, 209, 228
Democracy Schools Initiative, 23
Democratic Education (Gutmann), 126
Democrats, 6, 28, 105–8, 112–13, 123, 203, 231
Des glaneuses (*The Gleaners*), 232

DeSantis, Ron, 79, 83, 108, 118, 168–73, 176–81, 184–85, 190, 222–23, 226
Deschooling Society (Ilich), 43
Descovich, Tina, 179
DeVos, Betsy, 134
Dewey, John, 33–38, 41–43, 51–53, 56, 82, 111, 125, 135–36, 146, 228–29, 235
DeWitt, Sarah, 158–59
DiAngelo, Robin, 74
Diaz, Manny, 169, 184, 222, 226
Diercks, Adrienne, 193–94
Dietzen, Brad, 64, 250–51
"discriminatory equity ideology," 87, 185
dispositions, civic, 7–8, 23, 66, 99, 124, 126–28, 132, 248, 253
DiTella, Mike, 233–34
Dodd, William, 69
Don't Say Gay law (FL), 176
Dorfman, Alisa, 101–3, 224–25
Douglass, Frederick, 75, 178, 201, 246, 254
Drechsler, Kimberly, 53
Dred Scott case, 132, 160, 225
Du Bois, W. E. B., 102, 111, 137, 201, 221
Dubé, Louise, 142–45
Dudley, Elizabeth, 103
Duebel, John, 172
Dunning, William, 70
Dyche, Adam, 11, 14, 15, 229, 231

"Ed Scare, the," 174
ed school (education school), 21, 37, 41–42, 45, 62, 103, 113–14, 236
  the "lab school" at the University of Chicago, 135–36
  professional development, 23, 90, 93, 103, 134, 149, 158, 165, 169–70, 173, 209
  Teachers College at Columbia University, 42, 135
Eden, Max, 220
Educating for American Democracy (EAD) Roadmap, 10, 134–52, 154, 157–58, 166–67, 256
Education and Equality (D. Allen), 128
Education for Democracy, 191
education policy. *See* state standards; U.S. federal education policy
Educational Wastelands (Bestor), 41–42
Eduham (Hamilton Education Project), 89–104, 124
elections
  learning about, 22, 28, 171, 205
  recent presidential, 2, 8, 78–79, 203, 205, 258
  school board, 184
electives, 14, 44, 47, 57, 127, 188, 216, 232, 233
Eliot, Charles, 29, 135
Emile (Rousseau), 56
"End of History, The" (Cheney), 140
"Ending Radical Indoctrination in K-12 Schooling" executive order, 87
English class. *See* literature
equality, 21, 72–73, 75, 80–81, 85, 112–13, 129–30, 148, 229–30
Equality's Call (picture book), 241
equity, 87, 112–13, 147–48, 174, 185, 188–89, 194, 205–8, 209
Essays (Montaigne), 213
ethics, 24–25, 102, 171, 259–60. *See also* values; virtue
Ethics (Aristotle), 217, 247, 253
Ethnic Studies program in Minneapolis, 74, 187–208, 211
ethos, 62
eudaimonia (happiness), 7, 57, 66–67, 80, 128, 174, 249
European history
  AP European History, 15–16, 232
  Holocaust, 21, 116–17, 176
  Knights Templar, 249–50, 257
  Magna Carta, 46, 97, 171
  Renaissance, 16, 46
  World War I, 38, 116, 138, 232–33
exceptionalism, 5, 7, 80, 82
"Experience and Education" (Dewey), 37
experiential learning, 19–22, 98–100, 124, 146–48, 162, 170–71, 211, 257–58
  Deweyan underpinnings of, 37–38
  Hamilton Education Project (Eduham), 89–104, 124
  Legislative Simulation class (West Chicago High), 21–22, 28, 98, 123–33, 229, 248, 257
  See also participation

facts. *See* knowledge
faculty. *See* teachers
fascism, 82, 196
federal funding, 87–88, 141–42, 163, 185–84. *See also* U.S. federal education policy
Federalist Society, 79
Fifteenth Amendment, 230
Fikis, Candy, 27–28
financial literacy, 178, 239, 256
Finn, Chester, 46–47, 139–40
First Amendment, 169, 183–84
First Liberty Institute, 172
Flexner, Abraham, 135
Florida, 10, 79, 110, 168–86, 222, 226–27
  banned books, 181, 184–85
  Brevard County, 170, 175, 179–86
  Civic Seal of Excellence course, 169, 172–73, 227
  Don't Say Gay law, 176
  financial literacy program, 178
  "Parents Bill of Rights," 168, 174
  "Stop Woke Act" (HB 7), 174, 185, 222, 226
  "transparency" laws, 173–74, 176, 185–86
Florida Council for the Social Studies (FCSS), 168, 170, 172, 175
Florida Education Association, 184, 226
Florida Freedom to Read, 178

Floyd, George, 74, 77, 187–88, 191, 195, 197, 207, 219, 233
Foner, Eric, 71
Fonte, John, 150–51, 157, 166, 220
Ford, Constance, 211–12, 214
Ford, Gerald, 254
Fordham Institute, 5, 8, 13, 18, 111, 113, 121, 122, 157, 191
Foundations in Personal Finance, 178
Founders Academy of Mesquite, TX, 243–48
Founders Classical Academy of Lewisville, TX, 48–54, 58, 60–67, 84–85, 99, 209–10, 215–16, 243–53
Founding Fathers, 30, 49–50, 69, 81–82, 111, 147, 150–51, 173, 247, 250–51, 258–59
  nonchalant treatment of, 115–16
  views of citizenship, 7–8
  See also specific Founders
"four-corners exercise," 229
Fourteenth Amendment, 20, 129, 230
Fourth Amendment, 146
Fox News, 13, 78, 125
France, 16, 135, 250
free or reduced school lunches, 13, 25, 60, 88, 93, 211
Frey, Jacob, 200
Frey, Jennifer, 211
Friedman, Milton, 254–55
Friess, Foster, 211

Gallup polls, 139
Garcia, Jamie, 132–33
Garrison, William Lloyd, 70, 178
Gates, Henry Louis, 201, 223, 224
Gaza, war in, 131, 199, 250
Gecker, Dan, 114, 117, 121–22
gender identity, 61, 168, 176, 182–83, 206
Gender Queer (Kobabe), 182–83
Generation Citizen: The Power of Youth in Our Politics (Warren), 161–62
Generation Civics (organization), 99–100, 154, 161–63
Georgetown Elementary, DuPage County, IL, 238–42
Gerges, Nicola, 170, 175, 177
Giacometti, Alberto, 232
Gilder Lehrman Institute of American History, 90–95, 103, 124, 246
Gillett, Kevin, 54–58, 127
Goffman, Erving, 231
Goldwater, Barry, 3, 254
Gonzalez, Laura, 239–40
Good Citizen, The (Schudson), 259
"good society," 127–28
Goodlad, John, 44–45, 47, 235
Goodwin, David, 125, 214
Gorny, Brian, 158
graduation, expectations upon, 21, 23, 25, 39, 42, 46, 154, 248
graduation, rates of, 2, 30, 36, 93, 133, 194
"great books," 209–18. *See also* reading
Great Depression, 95, 99, 137, 203
Great Hearts classical charter schools, Phoenix, AZ, 59–60, 209–18, 243
Great Migration, 196
Great Society, 76, 86, 95
Greene, Tamar, 89
Groettum, Andrew, 203–5
Grossman, James, 134
"group rights," 80–82
"Guardian of Democracy" report, 141
Guelzo, Allen, 143
guerilla warfare class (Scarsdale High School, NY), 43–44
Guevara, Che, 194–95, 207–8
Guidera, Aimee Rogstad, 114–17
Gullah people of South Carolina, 236
Gutmann, Amy, 126

Haidt, Jonathan, 234
Hakim, Joy, 65
Hall, G. Stanley, 33
Hamer, Fannie Lou, 251–52
Hamilton Education Project (Eduham), 89–4, 124
Hammond, Zaretta, 236
Hannah-Jones, Nikole, 72–73, 75–76, 145
Hansen, Bill, 113
Harkness Discussion Circles, 101, 225
Harlem Renaissance, 104, 199, 201
"harmonious community," 24, 125
Harris, Kamala, 2, 226–27
Hart, Albert Bushnell, 31, 34
Healy, Shawn, 18–23
Hegseth, Pete, 125, 214
Heiler, Jay, 214
Heritage Foundation, 79, 167, 182, 210
Heseltine, William B., 39
Hess, Frederick, 220
Heston, Charlton, 254
Hewlett Foundation, 154
Hillsdale College, 60, 64, 77–88, 99, 109
  Barney Charter School Initiative, 60, 84, 86, 214
  ubiquity of, 111, 117, 146, 171–72, 191, 213–15, 250
  views of, 125, 171, 213–15, 250–51
Hirsch, E. D., 51–52, 84, 86, 120–21, 149, 211, 216, 230, 256
"historical thinking" skills, 20, 139, 141
history
  agency in, 126, 128, 131, 229–30, 259
  chronological, 9, 11–12, 20, 32, 39, 120, 139, 167, 216–17, 225, 257
  the fallacy of "presentism," 76

history (*continued*)
immersion in the material of history, 20, 47
marginalized people and voices in, 20, 70, 115, 126, 128, 149, 183–84, 190–91, 229–30, 241–42
monocausal history, 72–73
narrative history, 5, 9, 16–17, 44, 52, 144, 165, 250, 255, 258
national narratives, 5, 68–69, 72, 82, 143–44, 147, 191–92
overemphasis on the nation-state, 16, 145
revisionism in American historiography, 69–71, 74
social studies vs., 11–15, 18–19, 29–47, 51–52, 56, 84, 135–38, 242
as "stories," 257
thematic, 11–12, 16–17, 39, 70–71, 119, 147–48, 196, 249, 255
"World History," 12, 15, 91–92, 139, 158, 192, 202–3
See also culture wars; U.S. history; reading; textbooks
History of the Americas class (Washburn High School), 194–95, 207–8
History of the United States (Charles and Mary Beard), 69
Holocaust, 21, 116–17, 176
Holt, Jonathan, 43
Holton, Anne, 117–18, 121
Homer, 50–53
Homer, Winslow, 71
homeschooling, 53, 59, 245
Hoogheem, Christian, 205–6
Hopkins, Gerard Manley, 216, 217
Hosseini, Khaled, 182
How Children Learn (Holt), 43
How to Be an Antiracist (Kendi), 74, 108, 188–89, 201–2, 207
Howard, Donald, 59
Hughes, Troy, 244–45
Human Geography class (Waubonsie Valley High School), 12, 15, 229
Humane Letters class (Great Hearts schools), 216–17
Hunter, James Davison, 57–58, 67
Huster, Jennifer, 199–200
Hutchins, Robert Maynard, 41, 42

IB (International Baccalaureate), 194, 196, 202–5, 196
iCivics, 20, 93–95, 142–44, 149, 154–58, 163–67, 168, 210, 255
Idea of America, The (Wood), 258–59
identity
American civic identity, 7, 26, 64, 68–69, 122, 125–26, 189–90, 248, 259
gender identity, 61, 168, 176, 182–83, 206
identitarian perspectives, 26, 122, 144–45, 190, 241–42
politics of, 82–83, 86, 114, 117, 258
ignorance, 4–6, 39, 46–47, 190. *See also* knowledge
Ilich, Ivan, 43
Illinois, 9, 173
C3 Framework, 19–20, 26, 110, 145–46
Democracy Network, 12–13, 18, 23–24, 64, 66, 209, 228
"lab school" at the University of Chicago, 135–36
law requiring participatory activities in school, 109
mandate on "culturally relevant teaching," 190
Metea Valley High School, IL, 16–18, 21, 24, 56–57, 124–25, 238
Waubonsie Valley High School, Aurora, 11–21, 26–28, 56–57, 99, 103–4, 127, 132, 192, 218, 228–35, 238, 253
"Illinois Civic Blueprint," 23
Illinois State University, 21
immigrants, 2, 33, 255
citizenship and, 132, 144–45, 165
immigrant students and children of immigrant parents, 25–27, 123–24, 132, 164, 173, 194–95, 203–4, 237–38
Native Americans as America's "first immigrants," 118
parents choosing classical charter schools, 60, 93, 102, 210
Imprimis (newsletter), 83
"inclusiveness," 115, 128
Indigenous peoples. *See* Native American history; westward expansion
individualism
agency and, 126, 128, 131, 229–30, 259
as American tradition, 207–8, 236, 259–60
autonomy, 58, 125–27, 259
limits of, 259–60
indoctrination, charges of, 7, 87, 109–10, 126, 137, 151, 157, 170–72, 186, 190
Inferno (Dante), 249
"informed patriotism," 142
"inquiry-based learning," 15, 19–20, 44–45, 105, 113–14, 119, 143–44, 147–48, 154–55, 158, 164–65
institutional racism, 189, 197
instructional materials providers, 10, 20, 74, 90–94, 108, 149, 159, 168–69, 172, 210
International Baccalaureate (IB) classes, 194, 196, 202–5
Iran hostage crisis of 1979, 15
Israel, 131, 199, 250

Jack Miller Center, 93, 115, 169
Jackson, Andrew, 82, 94, 259
January 6 insurrection, 83, 146
Jefferson, Thomas, 2, 32, 98, 173, 246, 256

Jenkins, Jennifer, 179–81, 183–84
Jim Crow laws, 6, 69–70, 73, 195, 225, 226–27
Jirsa, Jason, 201–3, 206
Johnson, Lyndon, 76
Jolley, Jennifer, 175
Jones, Chris, 122
Jordan, Jim, 79
judicial review, 159–60
Juneteenth, 121
justice
  in a deeply unjust society, 43, 71–74, 125–26, 132–33, 188
  equity, 87, 112–13, 147–48, 174, 185, 188–89, 194, 205–8, 209
  neo-Marxist "social justice" regime, 109–11
  "restorative/redistributive" justice, 71, 127–28
  social justice, 109–11, 114, 124–28, 162, 187, 214, 240
Justice by Means of Democracy (D. Allen), 128–29

Kamensky, Jane, 142–43, 146, 151
Kaur, Rupi, 182–83
Kawashima-Ginsberg, Kei, 142–43, 144–45
Kazin, Michael, 94
Kendi, Ibram X., 74, 108, 188–89, 201–2, 207
Kennedy, Ann, 162–63
Kenosha, Wisconsin, 77–78
Kimball, Roger, 83, 109
kindergarten, 50, 191–92, 216
King, Arianna, 50–51
King, Martin Luther, Jr., 82, 118, 251–52
Kirk, Russell, 62, 251
Kirkpatrick, Jeane, 255
Kite Runner, The (Hosseini), 182
Knights Templar, 249–50, 257
knowledge, 1–10
  "democratic knowledge," 130, 132
  the scale of ignorance, 4–6, 39, 46–47, 190
  subject-matter knowledge and teaching, 8–9, 15, 20–21, 24, 34, 37, 41, 44, 53, 57, 62, 103, 107
  teaching civics without history, 11–28
  See also specific disciplines and topics
Kobabe, Maia, 182–83
Kozol, Jonathan, 43
Ku Klux Klan, 140
Kurtz, Stanley, 109–11, 174, 178, 190, 193, 220–23

"lab school" at the University of Chicago, 135–36
labor history, 121
Land of Hope (McClay), 85
language
  bilingualism in schools, 236, 245
  "code-switching," 26
  learning Latin, 216, 245
  "linguistic empowerment," 256
  linguistic skills, 129, 166, 245, 255–56
  phonics, 50, 107, 216
  vocabulary, 9, 13, 16–18, 52, 94, 132, 171
  See also reading
Las Casas, Bartolomé de, 194
Latino people
  Chicanx/Latinx history, 203
  Latino vote for Trump, 207
  students, 13, 15, 17, 25, 27, 60, 91, 129, 154, 155, 157, 164, 165, 194, 197, 204, 236–37, 283, 243, 248
  "white Latinos," 207
League of Women Voters, 38
learning. *See* content; pedagogy; skills
Left, the
  Democrats, 6, 28, 105–8, 112–13, 123, 203, 231
  "left-wing social engineering," 13
  New Deal social democracy, 137, 173
  socialism, 137, 169, 172–73, 196, 221–22
  wokeness, 56, 106, 108–10, 118, 150, 157, 169–70, 254
  See also liberalism; progressivism
Legislative Simulation class (West Chicago High), 21–22, 28, 98, 123–33, 229, 248, 257
Lessons from History (Nash), 140
"Letter from Birmingham Jail" (King), 251–52
Levine, Peter, 142–43, 145
Levinson, Meira, 26, 125, 132
Lewis, John, 200, 251
LGBTQ+ issues, 61, 108, 157, 180
liberalism, 3, 6–8, 124–29, 144–45
  classical education for the benefit of progressive liberalism, 6–8, 212–14, 217–18, 231–32, 256–60
  cultivation of the individual, 57, 67, 126
  defining a "liberal education," 42, 108–9, 211–14, 248, 260
  discomfort with virtue ethics, 126–28, 210–11
  liberal consensus of the 1960s, 71–76, 85, 227
  "liberal moralism," 126
  patriotism and, 66, 115
  secularism, 1–2, 31, 57–59, 125, 214, 235
  view of the culture wars, 49, 190
  See also individualism; progressivism
libertarians, 128, 137, 168–69
Liberty Common School, Fort Collins, Colorado, 84
liberty, 7, 49, 62, 72–73, 77, 80–81, 128, 171
libraries, 32, 87, 97, 181–85, 202, 235
Library of Congress, 38
"life adjustment" programs, 42, 57, 193, 200
Lightfoot, Lori, 110

Lincoln, Abraham, 71–73, 75–76, 85, 95, 133, 199, 230, 246–47
"linguistic empowerment," 256
literature, 209–18, 217, 247, 249, 253
Liu, Mark, 24–25, 124–25, 127
Logevall, Fredrik, 94
logos, 62
Los Angeles Times, 223
lottery-based admissions, 52, 60
Lou Frey Institute, University of Central Florida, 173
Loudon County High School, VA, 107–8
Louisiana, 149, 166
Lynd, Albert, 41, 45

MacIntyre, Alasdair, 259
Madame Bovary (Flaubert), 211
Madison, James, 7, 96, 97, 106, 190
MAGA activists, 142, 162, 206
Magna Carta, 46, 97, 171
Magritte, René, 232
Mahmoud, Rachael, 238–42
Malcolm X, 132, 251–52
"Man and His Changing Society" curriculum, 135–39
Manhattan Institute, 78
Mann, Horace, 1–2, 4–5, 31, 47, 256
Manor, Mary, 203–4
Mansfield, Harvey, 109
Marbury v. Madison, 159
Marshall, Thurgood, 182
Marx, Karl, 63, 72
Marxism, 109, 125
Mary Golda Ross Middle School, OK, 163–66
mask compliance, 179, 181
Massachusetts, 1, 9, 43
Masyada, Steve, 173
Matthewson, Robert, 164–65
Mayflower Compact, 77
McAuliffe, Terry, 112
McCann, Arlen, 229
McCann, Melissa, 198–99
McCarthy, Joseph, 3, 140
McClay, Wilfred, 85, 86, 191–92, 199, 204
McCormick Foundation, 13, 18, 23
McDavid, Maurice, 235–37
McGuffey readers, 30
McPherson, James, 75–76, 85
McWhorter, John, 76
"media centers," 32, 87, 181–85, 235
"media literacy," 21, 54
"media specialists," 184–85
"melting pot," 25–26
memorization, 30, 31, 39, 45, 52–53, 120, 153, 215–17, 242, 248–49
meritocracy, 174, 185
Metea Valley High School, IL, 16–18, 21, 24, 56–57, 124–25, 238
Michelangelo, 232
Michigan, 60, 79
Milk and Honey (Kaur), 182–83
Miller, Arthur, 11–12
Millet, Jean-Françoise, 232
Minneapolis, MN, 9, 74, 108, 187–208, 211
  Northeast Middle School, 194, 197–1
  Parnassus Prep School, 211, 214
  Washburn High School, 187–89, 194–97, 199, 201–8, 238
Minnesota Department of Education, 192
Miranda, Lin-Manuel, 90–91, 98, 100
Missouri, 36–37, 178
Mitchell, Beatrice, 157–58, 164
Moms for Liberty, 179–85
Mona Lisa, 232
Montaigne, Michel de, 213
Montás, Roosevelt, 212–14, 243, 246, 248
morality, 7–8, 25, 30–33, 125–28, 210–11
  legislating, 70
  moral philosophy, 63–65, 249
  See also culture wars
Morrisey, Will, 111
Morzenti, Jason, 196, 206
Mount Rushmore, 38, 49
Mullins, Mark, 181
Munch, Edvard, 232
music education, 165, 216, 238–39
Muslim students, 240
Mussolini, Benito, 82
Muzzey, David Saville, 69

narrative history, 5, 9, 16–17, 44, 52, 144, 165, 250, 255, 258
Nash, Gary, 138–40
"Nation at Risk, A" report, 46, 106, 138
National Assessment of Educational Progress (NAEP), 4, 6, 45–46, 138, 142
National Association of Scholars, 77, 109, 190–91
National Black Republican Association, 226
National Bureau of Economic Research, 123, 132
National Center for History in the Schools at UCLA, 138
National Conference of State Legislatures, 22
National Constitution Center, 93, 168, 210
National Council of Education Standards, 139
National Council of Social Studies, 19
National Education Association (NEA), 29–33, 35–36, 42, 73, 135, 193
"national efficiency," 35–37, 42, 46
National Endowment for the Humanities (NEH), 134, 138, 142
National Experience, The (Blum), 70
National Garden of American Heroes, 254
National High School Ethics Bowl, 24
national narratives, 5, 68–69, 72, 82, 143–44, 147, 191–92
National Review, 110, 221
National Right to Life Committee, 61

nationalism, 16, 49, 58–59, 145, 193
Native American history, 21, 110, 118–19, 160–61, 190, 220, 240, 241
natural law, 80–82, 171–72, 250–51
"natural philosophy," 210–11
Near Andersonville (painting), 71
neo-Marxist "social justice" regime, 109–11
neutrality
  as anathema to the populist imagination, 181
  antiracist challenge to, 74
  "divisiveness" and neutrality in content, 108, 115, 146–49, 157, 161
  pretenses of neutrality on both sides, 109–10, 125–26
  principled neutral positions expected of teachers, 169–70, 200–202
  value-neutrality, 126, 144
Nevins, Allan, 39–41, 46
"New Civics," 109
New Criterion, 83, 109
New Deal, 72, 86, 95, 118, 137, 173
New Hampshire, 178
New York City, 6, 89–93, 103
  Academy of American Studies, Queens, NY, 89–93, 95–104, 224–26, 253
  Hamilton Education Project (Eduham), 89–104, 124
  Vertex Prep, the Bronx, 213
New York Times, 5, 39, 44, 68, 73, 75–76, 83, 134, 167, 223
newspapers, 1, 4, 38–39, 41, 102, 172, 253
Nicomachean Ethics (Aristotle), 217, 247, 253
No Citizen Left Behind (Levinson), 26
No Property in Man (Wilentz), 85
"No to Conservative Accommodationism" (Fonte), 150
Noem, Kristi, 111, 114, 170
Nolde, Emil, 232
nonprofit organizations, 10, 93–95, 134, 169
Northam, Ralph, 105, 112–21
Northeast Middle School, Minneapolis, MN, 194, 197–201
Northern, Amber, 13, 18, 121–22
Norton, Mary Beth, 71

O'Connor, Sandra Day, 94
O'Donnell, Katie, 86
O'Neill, Tip, 6
Oakes, James, 75–76
Oklahoma, 153–67, 177–78
  Belle Isle Middle School, Oklahoma City, 155–56, 160, 166, 253
  the Educating for American Democracy (EAD) Roadmap in, 134–52
  Mary Golda Ross Middle School, 163–66
  Parental Choice Tax Credit Act, 159
  Tulsa Massacre of 1921, 159
  U.S. Grant High School, 157–58, 166
Oklahoma City Public Schools, 153, 159, 161–62
Oklahoma Council of Public Affairs, 162
"open schools," 43–45
Oyez (website), 160

Pageau, Jonathan, 210–11
"Paideia" class (Lewisville Founders Academy), 63–64, 125, 247
Palmer, Emily, 187–89, 194, 201–8
pandemic of 2019, 108, 112, 170, 174, 179–81, 188, 196
Panic of 1819, 94
Pankuch, Don, 21, 24
Paradiso (Dante), 217
parents, 12, 133, 137–38
  communicating pedagogy to, 49, 52–53
  Florida's "Parents Bill of Rights," 168, 174
  immigrant parents choosing classical charter schools, 60, 93, 102, 210
  "parental control," 106, 108, 111–12
  partisanship among, 107–12, 170
  perspectives of Black parents, 207, 236
  "school choice," 125, 159, 166–67, 214, 244
Parnassus Prep School, MN, 211, 214
participation, 7, 11–13, 23
  active citizenship, 66–67, 126–29, 144, 147–50, 228–29
  in the classroom, 11–13, 23, 91, 98–99, 109, 154, 197–201
  "participatory readiness," 7, 128, 258
"Partisanship Out of Civics Act" (Kurtz), 109–10, 174, 178–79
"Passport to Social Studies" curriculum, 103
pathos, 62
Patriot Day, 48, 64
patriotism, 5, 7–8, 29–32, 35–39, 78–79, 82–88, 108, 115–20, 254
  classical liberal formulation of, 115
  hostility to, 43–44, 73, 126
  "informed patriotism," 142
  Pledge of Allegiance, 14, 38, 155
  "reflective patriotism," 7, 66, 145
Patriot's History of the United States (Schweikart), 196–97
Peculiar Institution, The (Stampp), 70
pedagogy, 5, 8–9, 18–23, 250, 253–57
  child-centered pedagogy, 37, 43, 53, 193, 253

pedagogy (*continued*)
communicating pedagogy to parents, 49, 52–53
culturally responsive teaching, 21, 112, 228–42, 256
"inquiry-based learning," 15, 19–20, 44–45, 105, 113–14, 119, 143–44, 147–48, 154–55, 158, 164–65
traditional learning through memorization, 30, 31, 39, 45, 52–53, 120, 153, 215–17, 242, 248–49
"whole language" or "balanced literacy" pedagogies, 50
See also classical education; neutrality; progressivism; skills
Peede, John, 134, 142
peer culture, 57–58
PEN (organization), 174, 181–83
Pennsylvania, 181
People and a Nation, A (textbook), 71
People's History of the United States, A (Zinn), 71–73, 84, 125–26, 148, 196
Person, Rakeem, 214
phonics, 50, 107, 216
Pippin, Jennifer, 184
Place Called School, A (Goodlad), 44–45
Plato, 50, 86, 212, 250, 256
Pledge of Allegiance, 14, 38, 155
polarization, 3–6, 207, 258
illusions shared by both sides, 86–88, 125–26
pretenses of neutrality on both sides, 109–10, 125–26
"political correctness," 139
"political socialization," 14
politics
bipartisanship, 10, 80, 134–35, 142–43, 151, 255
as "downstream" from culture, 108
national politics vs. local control, 87–88
parents made into partisans, 107–12, 170
pluralism in America, 143–47
See also civic engagement
populism, 180–81
Prager, Dennis, 167, 178
PragerU, 159, 177–78
Prairie Restoration class (Waubonsie Valley High), 12–14, 120, 228
"presentism," 76
Presley Rice, Frances, 226–27
primary sources, 19–20, 84, 95, 97, 119, 146, 158–59, 196, 220–21, 233
private schools, 58–59, 154, 159, 235
classical, 48–49, 214
privatization / school vouchers, 125, 159, 166–67, 214, 244
teacher hiring practices at, 103
professional development, 23, 90, 93, 103, 134, 149, 158, 165, 169–70, 173, 209
progressivism, 8–9, 15, 18–20, 26–27, 37, 69–74
"administrative progressivism," 42–43, 57
allegedly progressive doctrine of "group rights," 80–82
commonalities with the classical approach, 217–18
in the history of school reform, 33–47
"inclusiveness," 115, 128
reactions against, 50, 52, 55–58, 64, 81–87, 211, 214–15, 250
the rise of social studies, 38–45
view of civic identity, 189
Waldorf schools, 182
Project 2025, 167, 203
Project Success, 193–94
Pronley, Matthew, 196
Prophet (Nolde), 232
prostitution, 130, 131
Protestant Ethic, The (Weber), 16
Protestantism, 16, 25, 30, 59
public libraries, 97, 202
public schools, 1–10, 254–60
"application schools," 155, 159
"inner-city," 43, 101, 146, 243
See also charter schools; classical schools
Pulitzer Center for Crisis Reporting, 73–74
purple states. *See* Virginia

race
affirmative action, 74, 82, 85, 129, 204, 213
critical race theory (CRT), 56, 78, 108–15, 122, 159, 168, 174–75, 177, 184–85, 190, 222, 236
DEI, 114, 167, 190, 240
Ethnic Studies program in Minneapolis, 74, 187–208, 211
identity politics, 82–83, 86, 114, 117, 258
mixed ethnicity, 24, 240
racial particularism, 26
whiteness, 174–75, 204–5
See also specific groups and communities
racism
antiracism, 74, 108, 113, 187–8, 224, 238
"discriminatory equity ideology," 87, 185
"inherently racist," 87–88, 129, 189
institutional racism, 189, 197
Red Summer of racial violence (1919), 196
structural racism, 78, 121, 195, 197, 207, 238
Tulsa Massacre of 1921, 159
white supremacy, 5, 70–76, 82, 117–18, 129, 213, 222
Ramsey, Dave, 178
Randall, David, 190–91
Random House, 73
Rankine, Claudia, 203–4
Rauch, Jonathan, 4
Ravitch, Diane, 46–47, 139–40

reading
  autobiographies, 47, 85
  banned books, 181, 184–85
  Bible study, 30–31, 107, 166–67, 210, 214, 230
  classics of literature, 209–18, 217, 247, 249, 253
  close reading of texts, 64–65
  poetry, 48, 50, 164–65, 182–83, 203, 216, 248
  primary sources, 19–20, 84, 95, 97, 119, 146, 158–59, 196, 220–21, 233
  scaffolding, 118–19, 158–59
  secondary sources, 19–20, 95, 119, 220–21
  whole books, 11–12, 235
  See also literature; textbooks
Reagan, Ronald, 6, 46, 115–16, 120, 220
Reconstruction, 46, 70–74, 85, 112, 229–31
"Reconstructionists" of the 1930s, 44
Red Summer of racial violence (1919), 196
"reflective patriotism," 7, 66, 145
reform, school, 1–3, 9–10, 22, 29–47, 193. *See also* charter schools; classical education; progressivism
religion
  secularism, 1–2, 31, 57–59, 125, 214, 235
  separation of church and state, 31, 173
  See also Christianity
Renaissance, 16, 46
reparations, 74, 82, 233
"Report of the Committee on Social Studies," 35, 135
Republic, The (Plato), 50, 86, 250
republicanism, classical, 7, 128
Republicans, 2, 28, 105–8, 123, 162–63, 203, 220, 231
Rescuing Socrates: How the Great Books Changed My Life (Montás), 212
Responsive Ed charter schools, MI, 59–60
"restorative justice," 127
Revolutionary War, 2, 241
Rhode Island, 74, 190, 191
Right, the
  MAGA activists, 142, 162, 206
  Republicans, 2, 28, 105–8, 123, 162–63, 203, 220, 231
  the term "constitutional republic," 171
  See also Christianity; conservatism
rigor, 16, 42–43, 45–47, 60, 116, 178–79
Roberson, Josh, 169–70, 175, 179
Rockefeller Foundation, 135
Rogers, Jonathan, 56, 57, 51, 62–63, 249–50
Rogers, Katie, 54, 67, 159
Romo, Eduardo, 194–95, 202, 206–7
Roosevelt, Franklin D., 64, 101, 137, 196
Roosevelt, Teddy, 33, 664
Roots of American Order (Kirk), 62, 251
Rose, Kelly, 15–16, 18–21, 103, 132, 192, 218, 230, 232, 253, 257
Ross, Mary Golda, 163–64
rote memorization, 30, 31, 39, 47, 48, 52–53, 120, 153
Rotherham, Andy, 113–14, 117–18, 120
Rousseau, Jean-Jacques, 33, 56
Rowe, Vernon, 194, 197–200
Rufo, Christopher, 78, 109
Rugg curriculum, 135–38, 224
Rugg, Harold, 135
Russell, Bertrand, 136
Rutherford, Mildred Lewis, 69

Sacagawea, 254
Sandel, Michael, 259
SAT scores, 45–46, 154, 219
scaffolding, 118–19, 158–59
Scarsdale High School, NY, 43–44
Scholasticism, 216
school boards, 5, 59, 106, 159, 179–84, 200
School of Civic and Economic Thought and Leadership at Arizona State University, 143
school uniforms, 58, 244
schools
  bilingualism in, 236, 245
  cell phone use in, 58, 61, 117, 123, 210, 234–35, 257
  during the pandemic of 2019, 108, 112, 170, 174, 179–81, 188, 196
  extraordinary schools, 67
  libraries vs. "media centers," 32, 87, 181–85, 235
  mask compliance in, 179, 181
  privatization / school vouchers, 125, 159, 166–67, 214, 244
  selective and lottery-based admissions, 52, 60, 93, 159
  "service learning," 23, 109, 163
  vacuity of schooling in general, 18, 43, 72–73
  vocationalization of schools, 36, 42, 56, 92, 101, 109, 111, 236, 260
  See also classrooms; students; teachers
Schudson, Michael, 259
Schweikart, Larry, 196–97
science education
  climate change, 176, 178
  Prairie Restoration class (Waubonsie Valley High), 12–14, 120, 228
  return to "natural philosophy" in classical schools, 210–11
  teaching creationism, 59
  teaching evolution, 80
  urban heat islands, 199–200
Scream (painting), 232
secularism, 1–2, 31, 57–59, 125, 214, 235
Seller, Jeffrey, 90–91
Semiquincentennial of the United States, 87, 254–55
9/11 (Patriot Day), 48, 64
"service learning," 23, 109, 163
1776 Commission report, 5, 9–10, 69, 73, 78–88, 146, 212–13, 227, 250–51, 258

"1776 Unites" project, 76–77
Shakespeare's Sonnet 65, 248–49
Shanker, Albert, 138, 140
Shaw, George Bernard, 136
Shklar, Judith, 126
Siebert, Alan, 118
Sikh people and communities, 117, 118
Silberman, Charles, 43–45, 47, 235
Silverstein, Jake, 76
"1619 Project," 5, 9–10, 68–88, 95, 108, 109, 134, 143–45, 191, 204, 207, 212–13, 224
1620: A Critical Response to The 1619 Project (Woods), 77, 109
skills
  civic, 7–8, 22–23, 66–67, 128–29
  content-neutral skills, 9, 18–23, 51–52, 111–20, 255–56
  "critical thinking," 9, 126, 253, 256
  decoding skills vs. vocabulary, 52
  financial literacy, 178, 239, 256
  "historical thinking" skills, 20, 139, 141
  "life adjustment" programs, 42, 57, 193, 200
  linguistic, 129, 166, 245, 255–56
  pedagogical skills, 41, 62, 103
Slaughterhouse Five (Vonnegut), 182
slavery, 16, 68–88, 111, 118, 121, 128, 129, 147, 150, 173, 212–13, 225–27, 255
social change, 34, 161–62
"social efficiency," 35–37, 42, 46
social justice, 109–11, 114, 124–28, 162, 187, 214, 240
social media, 4, 231–35, 257
social studies, 11–15, 18–19, 29–47, 51–52, 56, 84, 135–38, 242
  current events, 101, 109, 132, 196, 199, 233, 250, 253
  history vs., 11–15, 18–19, 29–47, 51–52, 56, 84, 135–38, 242
  the "new Social Studies," 44
social-emotional learning (SEL), 238–39
socialism, 137, 169, 172–73, 196, 221–22
sociology, 231–32, 257
"soft bigotry of low expectations," 236
Solzhenitsyn, Alexander, 251
South Carolina, 227, 236
South Dakota, 110–11, 116, 120, 122, 170
Sowell, Thomas, 227
Spalding, Matthew, 78–79, 82, 86, 99
Sphere (organization), 168
Stamped: Race, Antiracism, and You (textbook), 201–2
Stampp, Kenneth, 70
standardized testing, 4–6, 8, 13–14, 22, 40, 45–47, 51, 139
  memorization for, 45
  in selective admissions, 93
  time for "test prep," 65, 256
  See also College Board
state standards, 5, 9–10, 105–22
  local school boards, 5, 59, 106, 159, 179–84, 200
  mandates, 21, 26, 167, 173, 178, 190, 239
  prohibiting the teaching of colorblindness, 222
  the vague generalizations that plague, 5, 18–19, 41, 107, 114, 146, 190, 192–93
  See also specific states
Steele, Shelby, 227
Stoner, James, 150–51
"Stop Woke Act" (HB 7), 174, 185, 222, 226
Strange Career of Jim Crow, The (Woodward), 70
Strauss, Leo, 80
structural racism, 78, 121, 195, 197, 207, 238
structuralism, 44
subject-matter knowledge, 8–9, 15, 20–21, 24, 34, 37, 41, 44–46, 53, 57, 62, 103, 107
Sunbelt, 49, 60
Sykes, Lindsay, 206

Tale of Two Cities, A (Dickens), 50, 217, 253
Talking to Strangers (D. Allen), 127
Tampa Bay Times, 172–73
"Task Force 250," 87, 254
Tawney, Jake, 215–18
teachers
  ed school, 21, 37, 41–42, 45, 62, 103, 113–14, 135–36, 236
  "guide on the side" vs. "sage on the stage," 57–58
  at private schools, 103
  professional development, 23, 90, 93, 103, 134, 149, 158, 165, 169–70, 173, 209
  professional ethos of, 26, 149
  subject-matter knowledge, 8–9, 15, 20–21, 24, 34, 37, 41, 44, 53, 57, 62, 103, 107
  See also classrooms; students
Teachers College at Columbia University, 42, 135
teaching material. *See* curriculum
Teaching White Supremacy (Yacovone), 70
television, 73, 234
Ten Commandments in schools, 159, 166
"test prep," 65, 256
testing. *See* standardized testing; state standards
Texas, 48, 60, 108, 110, 181
  Dallas, 60, 243
  Founders Academy of Mesquite, 243–48
  Founders Classical Academy of Lewisville, 48–54, 58, 60–67, 84–85, 99, 209–10, 215–16, 243–53
textbooks, 30, 32, 44, 69–77, 241
  The American Promise, 196
  Bible study, 30–31, 107, 166–67, 210, 214, 230

History of the United States, 69
the McGuffey readers, 30
A People and a Nation, 71
A People's History of the United States, 71–73, 84, 125–26, 148, 196
the Rugg books, 135–38, 224
Stamped: Race, Antiracism, and You, 201–2
Your Community and Beyond, 239
See also curriculum; state standards
thematic history, 11–12, 16–17, 39, 70–71, 119, 147–48, 196, 249, 255
Thirteenth Amendment, 230–31
Thomas, Clarence, 169, 213
TikTok, 131, 132, 234
Tinker v. Des Moines School District (1969), 183
Tocqueville, Alexis de, 4
"total institutions," 231
"transparency" laws, 173–74, 176, 185–86
Trinity schools, Phoenix, AZ, 59–60
Trump, Donald, 2–8, 66, 69, 77–83, 87, 108–9, 152, 189, 195, 203–8, 254–60
in the classroom, 170, 185, 195, 203, 206–8
elections of, 2–8, 78–79, 203, 205, 258
January 6 insurrection, 83, 146
National Endowment for the Humanities (NEH), 134, 142
Project 2025, 167, 203
"trusteeship" doctrine, 101
tu quoque, 54
Tucker Carlson Show, 78
Tulsa Massacre of 1921, 159
Turner Elementary School, Chicago, IL, 235–38, 242, 245
Turner, Frederick Jackson, 29
Tutuska, John, 63–64, 210, 249
Twitter, 118
U.S. Army, 3
U.S. Bureau of Education, 34
U.S. Congress, 102, 134, 140, 255
U.S. Constitution, 7, 17, 18, 38, 48–50, 66, 80–81
Bill of Rights, 27, 81, 146, 169, 183–84
in the classroom, 129, 183, 240–42, 250
Constitutional Convention, 75, 96, 156–57
as defense of private property, 69–77
in our founding mythology, 144–48, 151
Preamble to the, 48, 66, 241–42
Reconstruction amendments, 20, 129, 230–31
See also Founding Fathers
U.S. education policy
Common Core Learning Standards, 19, 103
Educating for American Democracy (EAD) Roadmap, 10, 134–52, 154, 157–58, 166–67, 256
federal funding, 87–88, 141–42, 163, 185–84
free or reduced lunch, 13, 25, 60, 88, 93, 211
U.S. Department of Education, 46, 87, 134, 139, 142
U.S. Grant High School, OK, 157–58, 166
U.S. history
abolitionism, 39, 70, 74–75, 81, 173, 178, 199, 225
AP Government, 91, 101–2
AP U.S. History, 20, 102, 196, 219, 223–24
Asian American history, 21, 117, 190, 209–10, 236
Boston Massacre, 17, 98
capitalism, 68, 69–71, 137, 171, 192, 195, 224, 258
civil rights movement, 69–72, 82, 99, 118, 175, 200–202, 227–30, 233, 251
Civil War, 2, 6, 46, 69–75, 83–85, 99, 111, 118, 121, 199, 225, 241
Declaration of Independence, 11–12, 38, 75, 81–82, 171, 240, 246, 253, 255
Great Depression, 95, 99, 137, 203
labor history, 121
Mayflower Compact, 77
national narratives, 5, 68–69, 72, 82, 143–44, 147, 191–92
Native American history, 21, 110, 118–19, 160–61, 190, 220, 240, 241
New Deal, 72, 86, 95, 118, 137, 173
Reconstruction, 46, 70–74, 85, 112, 229–31
Revolutionary War, 2, 241
westward expansion, 118–19, 120
World War II, 5, 39, 116, 137, 233
See also African American history; American culture; Founding Fathers
U.S. Supreme Court, 81, 166–67, 169, 225
Board of Education v. Pico (1982), 183
Brown v. Board of Education (1954), 233
Dred Scott case, 132, 160, 225
judicial review, 159–60
Plessy v. Ferguson (1896), 20
Tinker v. Des Moines School District (1969), 183
UCLA (University of California, Los Angeles), 138–39
"understandings," 119, 145
United Daughters of the Confederacy, 69
United States. *See* American culture; U.S. history; *various government bodies*
"universal voucher" laws, 159

values
equality, 21, 72–73, 75, 80–81, 85, 112–13, 129–30, 148, 229–30

values (*continued*)
  liberty, 7, 49, 62, 72–73, 77, 80–81, 128, 171
  meritocracy, 174, 185
  as sacrosanct, but unspecified, 58–59
  truth, 2–4, 49–50, 55–59, 100, 193, 211–12, 214
  value-neutrality, 126, 144
  See also justice
Veblen, Thorstein, 136
Veritas Prep Academy, Phoenix, AZ, 59–60, 215–17, 244, 247, 248
Versailles, Treaty of, 116, 232
Vertex Prep, the Bronx, NY, 213
Victims of Communism Day, 173, 178
Virginia, 74, 83, 105–8, 111–22, 169–71, 179, 190, 224
virtue
  in classical philosophy, 7–8, 23–24, 57–58, 64, 66–67, 210–11, 258–60
  liberal view of, 126–28, 210–11
  the study of history, 30–32, 35, 211, 259
  the teaching of, 95, 155
  traditional Protestant American virtues, 30–31
vocabulary, 9, 13, 16–18, 52, 94, 132, 171
vocationalization of schools, 36, 42, 56, 92, 101, 109, 111, 236, 260
Vonnegut, Kurt, 182
voucher systems, 159, 166–67, 214, 244

Waldorf schools, 182
Walker, C. J., 157
Walker, Clarence V., 174–75
Walters, Ryan, 159, 166–67
Warner, Mark, 113
Warren, Scott, 99–100, 161–62
Washburn High School, Minneapolis, MN, 187–89, 194–97, 199, 201–8, 238
Washington Post, 108
Washington state, 31
Washington, Booker T., 77, 111, 137
Washington, George, 89, 106, 113–15, 132–33, 140, 147, 150, 156, 173, 227, 240, 246
Waubonsie Valley High School, Aurora, IL, 11–21, 26–28, 56–57, 99, 103–4, 127, 132, 192, 218, 228–35, 238, 253
Weber, Max, 16
Welch, Joseph, 3
West Chicago High School, IL, 17, 21–28, 123–33, 258
westward expansion, 118–19, 120
What Do Our 17-Year-Olds Know? (Ravitch and Finn), 46–47, 106, 139
What Was Liberalism? (Traub), 6
"whataboutism," 54
Wheatley, Phyllis, 95
White Fragility (DiAngelo), 74
White House Conference on American History (2020), 78
"white Latinos," 207
white supremacy, 5, 70–76, 82, 117–18, 129, 213, 222
whiteness, 174–75, 204–5
"whole language" pedagogy, 50
Wiesel, Elie, 251
Wilentz, Sean, 74–76, 81, 85
Wilkins, Roy, 202
Wilson, Woodrow, 29, 34, 47, 102
"Windhover, The" (Hopkins), 216
Wisconsin, 77–78
Witness (Chambers), 251
"woke," 56, 106, 108–10, 118, 150, 157, 169–70, 254
Wolak, Chris, 14, 27, 231, 233–34
Wood, Gordon, 75–76, 81, 258–59
Woods, John, 61, 63–64, 77, 251–53
Woods, Peter W., 77, 109
Woodson, Robert, 76–77, 95
Woodward, C. Vann, 70
"workplace readiness skills," 119
"World History," 12, 15, 91–92, 139, 158, 192, 202–3
World Studies class (Northeast Middle School), 198
World War I, 38, 116, 138, 232–33
World War II, 5, 39, 116, 137, 233
writing, 12, 91, 157, 164–66, 202, 236, 257
Wyoming, 112

Yacovone, Donald, 70
Youngkin, Glenn, 83, 105–6, 111–22, 170, 177, 179–80
Your Community and Beyond (textbook), 239
Youth Participation Evaluation class (Northeast Middle School), 197–98, 200
YouTube, 235

Zahn, Lynne, 155
Zeman, Joe, 17, 27, 132
Zimmerman, Jonathan, 137–38
Zinn, Howard, 71–73, 84, 125–26, 148, 196
Zonnefeld, Kevin, 203